D0930171

THE SOCIAL MEDIA HANDBOOK FOR FINANCIAL ADVISORS

Since 1996, Bloomberg Press has published books for financial professionals on investing, economics, and policy affecting investors. Titles are written by leading practitioners and authorities, and have been translated into more than 20 languages.

The Bloomberg Financial Series provides both core reference knowledge and actionable information for financial professionals. The books are written by experts familiar with the work flows, challenges, and demands of investment professionals who trade the markets, manage money, and analyze investments in their capacity of growing and protecting wealth, hedging risk, and generating revenue.

For a list of available titles, please visit our web site at www.wiley.com/go/bloombergpress.

THE SOCIAL MEDIA HANDBOOK FOR FINANCIAL ADVISORS

How to Use LinkedIn, Facebook, and Twitter to Build and Grow Your Business

Matthew Halloran
and
Crystal Thies

BLOOMBERG PRESS
An Imprint of
WILEY

Published by John Wiley & Sons, Inc., Hoboken, New Jersey.
Published simultaneously in Canada.

For general information on our other products and services or for technical support, please contact our Customer Care Department within the United States at (800) 762-2974, outside the United States at (317) 572-3993 or fax (317) 572-4002.

Wiley also publishes its books in a variety of electronic formats. Some content that appears in print may not be available in electronic books. For more information about Wiley products, visit our web site at www.wiley.com.

Library of Congress Cataloging-in-Publication Data:

Halloran, Matthew.
    The social media handbook for financial advisors : how to use LinkedIn, Facebook, and Twitter to build and grow your business/Matthew Halloran and Crystal Thies.
       p. cm. — (Bloomberg financial series)
    Includes index.
    ISBN 978-1-118-20801-4 (cloth); ISBN 978-1-118-22864-7 (ebk);
    ISBN 978-1-118-24086-1 (ebk); ISBN 978-1-118-26582-6 (ebk)
       1. Financial planners—Internet marketing.   2. Investment advisors—Internet marketing.
    3. Financial services industry—Internet marketing.   4. Social media.   5. Internet marketing.
    I. Thies, Crystal. II. Title.
    HG179.5.H35 2012
    332.6068'8—dc23

                                                                                            2012010362

Printed in the United States of America

10   9   8   7   6   5   4   3   2

MIX
Paper from
responsible sources
FSC® C005928

I dedicate this book to my wife, Angela, for her support and patience; to my boys, Derek and Wesley; and to Dr. Victor Harms for teaching me that anything is possible if you work hard and set realistic goals.

Matt

I want to dedicate this book to my fiancé, Rich Seil, and my parents, Arnie and Donna Thies. Without their love and support over these past three years, I never would have had the courage, strength, and ability to launch myself into this unknown world of social media to create a business and now a book out of a few ideas, realizations, and predictions of how the marketing world was not only going to change, but how the entire paradigm was going to shift. It allowed me to finally capitalize on natural and innate skills, abilities, and passions that weren't recognized until long after my formal education.

Crystal

Contents

Foreword

Can I tell you a little story? About a year ago I was referred to a senior VP in a large financial services firm. One of his field managers liked the work I was doing with his advisors and thought the entire company should be taught my referral system. The introduction came in the form of an email, so my first step was to send an email to the new prospect—looking to schedule a brief phone call to get our conversation started. This simple strategy works for me about 90 percent of the time. In this case, I received no response.

Since "proactive" is my middle name, about a week later I sent another email to the prospect. Still no response.

Then I thought I'd see if this prospect was on LinkedIn. Sure enough he was. I sent him a LinkedIn message to which he responded, "I'm sorry I haven't responded to your attempts to contact me. Kirk has spoken very highly of you. Please call my assistant to get on my calendar. I'll let her know you'll be calling. She'll make it a priority."

I'm not proud to admit that I came to the new social media kicking and screaming. I avoided using Facebook, Twitter, and LinkedIn for as long as I could. My internal conversation was probably a lot like yours. "I don't have time for this. I already have enough on my plate. Social media looks like a sink hole of time to me." My staff begged me to "get with it." I still resisted. How would I monetize my efforts?

Then it hit me like a blinding flash of the obvious. Social media is one big word-of-mouth, referral, and introduction machine. Since 1995 I've been showing financial advisors how to generate more word-of-mouth, referrals, and introductions. How could The Referral Coach stand on the sidelines and watch everyone else use this tremendous new tool? How could I allow myself to miss the opportunities it presented to my business?

I'm not going to tell you that by *not* engaging in social media you'll be left in the dust. You don't need social media to be successful—at least not right at this moment in time. However, if you do not engage in social media, you'll be missing a huge opportunity to build stronger relationships with many of your clients and centers of influence and, ultimately, to build a thriving culture of word-of-mouth, referrals, and introductions for your business.

Creating a thriving referral-based business is all about being seen as a valuable resource and building strong relationships with clients and centers of influence based on that value. It's also about being proactive, not passive. Some advisors make the mistake of thinking, "All I have to do is serve the heck out of my clients and they'll provide me with a steady flow of new clients through referrals." That's only partially true. Yes, you must serve the heck out of your clients—to keep them loyal and to make yourself referable. However, this usually only generates a trickle of referrals and introductions—and not always to the right types of prospect for you. To *thrive* with referrals, you have to be proactive.

The good news is that social media allows you to do both—provide value for clients and COIs and be proactive for introductions. Even better news is that Matt Halloran and Crystal Thies have provided the road map for how to do this in their book *Social Media for Financial Advisors* (John Wiley & Sons). Whether you're brand new to social media or have been dabbling in it for some time, Halloran and Thies have much to teach you in this no-nonsense guide.

Spending only a few hours a week with social media, you'll be able to:

- Provide great value to prospects, clients, and Centers of Influence.
- Build stronger relationships with those same people.
- Be strategically proactive for referrals and introductions.
- Be as selective as you want in who you bring into your business.
- Reach hard-to-reach prospects you know you'll be able to help.

Maybe you're with me so far, but you're still thinking, "But what about my compliance department?" (sometimes referred to as the Sales Prevention Department). Social media has thrown compliance departments into a tizzy. It can aptly be called "The Wild West." With that said, most firms see the opportunity that social media presents and have worked hard to create an environment where you can tap into the value of social media, without violating the many rules that regulate our industry.

When Twitter, Facebook, and LinkedIn hit the scene, compliance threw up a big stop sign. "No way!" they said. Yet now they're coming around. It's getting easier and easier. With the help of this book, you'll be able to tap into the power of social media in a safe, effective, and efficient manner.

Start small and build from there. If you have staff, do as I did, and relegate as much as you can to them. Social media is here to stay and will only grow in importance and effectiveness as a way to provide value and generate new business. Follow the advice of Halloran and Thies. They'll show you the way.

BILL CATES
President, Referral Coach International
Author of *Get More Referrals Now*
www.ReferralCoach.com

A Perspective on Social Media

There was a very smart man who lived around 2,500 years ago in Athens, Greece. He was a philosopher, professor, scholar, and overall a well-thought-of individual.

There were many students he taught on a regular basis. He taught them philosophy, physics, debate, and politics. They would listen for hours, learning from a master.

One day while they were all in class, a student raised his hand.

"Socrates, are you the wisest man in all of Athens?"

"I do not know, but I intend to find out!" Socrates said, abruptly leaving.

He was rather impulsive it seemed. What a great question and why hadn't someone asked him that before?

How does one find out if he is the smartest? *Well, I assume one has to ask the others that are the smartest difficult questions*, he thought.

In Athens, at the time, they had these people called oracles. They were gifted by the gods with knowledge. There were not many of them, but the ones that were, were very spread out all over the greater Athens metropolitan area. So he set off on foot. He figured he would have time on his walks to think about their answers before he got to the next one. Furthermore, he could use the exercise.

He got to the first oracle.

"Come in," the oracle said. Socrates was happy he did not need an appointment.

"I would like to ask you some questions," Socrates said.

"If answers are what you seek, I will provide," the oracle stated with confidence.

"What is truth?" Socrates inquired.

"Well, the only way do discuss what truth is, is to first talk about . . ."

Hours passed. The oracle told Socrates the origin, history, and meaning of truth. By the end, his head was spinning. Socrates thanked the oracle and walked out.

On his journey, he went over everything the oracle said—over and over in his mind, until he arrived at the cave opening of the next oracle. There was no place to knock, so Socrates announced himself in the manner appropriate at that time, and was summoned in with a quiet voice.

"May I ask you a question, oracle?" Socrates said loudly, thinking the oracle was hard of hearing.

"I have been in this cave for the last 30 years. No need to yell, I hear all and see all from this spot. I am here to answer the questions that plague all in Greece. I have had many come and sit where you are; what can I help you answer?"

Man, it seemed like this guy had been alone for a long time. He needed someone to talk to. This was going to take a long time, Socrates thought. And it did.

"What is the meaning of life?" Socrates inquired.

"The meaning of life is easy to understand," he replied. "It all started . . ."

For six hours, the oracle went on, covering all things concerning life, physics, death, the gods, and even the origins of olive oil.

"Does that answer your question?" the oracle asked.

"Sure, thank you so much for your time. Enjoy the cave!" Socrates speedily headed out the door.

Holy gods, what the heck? There seemed to be a trend with the oracles, but two does not a solid trend make.

Days later, he arrived at the last oracle's house. He had visited every oracle that advertised in the Athens newspaper. It had been a long journey. He was glad that he was at his last stop.

Socrates's feet hurt and he did not smell too pretty. He had been walking for days. He was so deep in thought he had even walked off the road a few times. And he had forgotten to eat the rations he grabbed when he headed out the door to start this journey, so he was hungry. He paused before knocking at the palatial house where he then found himself.

He fixed his hair. He drank some wine, enough to wet his whistle but not too much to cloud his ability to listen and absorb all that this oracle had to offer. He ate some bread, dried meat, and dipped it all in olive oil, which brought him back to the oracle that waxed philosophic about olive oil for about an hour.

Socrates's mind was so full of information. He needed to file it away and freshen up. This could be the missing piece. This oracle could solidify it all. This journey could have purpose. He could go back to his students and tell them what he knew they wanted to know—and well, Socrates wanted to know if he was the smartest man in Athens, too.

Okay, I am ready, he thought.

He knocked at the wooden panel on the right side of the door. A person appeared wearing robes so white they were glowing.

Socrates was motioned to come in. He entered a courtyard with hanging plants. Everything was white. Socrates thought he must have died and was about to meet the gods. The man was walking a few steps in front of Socrates.

The courtyard smelled wonderful. The fragrances of flowers, wine, and perfume were perfectly balanced. It took a few moments for Socrates's eyes to adjust to the brightness. He realized the person guiding him was not a man but a young woman.

Not being sexist, Socrates inquired, "Are you the oracle?"

"No, we are going to see her now." Her voice was musical. Perfectly paced and inflected.

She pushed two doors open, which were the size of Hercules himself, with no effort. Her exposed forearms displayed rippling muscle.

"The oracle is here," she announced.

On a simple pillow sat a woman with pitch-black hair. It flowed over her shoulders in soft waves.

"Sit," she gestured, and then inquired, "How may I help you?"

This was going to be the best yet, Socrates thought. She is rich, beautiful, and has servants. She has to know something, probably everything. She will give me the best answer yet.

"I have a question. What happens after you cease living?"

"Well, that is a good question, most don't know, but I do . . ."

The sun started setting and she was still talking. Socrates had arrived just after sunrise. He was offered food during this sermon and wine, good wine. He was enjoying the surroundings and the smells, and during that brief moment of distraction from the oracle's message, it hit him.

"Thank you, oracle, you are so wise," he interrupted.

She looked appalled. "I am not done. Don't you want to know what happens after you die?"

"No," Socrates said. He made a quick exit for the door.

He was filled with so much energy he started to run. Now, Socrates was not a young man and running was probably not the best idea. But he ran all the way back to the university. Classes were just finishing up when he arrived.

He burst through the door. The students gasped! The professor moved aside. Socrates took the floor. A student offered him some wine.

He was panting and holding his chest. His students thought this was it; he was going to keel over before he told them what he found.

"Get the other students; they all need to hear this," Socrates gasped, still visibly winded.

All the students scurried. You could hear yelling in the hallway. In moments, the room was wall-to-wall with students.

"I was tasked to find out if I was the smartest man in Athens. It was a long journey. I walked for days meeting with every oracle I could find. I asked them the deepest questions philosophy has to offer. What is truth, beauty, life, death, and from where the gods came. They all waxed on and on for hours, definitively answering the questions with arrogance and wisdom all rolled into one. After careful consideration, I now know that I am the smartest man in all of Athens and probably all of Greece." He gasped for air.

There was dead silence in the room. Then, off in a far corner, a student asked, "How do you know that?"

Socrates was somewhat of a dramatist. He waited for the right moment to cut the tension.

"I know I am the smartest man in Athens and all of Greece because . . ." He took a large draw off the wine, and then continued, "because I know I do not know everything!"

A huge roar of laughter went up in the room! A cheer and a lot of high fives.

■ ■ ■

As you can probably tell, I paraphrased this story. High fives in Athens? Well, that is not the point of the story. I tell you this story because I, too, like Socrates, know I do not know everything. I know a lot about social media, how to set it up, and how to use it to maximize your marketing efforts.

But, it is an ever-changing landscape. I know that I do not know everything about social media. What you will get from this book is a lot.

This I promise. But, to think that this will be the definitive book on a medium that changes faster than I go gray . . .

There will be many editions of this book to keep up with the times. With all that said, I doubt the basic understanding of how to set up accounts, the philosophy, and the basic use guidelines will change that much.

Remember, there are many out there who claim to know it all. We do not. Since you are reading this, you do not think you do, either. So then, since our cups are not yet full, let's continue to fill them together. Enjoy.

Matt Halloran

Introduction

Here are some quick facts:

1. Social Media has overtaken pornography as the #1 activity on the web.
2. Facebook added over 200 million users in one year.
3. If Facebook was its own country, it would be the third largest behind China and India, respectively.

Financial advisors are always looking for a competitive advantage. There has been no greater competitive advantage in marketing and positioning than social media. Using Facebook, LinkedIn, and Twitter will unlock powerful direct marketing opportunities that have already changed the way many communicate and market to existing clients and prospects.

Many advisors have been quite terrified of the compliance issues surrounding social media. Compliance moves slowly but deliberately to protect the interests of the financial services industry and the clients we serve.

When email came out what seems like ages ago, compliance told advisors they could not use it. Some broker-dealers took years to approve the use of email because of their concerns surrounding archiving. Social media is no different. Broker-dealers, even the progressive ones, have dragged their feet using excuses like: *There are not enough people using social media at this point for us to use our resources to provide advisors with compliance services pertaining to social media.* Well, this archaic view of technology has changed. Broker-dealers are now allowing advisors to use social media in a limited manner, asking them to invest in archiving services to comply with their compliance regulations.

If you've picked up this book or are checking it out online, you're probably trying to decide if you should buy it. Yes, it has a pretty cover, it says it's about social media and it says it's for financial advisors, but is that enough? One thing the Internet has taught all of us, is that with the vast amount of information and resources available, we had better be clear and up front about our value proposition in order to keep people reading. Therefore, if you have any questions that are running around your head that start with "why," then we encourage you to finish reading the Introduction and we'll do our best to answer them.

Why This Book?

This book is designed to be a primer to help the tens of thousands of financial advisors, financial planners, wealth advisors, investment advisors, etc. who have not yet ventured into social media (out of choice or as a result of policy) to do so quickly and effectively. Technology has finally caught up with social media and it is now possible to technologically and cost effectively capture and preserve social media activity as is required by law. Additionally, the regulatory bodies (FINRA and SEC) have also been providing more clear guidance of where social media fits in its definitions of advertising materials and the appropriate oversight, prereview, and record keeping requirements of the many moving parts that are social media. Further, the largest broker-dealers have been beta testing the usage of social media by select groups of advisors for almost a year in order to develop appropriate internal policies and guidelines. The expected result is that the vast majority of financial advisors will be unleashed on social media to some degree by the end of 2012 (possibly mid-2013 at the latest). This book is created for them.

Bottom line—If you are regulated by either FINRA or the SEC and have not been using social media yet, then this is the social media book for you. To be honest, if you're not regulated and are still new to social media, then this book would still be beneficial—just ignore the parts that talk about compliance and that tell you that you're not allowed to do certain things.

If you're one of the financial advisors who were early adopters of social media and have been actively using it to grow your business, then chances are there won't be much new information in this book for you. Of course, that's not to say that you won't learn anything, but we literally start with walking you through creation of accounts. We start from an assumption that the reader has never looked at LinkedIn, Facebook or Twitter. Our hope and intention is to come back and provide a follow-up advanced strategy book for you and the financial advisors who will be ready for it further down the road after implementing what they learn in this book.

Why These Authors?

We do not claim to be the "be all" and "end all" of social media experts or even financial social media experts; there's simply too much to know and it changes too fast for any one person to be "the best." We definitely know our stuff and we bring a very unique perspective compared to other experts in our space.

As a business coach to financial advisors, Matt's perspective is based off of hundreds of offices', not just one advisor's, perspectives. He has worked with his clients to implement marketing and social media, helped them traverse the compliance waters, but never had to personally debate the compliance officer to get a letter or advertising piece approved (and he is happy not to have had to do that!). However, with his bigger picture perspective, when a compliance review appeared to kill a project, he helped his clients see another route to accomplish the same goal. With substanial success creating his own network of social media connections, he is regularly consulted by the media to weigh in on FINRA and SEC policy changes.

As a past financial planner turned social media consultant, Crystal brings the inside-looking-out perspective to this project. She has personally—and frequently—worked with compliance departments to create effective marketing materials to grow her own practice. So, she understands the frustration and extra planning required to uniquely market your financial advisory practice. She's been in your shoes. Financial companies such as Wells Fargo, UBS, and Fifth Third Bank, in addition to independent wealth advisors come to her because of the success and expertise she has had with LinkedIn in addition to her understanding of the internal challenges to implementing social media in financial services.

Our goal is to help financial advisors successfully grow their businesses using social media compliantly. Our combined experiences, expertise, and perspectives have allowed us to write this book while looking through the eyes of an RIA, registered rep, compliance officer, and broker-dealer, with the concerns of a small business owner, marketer, financial controller, and risk manager. We've tried to address all points of view to help you make the right decisions for your financial advisory practice as you begin to implement your social media strategies.

Why This Approach?

Much of what is available in terms of marketing strategy and business development for financial advisors comes from a place of "No." Given the continuum of oversight and compliance controls, most materials are written for what is allowed for the majority (registered reps of highly conservative broker-dealers) and not what is possible for the minority (independent RIAs). Therefore, if the majority of financial advisors are not allowed to implement a marketing or business development strategy (often due to the expense of the oversight by the broker-dealer), it is often stated that it's not allowed—period. Even though it is legal and able to be used by some who are applying proper policies and oversight.

We've taken on a difficult task because we want this book to be applicable to *both* RIAs and registered reps AND we want to come from a place of "Yes." That means that there are some strategies and recommendations included in this book that cannot be used by a large number of the financial advisors reading this book—though most of the book applies to all financial advisors. We want to show what is truly possible for financial advisors with social media.

We believe in customizing our advice to the audience we're speaking to. In this case, it's everyone, so we're sharing what's possible to anyone who is reading the book. When a broker-dealer hires us to work with their financial advisors, we share what's possible and allowed within the confines of their compliance policy. When a financial advisor hires us, we share what's allowed within their compliance policy, what's possible within the law, where the gray area is between the two, and they decide how to apply social media to their practice.

Our approach is based on some important assumptions—you're an adult, you're smart enough that you were able to pass some very difficult licensing tests, and you're being monitored by a licensed authority or are smart enough to have been able to pass an even tougher test that allows you to monitor yourself. Therefore, you should be smart enough to apply your compliance policy to our suggestions to determine if you're allowed to do them, and you're smart enough to understand the implications and repercussions if you decide to act contrary to your compliance policy.

How This Book Is Organized

This book is written by two authors and broken down into four main parts. At the start of each chapter, the author or authors that wrote or contributed to that chapter will be identified to help you understand from whose perspective and experience the material is coming.

The first part of the book is a basic introduction to social media and includes the only chapters with the authors writing in tandem. The material covered in these chapters include basic philosophies, approaches, and strategies to social media in general. It also includes tips and suggestions on how to be more effective and efficient in implementing social media into your financial advisory practice.

The title of the book lists the social networks in the following order: LinkedIn, Facebook, and Twitter. However, they are covered in the opposite order in the book with Part II on Twitter, Part III on Facebook, and Part IV on LinkedIn. This was done on purpose. Financial advisors may be more comfortable with LinkedIn so we wanted to emphasize in the title that the largest part of the book covers the use of LinkedIn. However, it is also the most complex of the three social networks, so we covered that material last. Essentially, the three social networks are covered in the order of simplest to set up and operate to most complex.

If you're not ready to take on all three social networks right away, then pick one and start there. It's much better to do one social network well than to do all three poorly. If you decide not to do Twitter, then just jump over that section to the social network that you want to start with. There are unique benefits to each social network, so if you're not sure what you want to do, then read through the entire book before making any decisions and taking any action.

When it comes to the three social networks, don't confuse the terms simple and easy. Twitter is simple to get going and implement because it has so few moving parts. However, it is far from easy to use effectively. LinkedIn has the most moving parts of all three social networks and we didn't even cover the addition of the new Company Page features because only a small subset of financial advisors can have LinkedIn Company Pages (due to LinkedIn's restrictions on who they want to have a Company Page).

Matt explores and explains Facebook and Twitter and Crystal delves deeply into LinkedIn. Throughout this book, we will walk you through setting up accounts, creating profiles, building networks and implementing strategies to help find prospects and build awareness of your expertise. In addition to the social networks themselves, there are other third party tools and services that can be used to enhance your activity and make it more efficient. We will also share the tools that we know of and have used.

The final conclusion chapter wraps things up by acknowledging that there is much we have not yet touched. We also provide you with contact information and our website to get more information, tools and resources. We would love to hear from you, so feel free to connect with us.

We hope you enjoy the book!

PART I

Introduction to Social Media

CHAPTER 1

Compliance

Crystal Thies

Yes, that's where we're starting, and I feel very strongly about starting here. I was reading a *Wall Street Journal* (WSJ) blog article by Josh Brown, who was making fun of the concept of "*financial* social media experts," and I knew we had to address this issue first to prove that there is such a thing and that we *are* qualified.

Now, Matt's a little more timid in this space because as a financial practice coach, he's mostly been on the sidelines of the compliance war. I, however, have fought several compliance battles and reigned victorious! By victorious, I mean I ended up with a marketing piece that did work, but that was not necessarily my original glorious vision. Of course, that was after many rounds of back and forth editing and negotiating the use of adjectives.

To this day, it's still hard for me to not see a compliance officer as the enemy—at least until the next securities fraud story hits the news. We have to remember that in the terms of history, Bernie Madoff just happened. And, in terms of securities fraud, that's the biggest name since Charles Ponzi. We like to think that financial services and securities has become a better, more ethical profession. Unfortunately, it only takes one person to spoil it for everyone. I can only imagine what could have happened if Bernie hadn't gotten caught when he did and had gotten his hands on social media! How many other people and organizations would have lost their money?

So, as much as they frustrate the heck out of me, we do need our compliance officers. It's taken some time, but I believe that most financial advisors will be seeing their companies opening up to social media in 2012. That's because two things are happening. First, the broker-dealers are realizing that they are losing out on business by not participating in the *conversation*. Second, technology has finally caught up and there are affordable solutions to properly and legally archive the activity.

I'm going to be completely honest with you. As a practicing financial planner, I did not follow my broker-dealers' marketing and communications policies 100 percent of the time. I did knowingly do things that were not allowed. I also took advantage of gray areas where you knew that the broker-dealer likely meant one thing, but the way it was written was ambiguous and an argument could be made that what I was doing was allowed.

I bet that's not a complete shock to most of you. One of the most interesting things I found when I returned to financial planning in 2008 after being out of the industry for just under a decade was that not much had changed in the helpful advice offered by experienced advisors in my office. Many experienced financial advisors would confide that if you wanted to succeed, you had to bend some compliance rules. Not lie, not deceive, and not break the law—just bend some of the rules.

Now, I'm sharing that with you because I want you to know that I've been in your shoes and I understand your frustration. However, as you will read in the next section, I'm not advocating bending or breaking your broker-dealers' or firms' compliance policies in regard to social media going forward due to some very important changes. Besides which, I was wrong to do it in the first place and so were the others.

Compliance and FINRA Licensed Advisors

The vast majority of broker-dealer compliance policies are much stricter than the law established by the Financial Industry Regulatory Authority (FINRA). So, it is not difficult to bend and even break some of their rules without breaking the law. You're risking losing your contract, but not going to jail. In the past, I have worked with some of those advisors who were more interested in playing in the gray areas of their compliance policies in regard to social media, but I've changed my tune since August 2011, when FINRA released Regulatory Notice 11-39 Guidance on Social Networking Websites and Business Communications (www.finra.org/Industry/Regulation/Notices/2011/P124187).

Regulatory Notice 11-39 clearly states that if your broker-dealer says that you cannot use social media for business purposes, then you cannot use social media for business purposes. They've removed the gray; we're in black and white territory now.

As part of this responsibility, a registered principal must review prior to use any social media site that an associated person intends to employ for a business purpose. The registered principal may approve use of the site for a business purpose only if the registered principal has determined that the associated person can and will comply with all applicable FINRA rules, the federal securities laws, including recordkeeping requirements, and any additional requirements established by the firm.

However, another important point that has come out of Regulatory Notice 11-39 is that whether or not the social media communication is personal or business is not determined by the device used (meaning that you can't go home and use your home computer or use your smart phone to send out financial-services-related status updates and messages and call it personal), but by the actual content in the communication.

SEA Rule 17a-4(b)(4) requires a firm to retain records of communications that relate to its "business as such." Whether a particular communication is related to the business of the firm depends upon the facts and circumstances. This analysis does not depend upon the type of device or technology used to transmit the communication, nor does it depend upon whether it is a firm-issued or personal device of the individual; rather, the content of the communication is determinative.

Therefore, only social media activity that is clearly business related must be supervised and archived. If you're mixing the two, then chances are that all will be reviewed and archived, so make certain you're comfortable having your manager reading the personal social media activity. I say that because 11-39 also states that if it is cost prohibitive, your broker-dealer can treat all communication on a device used for business communication as business communication—*no matter who owns the device.*

FINRA Rule 2210 ("Communications with the Public") is currently in process of being approved and should be approved by the final printing of this book. Full compliance and implementation of the new rules will be required sometime around March/April 2013.

FINRA Rule 2210 clarifies where social media falls in relation to other communications of regulated firms. At this point, posts in "online interactive electronic forums" (i.e., social media) are considered "public appearances" that do not require pre-approval, but do require filing and archiving. 2210 does away with the category "public appearances" and recategorizes such activities as "retail communications." The new "retail communications" category will not require pre-approval (accept for very specific types of communications) and will require oversight, monitoring, and archiving. 2210 also specifically exempts content in "online interactive electronic forums" from pre-approval. Therefore, tweets, status updates, comments, group postings, etc. in Facebook, Twitter, and LinkedIn will not require pre-approval simply because they are on an "online interactive electronic forum." However, the static profiles will require pre-approval as they will continue to be categorized as advertising content.

One final, important clarification from FINRA Rule 2210 is that retail communications that do not make any financial or investment recommendation or otherwise promote a product or service of the member, irrespective of the number of recipients, also is exempt from pre-approval. This also tells us that anything that *is* recommending or promoting a product or service – regardless if the communication will be on social media or not – will likely still require pre-aproval. Therefore, if the content you're planning on sharing on Facebook, Twitter, or LinkedIn is promoting your services as a financial advisor or something like a seminar that you're presenting that is meant to generate new clients, then that type of social media content will still need to be pre-approved. If it's an event you will be hosting, then pre-compose and submit the promotional status updates with the rest of the material you will already be submitting to compliance for pre-approval. If you're planning on regularly encouraging people to sign up for your newsletter or come in for a complimentary consultation, then put all of those status updates together and get them pre-approved. Once approved, you'll be able to re-use them as long as you make no changes to them.

We are still in the commenting phase on one last amendment to the new proposed rule, however, the bulk of 2210 has been well vetted and commented on and will likely be passed in its current state.

Compliance and SEC Licensed Advisors

For those of you out there who are only registered investment advisors (RIA) and not a hybrid with dual licensure with FINRA, you may be wondering what the hullaballoo is all about because you may have been using social media for quite some time now. In fact, I would hazard a guess that the majority of financial advisors who have been active in social media thus far are RIA. You haven't had someone telling you, "No!" because you're the person who is supposed to be telling you, "No!"

Actually, it's all right if you've been saying, "Yes," to social media if you've been doing everything that you're supposed to be doing when you say, "Yes." Unfortunately, the Securities and Exchange Commission (SEC) has recently learned that proper policies and procedures are often not in place for effective approval, monitoring, and preserving of social media usage in RIA firms of all sizes—solo practitioners and RIAs with many investment advisory representatives (IAR).

Therefore, *go no further* until you have put your policies, procedures, and archiving service in place that specifically address the use of social media by you, your IARs, and administrative staff. You can find the details of their concerns in the National Examination Risk Alert entitled, "Investment Advisor Use of Social Media" (Volume II, Issue 1, 1/4/12).

Of additional note in that Alert is their interpretation of the *Like* buttons used on websites and in social media. Depending on the facts and circumstances of what could potentially be liked on Facebook or on LinkedIn, it could be deemed a client testimonial, which we all know is prohibited by the Advisors Act.

Testimonials

Whether a third-party statement is a testimonial depends upon all of the facts and circumstances relating to the statement. The term *testimonial* is not defined in Rule 206(4)-1(a)(1), but SEC staff consistently interprets that term to include a statement of a client experience with, or endorsement of, an investment advisor. Therefore, the staff believes that, depending on the facts and circumstances, the use of *social plug-ins* such as the *Like* button could be a testimonial under the Advisors Act. Third-party use of the like feature on an investment advisor's social media site could be deemed to be a testimonial if it is an explicit or implicit statement of a client or clients' experience with an investment advisor or IAR. If, for example, the public is invited to like an IAR's biography posted on a social media site, that election could be viewed as a type of testimonial prohibited by rule 206(4)-1(a)(1).

Therefore, you will need to be more careful about what you include in a status update on Facebook and LinkedIn since your networks currently have the capability to click on *Like* of the status update without any control by you. Additionally, you will want to be careful of the website pages on which you use the Facebook Like plugin if you choose to use it. Specifically, keep it off any pages with biographies since that's the example the SEC used!

What Should I Do if I'm Not Allowed to Use Social Media?

As I said in the discussion on FINRA's latest regulatory notice on social media, your social media activities are only required to be supervised if they are business related. It is possible to take a 100 percent personal approach in engaging on social media and get business benefits from it. However, there are very fine lines that you will have to watch and be careful not to cross if you venture down this path.

So, what does this mean? My interpretation is that if you identify yourself as a licensed and practicing financial advisor affiliated with your broker-dealer or DBA on your social media profiles, then that is advertising content requiring pre-approval from your broker-dealer. Any status updates, shared content, messaging, and discussions in groups or forums regarding financial topics would be business-related communications. Any content that is not financial in nature and not directly business development for your financial advisory practice is non-business related. Bottom line: Sharing content about any financial topics is out.

What makes social networks so powerful is the ability to build and strengthen relationships. Once the relationship is created, then you can take business-related communications and activity away from the social network and use approved and authorized channels to actually communicate. Establishing a connection is the first part of the battle. Growing the relationship is the second, and converting the relationship to a client is the third. Just because your broker-dealer isn't allowing you to do the second and third on social media doesn't mean that the ability to do the first isn't valuable. And, to be honest, the freedom that you have by not being allowed to talk business on social networks could potentially be more beneficial because none of your activities are limited and the relationships you build may be stronger because the new people you're interacting with may feel like you have no ulterior motives.

How Does This Work?

It starts with building profiles that don't reference your current financial advisory practice. This is very easy to do with Facebook and Twitter. It's not so easy to do with LinkedIn. I've seen three successful methods of LinkedIn profile building without identifying yourself and your business.

First Method: Simply identify yourself as a *financial services professional* or *financial professional* working at an *undisclosed company* or *self-employed*. Because not all financial occupations require licensing and regulation, that should be generic enough; however if it isn't, then you can also call yourself a *business owner*. Additionally, in the summary or in your position description, mention that your current company and regulatory agency does not allow you to use social networking for advertising and business development purposes and that if someone is interested in learning more about your occupation or business they should send you their contact information and you will contact them through approved business-related channels.

Second Method: If you are involved in a leadership position in a non-profit or community organization that you are committed to, then use your profile to benefit them. List your leadership position as your current position. Then, in the summary section discuss your passion for that mission and your use of a social network profile to benefit their cause instead of promoting your business. If people are interested in learning more about your business, let them know you would be happy to discuss it in another forum.

Third Method: Use another declared business as the basis of your profile and interactions. I have a client who is both a financial advisor and a sales coach. Both are established, legal, and declared businesses. His profiles are all about his sales coaching business. His interactions in groups and status updates are all about helping others become better sales people. Once he's built the relationship, he'll mention to people that he is also a financial advisor. What this has allowed him to do is build a great niche client base of sales professionals and small business owners who saw his expertise in another field and made the leap in thinking that he was likely to be as effective in his main area of expertise—financial planning.

The second part of the non-business-related strategy is focusing on building a solid network of people who are willing to help you. Building that network is what is most important. Once you're connected to them, then you have other contact information you can use to communicate with the connections regarding business-related matters through approved channels. Now, I don't recommend that financial advisors be open networkers to find and connect with people just to be able to cold call them. We'll talk more about effective network building in another section. However, connecting with everyone you meet and have a significant interaction with is definitely the way to go.

The third part of the non-business-related strategy is to use this opportunity to promote and connect the people within your network to the rest of your network to help them with their businesses. Since you can't talk about your business, you're going to need *something* to talk about. Promoting your network, their businesses, and business activities gives you great content that is not self-serving. Additionally, the people in your network are going to be enormously grateful and much more likely to help you with your business through referrals and unsolicited third-party promotion (as long as it's not a static recommendation on your profile about your financial advisory practice). If someone decides to do a spontaneous status update on their profile that will disappear in two weeks about what a great financial advisor you are, then there are no compliance issues as long as you *don't* interact with it. Then, the hope is that some of the shared connections in your network see it, jump on the bandwagon by commenting or liking it, and *whoosh!*—social media works! Huge, viral, temporary, visibility that you weren't involved in, can't control, and can't get rid of until it completes its life cycle or the owner removes it.

The last part of the strategy is to build yourself up as an expert in a non-financial topic that correlates to the expertise you have as a financial advisor or that appeals to the target market you want for your financial advisory practice. That's what my sales coach/financial advisor client did. Another similar topic would be small business ownership (the nonfinancial stuff, of which there is a lot!). Topics of interest to your target market could be as simple as your passion for wine or other interests that may appeal to a wealthier market, or volunteerism that would appeal to those charitably inclined as well as the nonprofits themselves that could be referral sources. It just comes down to knowing your target market.

My final suggestion if you should decide to go the non-business-related social network strategy route (whether you're not allowed to use social media by your broker-dealer or you choose not to in order to not deal with the headache), is to personally invest in an archiving system. Even though you're not discussing business-related stuff, the only way to prove it is to preserve it. A few of the archiving platforms do have individual level accounts that are cost effective (Erado and Arkovi come to mind). These will record all of your social media activity and communications no matter which device you use and are a safety net you cannot afford to go without.

Final Thoughts

Before you go any further, pull out your latest compliance policy on the use of social media. Read through it and if you have any questions about what is meant by anything that appears to be ambiguous, ask your compliance officer to explain what is meant.

I would also recommend reviewing the regulatory notices on social media put out by FINRA and the SEC (depending on which are applicable to you). Although accurate at the time of writing, both FINRA and the SEC are working on more definitive guidelines so that less is up to interpretation. Hopefully, some more of those guidelines have come out by the time you're reading this book. If they have, then our understanding and interpretation may no longer be relevant.

If your policy is still very restrictive, inquire as to the broker-dealer's or firm's intentions and plans with social media. Take a proactive approach and let them know that your use of social media can only benefit them because you're committed to using it responsibly. The vast majority of financial advisors are independent contractors. Adding your broker-dealer's branding to your social media helps them more than it may help you (unless you're operating under your own DBA). They should want it there.

As you read through the book, we will address compliance issues and considerations from time to time. When we can, we will point out areas where there may be different interpretations and approaches by broker-dealers and RIA firms so that you know to take a closer look before taking action. While we strive to be as thorough as possible, only you can have access to your policy and only you are responsible for acting appropriately within that policy. Not every suggested strategy and approach will be deemed acceptable use by every compliance policy; however, our understanding and interpretation is that they do meet the guidelines established by the FINRA, the SEC, or both. This book is written for both solo RIAs and Registered Representatives of broker-dealers. Instead of going with what can be done by the lowest common denominator to be super safe, some of our strategies are designed for and can only be used by the highly ethical independent advisors who are following through with good policy management and recording of their social media activity. Because they fully own the liability of their actions they are able to use the social media tools to their full ability within the limits of the law. We realize that the vast majority of the readers are not in this category, however, we want to demonstrate what is truly possible.

CHAPTER 2

Creating Rapport Online

Matt Halloran

Crystal Thies

Once you have your social media pages up and running, you are posting regularly, and you are getting followers over the social media landscape, you need to follow some social media rules. The first rule is to build and maintain rapport.

What is rapport and why is it so important to create it online? Rapport can be defined as a feeling of connection, of trust, or simply that you are being understood. This is important not only online but also in your everyday activities with clients, prospects, employees, friends, and family. Please do not look at these tips as being just for social media and Internet interaction. They are applicable in all of your fields of business behavior.

The Three Cs

In order to remember how to create rapport, you need to remember what we call the *three Cs*:

1. Connect
2. Communicate
3. Comfort

Connect

Connection with social media—you might be thinking, "Duh, of course!" The type of people with whom you connect and seek to connect is why this part is important. In social media, you have to understand that connecting usually results in full visibility. If you're only using social media for business purposes, then that likely isn't a problem. However, if you're mixing business and personal, then your business connections will see the crazy party pictures posted by friends and family, your escapades in Farmville, and your political debates over the latest scandal. But, even if you're behaving yourself, you still may not be out of the woods. Most of the time, they can see what your connections are saying—particularly about you. Believe it or not, the people you're connected to and the things they say and do on social media does reflect back directly on you. Those prospects who don't know you well will make judgements on that basis alone.

Connecting means slightly different things for each of the three social networks we will talk about, so let's explain the differences.

Twitter. Twitter is the one social network that does not require permission of acceptance to halfway connect. For the most part, you can follow anyone on Twitter and see their tweets without them accepting you first. Additionally, people can follow you without permission. You can block someone from following you if you don't want that person to see your tweets. A full connection on Twitter happens when both parties follow each other; that's now called a Twitter Friend. This also opens up the ability to send private, direct messages. Anyone—whether they are following you or not—can publicly mention you on Twitter, but that message is not attached to your Twitter profile, it's attached to theirs.

Facebook. A Facebook profile has *Friends* and a Facebook fan page has *Likes* or *Fans*. In order for someone to be your friend on Facebook and see your status updates (depending on your privacy settings), you must accept his or her friend request. Facebook has introduced a concept similar to Twitter called *Subscribe*, which allows people to follow and see your activity without permission and without fully connecting and becoming a friend. You have to turn this function on if you want to use it. If you create a fan page, then anyone can like the page and follow the activity (though you can remove them if you choose). However, there is no way for you to connect back to them as a fan page. You can become friends at the personal profile level, but the fan page connection is only one way. Friends and fans can both post messages directly on your profile and page. What they post is attached to both their profile *and* your profile or page.

LinkedIn. LinkedIn has *connections.* In order to connect with someone, one party sends an invitation to connect and the other must accept it. LinkedIn's philosophy is that you should only connect with people you know. If you send an invitation to connect to someone you don't know, that person has the option to click on an *I Don't Know this Person* link and report your activity. If several people click on this link, then LinkedIn will restrict your account requiring you to have the email address of every person you want to invite to connect. Therefore, it's very important that you make appropriate connections in LinkedIn. When you're connected with someone, you see that person's LinkedIn activity and status updates in your news feed. Your connections cannot post directly to your LinkedIn profile; however, they can comment directly on your status updates. These comments are visible for the life of the status update, which is about two weeks. You also have the ability to send them messages directly to your connections through LinkedIn's messaging system.

Let's look at an example of how connecting to the wrong person could be harmful to you. So, let's say you are feeling a little nostalgic and you see that an old high school buddy is on Facebook and he has a fan page. So while you are using Facebook as your fan page, you like his page. He decides to like your page back. Let's also say your friend is a little left wing. He often posts all sorts of inflammatory language and opinions. Your compliance department may see what he is posting. If he decides to rant in a comment about one of your posts about the economy for instance, his post is now on your wall. It is part of your brand, because he is someone you are connected to. You can delete comments and posts to your wall, but not before they are captured by the archiving software you will be required to use. Please be careful of who you connect to.

There are a lot of spammers and they seem to be more prevalent on Twitter. Once you open your Twitter account, you will get a lot of people who will follow you. Many are Twitter parasites. Their goal is to gain as many followers as they can, then blast those followers with spam that they get paid for per click. We know this firsthand because we have had many of these people follow us. Avoid them; they will be an unwanted part of your brand. If you notice anyone particularly unsavory, you can immediately block that person from following you. The rest you can simply ignore because if you don't follow them back, they will usually stop following you within a week or two.

A great strategy to grow your Twitter followers is for you to find people who are your competition or are in your local chamber of commerce. Then, look at their followers and who they are following, and follow those people. Normally, about 50 percent of the people you follow will follow you back. Could you imagine looking on your local president of the chamber of commerce's page and seeing that he follows some quite questionable people? You may learn a lot more about him that you wanted to. People will do this to you, too. So be careful.

Being mindful of those who you are actually following or who follow you is just one aspect of connection. The next level of rapport is to decide on the level at which you connect. With LinkedIn, Facebook, and Twitter, you can specifically target those people who love the same things you do. Matt personally follows many charities, athletic events, and people who help him round out his brand but also feeds his intellect. It is quite easy to find these people who share your hobbies. A quick search in the search engine on any of the big three social media sites will yield a lot of people who you can connect with on a deeper level.

People like to talk about things they like. Pretty simple, isn't it? Wouldn't it be great to have clients that like the same things you like? There is a great rule of business: People like to do business with people they like and have things in common. Instead of always talking about finance, wouldn't it be great if you connected with people talking about, let's say, fly-fishing? Perhaps you are an avid fly fisherman. On your fan page, you may talk about your last trip and share some pictures of the large brown trout you caught. Oh, and by the way, when this is the type of stuff you're talking about on your social media, compliance isn't an issue since it's personal and not business related.

People like to know that there is more to their advisor than just facts, figures, and pie charts. They want to know that you are human and you have a life. So, you post the picture of a trout you caught and one of your clients responds to that post with a picture of the trout she caught. What a great opportunity to post a response and call that client to ask her to go fishing with you and have her bring along a friend who also loves to fish. This is a novel idea that works well. Now you are connecting with your audience (followers) on a personal *and* professional level. Your depth of connection has just increased substantially.

One last word on connecting. Be careful about connecting with competitors. Given the often cutthroat nature of competition between financial advisors—including those in the same office—you want to be certain that you can completely trust those with whom you choose to connect (particularly on

LinkedIn). If you connect with a competitor, they will be able to see your other connections and could go prospecting in your pool and get to a prospect before you. They will also see your status updates and activity and could copy business ideas and strategies from you. We have had it happen to us. So if there is any question of the competitor's level of trustworthiness and ethics, we would recommend against connecting with them.

Communicate

Now that you have made a deeper connection, you need to focus more on what you say, do, and how often you do it. This is how you are going to create a communication strategy to create better rapport. Consistency is key in social media. If you cannot commit to consistently posting information to a social network, then it's better not to do it at all. We can't tell you how many *dead* Facebook pages we see. You tell me what looks better to you: a Facebook page with five posts with the most recent being six months ago, or no Facebook page at all? If you're concerned about the time commitment involved in social media, the best decision is to pick one social network and do it very well, rather than to try and do all three at once and do them poorly.

Later in this book, we will discuss what you can say; most of that will be seriously governed by compliance. Make sure you are using approved materials because you never want to have to ask for forgiveness from your compliance department.

With that in mind, you're going to want to plan out much of what you want to communicate. Any status updates or links to information that is considered advertising material will require preapproval. We recommend planning out a month in advance. Depending on the turnaround time of your compliance department, that means regularly scheduling time in the third or fourth week of the month to compose and submit to your compliance department status updates for the following month. What's even better about thinking this far ahead is that when you get your compliance approval, there are tools that you can use to preschedule the status updates throughout the month so that you don't have to worry about posting them every single day. We'll talk more about those tools later in the time management section.

Several broker-dealers are creating libraries of preapproved status updates for you to use, as well. Such a resource can be great to take the pressure off of coming up with original content if you want to have a high frequency of posting. Now, the planned status updates are great for you to stay compliant and streamline your social media activity so that it doesn't interfere with your actual client work; however, real life interaction and responding to what is happening *now* is what makes social media so valuable. Therefore, you're still going to need to schedule some time every day to look for and reply to comments and responses to your postings. Additionally, you'll want to add non-business-related posts that may be of interest or share the posts of those in your networks to help them out and increase their visibility.

How you actually communicate using social media is a different story altogether. What you say and how often you say it will totally change your social media experience. Once you start posting something on social media you cannot stop, you cannot "unring that bell," as one of my coworkers used to say. If you start posting meaningful things once a week and then you skip a week, people notice! You will be surprised that you will lose followers or people will ask you if you are okay. You train your followers and con-nections to expect information from you at a certain time on a certain day.

As a financial services coach and consultant, Matt often talked to advisors about sending out weekly communications to clients. This is not a new idea created by the company he worked for, but it is a powerful one. His advisors used to send out a market commentary every week. Some would do it on Monday and some focused on Tuesday. They all called it different things because a compelling subject line was a huge part of marketing and branding their companies.

One of the advisors used to email a newsletter every week on Tuesday morning. He always asked Matt, "Do my clients actually read this?" Matt told him about programs that can track how many emails are viewed but he was not interested in actually getting the data. So he decided to skip sending out the newsletter one week to see what happened. His office was flooded with calls and emails asking if the advisor was okay.

These pieces of communication—social media—get legs, too. Remember, this is a web of information. Email content such as market commentary and newsletters end up with clients' CPAs, other advisors, and prospects all the time. So will the content that you share via social media.

So, how do you use this with social media? Well, an approved market commentary or newsletter is a great thing to post on your website and to link to and share with status updates. That is why we brought it up. That sort of pre-approved communication is a great way to get good and practical infor-mation out to your followers on a consistent basis. Use a URL shortener such as www.bitly.com so that you can track how many clicks these commentaries are getting (there will be a greater explanation of Bitly and URL shorteners later in the book).

On LinkedIn and Facebook, you can track how many people like or comment on your post. Status updates are a great way to communicate directly with clients, prospects, centers of influence (COI), or other connections. If a person who is not your client consistently likes or comments on your posts, please reach out to that person and ask if he or she would like to meet to continue the dialogue. You can do this on Facebook and you can also share that post on your page. That, in social media terms, is the most powerful way to see if people really like your posts. Thank anyone who posts, likes, or comments on your posts. This is how you will deepen and communicate effectively with your connections.

With Twitter, it is even easier to see who is liking, favoring, or retweeting your posts. You will be notified in your @mentions, and your retweets will show up there. You can also go to the retweets tab and see who and how many people are retweeting your tweets. This is a great feature to see how many legs your tweets are getting. This is the viral aspect of social media that is somewhat out of your control and can help you out or bite you hard if you are not watching what you are posting.

HASHTAGS

A (#)hashtag is a way to organize and brand your communication (tweets) on Twitter. It allows your followers to search that (#)hashtag to see all of your posts on one page.

Matt will talk about hashtags (#) in the Twitter section, but we would like to address it first here since we are talking about creating rapport with communication. When you are posting something on Twitter, using a # will help you stay organized and brand your Twitter profile. You can use # to search all of your tweets and you can tell your clients that, too. #s are a great Twitter organizational tool. There is no limit to #s; just understand your entire tweet must be 140 characters or less (including any links you want to share). Make them short, meaningful, and branded.

To close out communication, we want to focus on language and tone in your posts. Have you ever gotten a text message or an email that just got under your skin and made you angry? And when you confronted the person about it, perhaps she said, "Oh my stars, I did not mean it *that* way." Now, we know most people do not say, "Oh my stars," anymore unless they are 80 years old, but you get the meaning behind my point. The words you use, words you CAPITALIZE, and jargon can hurt you more than help you.

Keep your communication short and always in a positive tone. Here is an example of negative tone:

Obama does it again, the market tanked today. #markets

Here's another way to say it:

After Obama's speech, markets dropped significantly. #markets

We are not blaming our president here and even if you want to, don't. You can and will lose clients over this post and you can attract some very negative attention surrounding posts like this.

Never post in all capitalized words unless you want to come across as if you are yelling directly in the ear of the person who is reading it. Our professional opinion based on working in this industry for years is that advisors should not ever yell. You want to come across as a steady, even-keeled professional. Professionals in the world of business do not yell, especially in our industry. Jim Cramer aside, you should not capitalize an entire status update, tweet or comment. Given that most social media is in plain text, it is appropriate to capitalize an individual word for emphasis, but stop at one word.

Jargon is always dangerous in social media because you're speaking to everyone. You want everyone to understand you — particularly clients and potential clients. If you fill your social media with industry jargon, the only people who will understand you are your competitors — what good is that?

Here is an example of jargon that can be said another way:

The beta of the S&P is inversely related to the support level of the last two weeks. #markets

You could say:

The S&P seems to be holding at 1250, a number analysts say is a support level. If it goes below that number, the next support is 1129. #markets

Now, we totally made that first sentence up. But we have seen advisors post similar jargon-filled statements in an attempt to look smart. The smartest advisors are able to take complex ideas and terminology and make the average investor understand them.

Remember: Know who your audience is in all your social media communications. Your audience is most likely the general public. Always read every communication aloud before you post (and/or send it to compliance for approval). This goes for both personal and professional communication on social media outlets. If you are concerned your post may have too much jargon, have your assistant, friend, spouse, or office neighbor read it first. Once you type it into a computer and hit *send*, the post will live forever!

Comfort

The last piece of rapport we want to address is comfort. This might seem foreign to you. It did to us at first. When Matt teaches this to people for face-to-face interpersonal communications, this is the most powerful piece he wants his students or clients to learn. But, how does one do this over a cold-hearted medium such as social media?

First, you have to look at how your profile is viewed by others. Using calming colors such as earth-tone colors communicates a sense of comfort. There have been huge and in-depth sociological studies on this. Following are some additional tips:

- Don't use red. Studies show that red can increase whatever emotion a person is feeling. It is also associated with danger, war, blood, and fire. Not things an advisor wants to communicate directly or indirectly with a profile page.
- Not far on the color spectrum from red is orange, which has a very different feel and response. It is associated with joy, warmth, and comfort. This is a great color to use on your pages or in your logo. The Three Cs again are *connection*, *communication*, and *comfort*. Orange is a home run.
- Yellow signifies intellect, cheerfulness, warmth, and warning—a mixed message. If paired with blues and greens, it can be very inviting, but with darker colors such as purple or black it immediately elicits a feeling of warning.
- Green is the color of nature and money. It symbolizes harmony and safety. Green is another home-run color. I know it is the color of money, but you

live in the world of money. It is your tool to help clients live their lives in line with their goals, right?

- Blue represents wisdom and stability. Having a solid or gradated background on your pages can set people at ease and change the tone of your messages. Blue is one of the most powerful colors you can use.

I have worked with many graphic designers and they cannot stress enough how much color plays a part in the perception of brand communication. Remember that you are communicating your brand here, so we want the colors to represent the level of comfort you want to communicate.

LinkedIn does not have the capacity at the time this book was written to change overall color schemes or add graphics, but Facebook profiles and fan pages as well as Twitter backgrounds do. Consider the previous color recommendations when you are setting up your Twitter and Facebook pages.

The last aspect of comfort I want to address is what you want your messages or profile copy to convey. Intention is really important here. Before you write or design anything, make sure you have the right intention. Have you ever listened to a song and you can feel what that person is feeling when she sings? Or, and I assume you are alone so don't worry about answering this aloud, have you ever read a book and been so moved by the words on the page that you started crying (or however you allow yourself to express emotionally)?

Ernest Hemingway said something like, "If I ain't crying when I write it, how can I expect anyone to cry while they are reading it?" Of course, we do not want you to be sobbing during every post because you want to see if you can exercise strong emotional control over all of your followers. We want you to check yourself to see where you are mentally before you post.

With LinkedIn, the comfort comes in the verbiage you use in your profile — particularly your profile Summary. Does it clearly explain what you do, who you are, and who you help so that a non-financial person would understand it and be able to tell others about you? This is a part that many people don't think about. You want to make your message as easy for others to understand, remember, and share with others who need your services.

Another important piece of communicating comfort is spelling. Yes, that means getting back to your roots in elementary school grammar. Watch out for the autocorrect function or over-reliance on spell check. Look words up. Read every post aloud. People get very frustrated when people in verbal communication use the wrong words. When you post something online you do not have the same feedback like you do in face-to-face communication. Making posts positive and plain vanilla is the best thing you can do to increase comfort.

As a sidebar, this applies to all interactions, especially those pertaining to sales. Here is a freebie:

Have you ever watched the Winter Olympics? I know it is not the most popular Olympics, but for those of you who don't watch it, skiers are at the top of the hill, crouched over and moving back and forth. Their eyes are closed; they are all geared up. They are visualizing all the turns and moves they have to make before they hit the starting gate. It has been proven in all forms of athletics (and life) that if you visualize winning and can see yourself on that podium with that gold medal around your neck, you have an exponential increase in the probability of that happening.

You want to do the same sort of visualization with your communications to build rapport. Intention is everything here. If you are trying to be comforting but you are really upset about something, guess what comes through—being upset. Check your frame of mind at the door. Not just with social media but with everything.

If one of the recommendations you made tanks and you made a bad call, but you have a prospect meeting in 15 minutes, do you think that meeting will go well if you are thinking about that decision during the meeting? *No!* Clear your mind and get into the emotion you want to convey when you are trying to build rapport, whether it is face to face or screen to screen.

Final Thoughts

If you always keep the three Cs in mind with all of your online or offline communications, your ability to communicate effectively will increase exponentially! In the next chapter, we will discuss the life lessons we have learned while using social media and how it has changed the way we communicate.

CHAPTER 3

Lessons Learned from Social Media

Matt Halloran

Crystal Thies

Social media has been a very humbling and invigorating part of our life. We have both met some wonderful people who we would now consider friends through social media. Have we ever met them face to face? No. Have we had meaningful conversations over the phone and email? Absolutely. In fact, WE—Matt and Crystal—met via an introduction on LinkedIn and have yet to meet face-to-face. And, we've written a book together!

This is how social media has been humbling; there is always someone out there who has a more engaged follower base and more followers. You will not be number one and you have to be okay with that fact. Matt resigned himself to this reality when he found out there was a snake in New York City that got loose from the zoo. Within days, it had a million followers on Facebook and Twitter. He was overtaken by an animal that cannot talk and that conjures fear in most people? Very depressing until you realize you can look at social media in two ways—as a game of numbers and as a business building tool. Social media has changed the way we communicate. It will change the way you communicate, too, and we believe it's for the better. We will discuss more principles of communication and give you the mindset to use social media effectively.

Lesson #1: People Can Only See Words

The first rule of communication is so important to remember when you are working with a screen and characters. All that people have to judge you by are the words they are reading. Of course, they are reading those words through their own lenses of experience, culture, beliefs, and knowledge. They can't see the twinkle in your eye and your sly smile to know that your message is meant with a hint of sarcasm or playfulness. I touched on this earlier, but it is worth repeating. Once you hit send, your message is out there in the world for all to see, permanently (the Library of Congress is archiving the Twitter stream to preserve it in perpetuity). Even if you delete the post, it can and will be found. This is not to scare you; it is to make you think about what you write before you send it.

Proofread everything, spell check everything, and do not rely on spell check or auto correct. These things can put horrible words in place for you when their intentions are usually great. Not sure that the right message is being conveyed? Then send it to some friends first and ask their opinion. Testing a message first is particularly helpful if your message could be controversial or if it uses obscure humor or double entendres.

Even with the greatest intentions, you need to be ready for misinterpretation. You can use this for a deepening of relationships or you can let it crush you. If you find yourself in a situation where a message has been misinterpreted, it's extremely important that you stay engaged, apologize for the misunderstanding, and do everything possible to try and explain yourself to clear up the wrong interpretations.

When you have hundreds (or thousands) of followers, you have no idea how your message will be received. This is why you need to be prepared for your message to be taken differently than you intended. In fact, social media loves when this happens. It gives you a great opportunity to engage your audience and discuss their opinions, in a compliance-friendly manner, of course. Sometimes the best thing that can happen is someone misreads your post. How you handle this can make your followers stick to you even more. If you say something that is not received in the way you want it, it is not the end of the world. Learn from it and address concerns.

Lesson #2: Social Media is More About Listening

Social media is all about posting and sharing and liking. So, it's all about talking, right? Not necessarily. Believe it or not, it's possible to successfully use social media for sales and business development without massive frequency in posting content. Listening in social media is equally—if not more—important.

Listening in social media is all about seeing and finding opportunities. The types of opportunities that you can uncover by listening include sales opportunities, expertise opportunities, and visibility opportunities. By listening first and talking second, the things you say on social media will have greater weight and lead to a greater return on investment.

First, you should always be listening and paying attention to what is happening with your connections. Your networks will be telling you about those key life moments when they could use your services. When your LinkedIn connections update their profile with a new job or identify themselves as *in transition*, there's an opportunity for a 401(k) rollover. If one of your friends on Facebook changes his relationship status to divorced or married, we know that changes need to be made to their finances and you may have an opportunity. If someone announces a new baby or grandchild on Facebook or Twitter, there could be an opportunity for new life insurance or education funds. If you're not listening for these opportunities, you're going to miss them or someone may beat you to it.

Second, there are tools available where you can monitor keywords that are used in social media posts across all three social networks. By setting up such keyword monitoring, you'll be able to see and find those opportunities where people are literally asking for your help. They could be asking a question about a financial topic and you can answer it. They could also be asking their network to recommend a financial advisor.

The third method of listening is to be aware of what content is being heavily shared so that you're the person who brings it to your network. News articles on developments in the financial markets and economy in addition to other articles of general interest are ideal. If you're one of the first in your sphere of influence to share a super popular article, then your network will retweet, like, or comment on your post, giving you more exposure to their network. If it's spreading like wildfire, then you want to be the person bringing it to your people.

A fourth method of listening is to know what your competition is sharing. The goal is not to copy or share their content, but to do it better and look for opportunities to position and differentiate yourself. If all of your competitors are repeating the same comments and opinions on a current news item, can you bring a unique or different angle to the conversation? If your competition is getting a great response on a particular topic, is there a way that you can do it better or different to get the same benefit?

We have found that strategic listening really is the differentiating factor between exceptional results from social media and average results. That's because you actually have more control. Although you are responding and reacting to something posted by someone else, you are the person who is fanning the fire. Crystal once got a stream of 34 comments going on a LinkedIn status update that belonged to one of her clients. Every time a new person joined into the conversation, she got visibility to their entire network.

Lesson #3: To Be Successful, You Must Be A Social Media Giver

In order to be successful in social media, you have to be a social media giver. A social media giver is someone who retweets, likes, shares, and comments on the status updates of the many people in their network. They are also people who are proactive in referring and introducing people in their network to each other. Think about it; you're going to want your network to do those things for you. The best way to get them to do that is to generously do the same for them.

When you are constantly reaching out and helping the people in your network grow their businesses, then it's going to be a no-brainer for them to reciprocate when you ask. People take notice of who helps them get visibility with their social media efforts and a debt of gratitude can grow as long as the activity is genuine. It's not always going to be a quid pro quo and you will likely be seen as giving a lot more than you get, but is that a bad thing? Being seen as an overly generous person?

Getting others to share content around your business, services, and products is the ultimate goal of social media. Yes, we can and should share our own information, but if others share it about us, then it often has more credibility. Additionally, as a highly regulated financial advisor, your Holy Grail is to have people in your network share original status updates about you and your business that were initiated 100 percent on their own.

Your clients can't post testimonials or recommendations on your LinkedIn profile, Facebook wall, or Facebook page, because they are attached to you and become part of your advertising material. However, if they give a testimonial in a status update or tweet that is only attached to their personal profile and that you didn't initiate by asking them to do it, then you're not responsible from a compliance standpoint. The key is to make certain that if it happens you don't become entangled in it, which means no clicking on the *Like* button or adding a comment thanking them for it.

I've found that the only way to get people in your social networks to become big enough advocates that they would do something like recommend you spontaneously in a status update is for you to already be doing those types of social media activities for them and doing them often.

In addition to creating active advocates of your network, there are some secondary benefits to this type of activity. First, because these status updates aren't business related, it's great content that shouldn't have to be passed by the compliance department first. Second, it gives you great nonfinancial content to share. There is a danger to people not paying attention to your social media if everything is 100 percent financial and business related. When you mix it up and provide a variety of different types of content, people won't assume that you're always pushing a financial message and will read it to see what you have to say.

You have to be a super social media giver. Instead of following the Golden Rule (do unto others as you would have them do unto you), follow the Platinum Rule (do unto others as they would *want* you to do unto them). Before you know it, you'll have a mini army of advocates helping you grow your business.

Lesson #4: Keep Sales Messaging to a Minimum

One last quick lesson is to be careful about the sales messaging. People who do nothing but post overt and subtle *buy* messages will soon find that people stop listening and disconnect. Social media posts that are offering special sales opportunities and free consultations, as well as access to marketing materials like seminars, newsletters, and so on, should comprise no more than 25 percent of the status updates you send into social media.

The scary part is that you might not even know you're turning people off. There are some people who will disconnect/stop following/unlike/

unfriend, but LinkedIn and Facebook both have the ability to *hide* the social media content from specific people without disconnecting. You'll never know if they've hidden you in their news feed. However, if they do, then *game over*. You just lost.

Your network won't mind seeing *buy* messages if they are balanced with other great content and sharing. You'll also find that they will jump in and help get the word out when you have something special—like a financial planning seminar—you are trying to get new people to attend.

People don't want to connect just to be sold to. Yes, I know that your goal in using social media is to get new clients. However, if the only value you see in every person you connect with in social media is their potential to become clients and make you money, then you will soon find yourself in a network of one. Additionally, if this rings true for you, you should really reconsider your decision to be a financial advisor.

Final Thoughts

Since social media is ever evolving, you are certain to continue learning new lessons every day. The most important thing to keep in mind is that it's impossible to completely erase anything posted, so make certain that what you are posting is what best reflects you and your brand. Always assume that everyone can see everything. Yes, there are some privacy settings to hide content from certain eyes, but those settings can be complex and may not work the way you think. Additionally, someone in your network can always take what you've posted and post it somewhere else. It is possible for you to lose your license, your job, get heavily fined, and even go to jail for what you post on social media, so be certain you never say anything that could cause any of those consequences.

Lastly, you get out of social media what you put into it. You have to be involved, you have to be strategic, and you have to be generous. If you keep those three things in mind, you'll never go wrong.

CHAPTER 4

Give Something for Nothing

Matt Halloran

In order to get attention online, especially using social media advertisements, you need to give away something for nothing. We call this intriguing but incomplete information. This does not have to be incomplete planning or financial advice, in which they can only get the full thing if they become a client. In fact, I would recommend just the opposite. Give out meaningful and beneficial information. If you are not going to give it to them, well, they will go somewhere else. There are many different things you can give away, but make them unique. Everyone has retirement calculators on their site; that is not unique. This is where you can share articles, opinions, broker-dealer (BD) approved commentary, or free basic advice. The important thing is, there are so many people who are willing to give away information for attention you need to do the same.

Internet Resources

The advent of the Internet has changed the way we view the value of information. We can find out just about anything we want with simple searches. Before, you had to tolerate that poorly dressed and sometimes smelly *Encyclopedia Britannica* salesperson or you had to go to the library for the information you needed. You can do it now in seconds from the privacy of your home. When I grew up I had to go to my grandparents' house to borrow the encyclopedia to do research for my papers in school. Kids now can find out reliable, and yes, I said *reliable*, information from the Net. Wikipedia can be as accurate as our old encyclopedias. It is strange, but very true.

If I want to find simple financial planning techniques, I can go to hundreds of different sites for free. What will you bring to the table? We will discuss how using social media will allow you to get targeted information to those who want and need to see it. That is the difference between those old moldy encyclopedias and the Internet: Before, I had to hit the books to find the information I was seeking; now, the information can find me.

There is so much out there about saving for retirement, retirement calculators, saving, saving, and more on saving. What else can you offer? Can you offer planning advice? Maybe you can offer a sample plan that people can plug in and play? Make it a skeleton type plan, and of course, if they want more then they have to inquire about your services.

Some of you do this already with your seminars. You provide good but not great information about whatever your education is focused on. This gets people interested in you and makes them want to meet you. They get to see who you are and that you are real and intelligent. We can do that with social media, too. It will be a fun journey!

You need to do this. You need to give people a reason to visit you on social media. Since you are not a star (because if you were you would not be reading this book and you would have a person or team handling your social media), you will need to get their attention.

If you have access to ghostwritten material from your BD or General Agency (GA), that stuff works great. Post a ghostwritten article online and then at the end put something like: For more information or if you have further questions, please call to set up an appointment to talk to a financial services' professional. This ghostwritten material is already compliance approved!

One great resource that I recently learned about for great ghost written content is from Advisor Products Inc. Their website content platform will add eight to twelve new articles per month that you can use on your website and share via social media. Each article is submitted for FINRA approval with three social media updates. The FINRA approval letter is included for you to provide to your compliance department. The best part is that with this content service you get a dashboard that will automatically add the newest articles to your website and automatically send updates with links to the stories on your website to your LinkedIn, Facebook and Twitter accounts. You can manage these processes manually, but the set it and forget it option is great and with writers like Andrew Gluck (CEO of Advisor Products), it's one of the few companies I would trust for set it and forget it content. They will even write custom blog articles for you. For more information visit www.advisorproducts.com.

The best thing I have seen an advisor do is come out with a series of about 20 tips. Each tip builds off the last one. So your readers get hooked. They willingly come back to your pages or your Twitter feed. Later in this book, we will talk about how to set up messaging like that using things like hashtags on Twitter and Notes on Facebook.

We will show you how to set up free events on LinkedIn and Facebook to hold virtual seminars! This will save you a lot of money on those steak dinners you so fondly use to get people in the door. Your conversion ratio will be as high, your costs will be down, and your profit margin per client will go up. How does that sound? More profits, more clients, less time in steak houses? Well as good as a steak sounds to me, I would rather scale my time and maximize technology to get people to make appointments.

Following are some examples of things others have given away for free on social media.

Tweet

Insider Trading by Members of Congress? http://t.co/DrzPIdLs

This is a great example of a tweet because it is a link to a story with an intriguing title. It seems like it is the tweeter's opinion, but it is actually the article's title. It also shows that you are paying attention to topics your clients are interested in.

There is so much to worry about these days—clients really need our help navigating this market!

I like this one because it might not seem like there is free information here, but there is. You are tapping in to client concerns and telling them that you can help them navigate their way through this. Short, sweet, and a powerful tweet.

big bond funds with lots of derivatives in them . . . http://t.co/XLWcsDU0

This one is a little slippery unless you are your own registered investment advisor (RIA). This one slams the BD's tweet. A great and informational marketing tool if you are your own shop.

> Market soars on Europe plans to bail out Greece. We could've seen market bottom at 1074 . . . but it's probably time

There is opinion in this tweet, but it is ambiguous enough to pass a very large BD's compliance scrutiny. Again this shows that you are paying attention and you have an opinion.

Facebook

Most advisors I know post their commentary on the markets on their Facebook page. These are either written by the advisor or a third party. Since Facebook allows a longer stream of characters, it is a better medium to post longer ideas. It also shows how willing you are to give away a lot of information. I would show an example here but you should know what a market commentary is; I am sure you get 20 in your email inbox every Monday.

> "How the Rich Avoid Taxes" . . . and how to fix the problem
> "How the Rich Avoid Taxes" . . . and how to fix the problem October 20, 2011 By Ada . . .

Now these are links to articles this advisor wanted his clients to know. As you know, no matter what side of the line you are on when it comes to your client base, clients like to see if you stand with them.

> An article like this can create good discussion on your Facebook fan page. It is a great way for you to engage your audience (followers) and show responsiveness. Social media is so powerful because it shows that you are not one of those advisors who is sitting on her yacht and not paying attention, all while rolling on a bed of your clients' money. The new way to #invest—not "buy and hold" but "buy and keep buying." Otherwise known as dollar cost averaging.

This is a Facebook post that is mirrored on Twitter. We will talk about how you do this, but it is another great example of a post that shows your willingness to tell people your position on things without raising the compliance eyebrow.

LinkedIn

Well, unlike Twitter and Facebook, people post a lot of free information on LinkedIn. LinkedIn is the place for business and it is done freely. LinkedIn, the site, will show articles based off your professional profile tailored to you. They do this to your clients, too. It is a very crowded place for information. Most people on LinkedIn mirror their information across all their social media sites. We are going to discuss this in each chapter that specifically focuses on the sites themselves.

Most people post articles on LinkedIn. They will go to their favorite news site and click on the *share* button and share the article on their LinkedIn page. Since many and most professionals are on LinkedIn, this is a common practice.

The examples I would show are either reposts of Facebook or Twitter tweets, or article rebroadcasts.

Final Thoughts

There are great examples everywhere on the net of this something for nothing, intriguing but incomplete information. AllExperts.com is a great example. This website is comprised of experts that use their free advice to get clients. Yes, some of it is pro bono work but, again, you have to give to receive.

Make sure that whatever you post—the information you are giving out for free—is compliance approved. Engage your audience, even if it is a comment like, "I would be happy to discuss this with you over the phone, please call. . . ."

You have to get the attention of those who are cluttered with noise using social media. It has to sound and feel like you are talking to them. This does not happen overnight. Look at those who have hundreds if not thousands of followers and see what they are doing right.

The next chapter will focus on the disciplined approach to social media. Social media can be a black hole. I want to make sure you do not fall in and lose productive time.

CHAPTER 5

The Disciplined Approach

Matthew Halloran

Crystal Thies

One of the major concerns we hear from advisors is that social media can be a huge time waster. Most advisors can do a great job wasting time on their own and they do not need another excuse. Time management for any business owner is a challenge. Matt has coached hundreds of advisors on time management to build successful practices. Crystal understands the technology tools that can increase your reach and efficiency with social media within the same amount of time. When you combine Matt's time management techniques with Crystal's technology tools, you can find great benefit from social media marketing without it costing huge amounts of time.

Streamlining Use of Social Media

Have you ever been on Yahoo, Google or other online news sites, saw an article you found interesting, and before you knew it, you were 14 articles in and you forgot what the first article was that you clicked on, and so you wasted an hour? Since you are reading this, we assume there is no one around, and we want you to say, "Yes," out loud to acknowledge this tendency. The linking of online content can take you down unexpected paths resulting in loss of time not in the plan.

Most advisors are on an island and that can be a boring place to be sometimes. Social media can be that thing that makes you feel like you are connected to others like you, who want to feel less alone. This can be a trap.

Compliance specifically states that real time instant messaging (IM) (since it cannot easily be archived) is prohibited. This will quell that desire to IM clients, prospects, or centers of influence. If you want to chat with old high school classmates, friends who are great distances away, or family, do not use your professional social media pages. Create your own personal Facebook or Twitter page for those purposes. You can IM or chat your brains out there; just make sure you are not connecting with clients on those sites, even if they are friends. Separate your social from professional life here. It is safer that way.

It does not matter if clients are friends when it comes to how compliance will view a personal Facebook or Twitter page. They are clients first, in the mind of most compliance officers. Keep them separate. If you want to talk to them, use your official channels or call them on the phone. Yes, that archaic thing called the phone—many people like to use it still; we know it seems strange.

There are many tools that you can use to streamline your use of social media. In this chapter we'll address comprehensive tools that can help you manage the entirety of your social media activity. Sprinkled throughout the remainder of the chapters will be recommendations of third party tools and built in features that can help with specific actions and activities. These tools will do two things for your social media presence. Some of the tools will increase reach and multiply activity without adding to the social media workload. Other tools will provide insight, tracking, and information to help you be more targeted and take advantage of opportunities found on social media.

We can make Facebook, LinkedIn, and Twitter feel more time-friendly by instantly connecting with them through what is called RSS feeds. RSS stands for "Really Simple Syndication." Your clients can use this RSS to keep up with you by subscribing to your RSS feed to receive your content. You can use RSS feeds to read news and keep your pulse on what is going on in our industry without having to spend a lot of time searching for it. Instead of you having to find the news, the news finds you. You can set up RSS feeds on most home pages or use tools like Google Reader and Google Alerts. We bring this up because we want you to streamline your use of not just social media but also of the computer.

Some programs use API (Application Programing Interface), but either programing application they use, it basically works the same. You know you're working with an API when you see "share buttons" attached to articles and other online content you want to share. Share buttons allow you to do an immediate one time post of content your network would like. RSS feeds automate content without you having to initiate it; that's the main difference.

Setting up RSS feeds means that you are syndicating—or sending—your posts to other sites. It can include the full text, images, videos, links, and summarized text (in case it is over 140 characters on Twitter), and can include authorship. Essentially, this means that you can pick one social network to post your updates to and they will automatically show up on the other two social networks without you having to post the update three different times. We will continue to talk about this over the rest of the book based on the type of medium we are using. However, you do have to be careful about how you set up your RSS feeds for sending content to the other social networks because it's very easy to create multiple and duplicate postings. Connections who double post can become irritating and can result in your connections disconnecting or hiding you in their news feeds, so you want to be careful not to do that. RSS feeds and APIs can be great friends when you know how to use them correctly. However, they can also make you look foolish if you use them incorrectly and cost you social media credibility within your network.

Managing Time

There are two different aspects to the managing time equation of social media. First, there's how much time it takes you to do social media. Second, is the timing of when you do social media. Posting to social media is much like a tree falling in the woods—is anybody hearing you? The trick is the coordination of the amount of time you want to spend with the right time to be spending it.

As for your amount of time expectations, what should you expect? How much time should you spend on social media? Is there an average? How much do you want to do? We get asked all the time how much time we spend on social media. We are disciplined with our time and we ask the same of you.

There is no average, or at least in a study we can find, on the amount of time financial advisors spend using social media. We can tell you that there is a learning curve that results in you spending a lot more time when you're first getting started than you will spend on a regular basis once you know what you're doing. That's because you don't know the navigation of the programs and the tools so you have to think about where you need to go, what you need to do, and spend the time looking for it. Once you know that, then you can quickly click through, scroll down, and jump to the parts of the social network platforms you need. If you're new to social media, you can estimate that it will take you half as long to do what you're trying to do today once you know how to use and navigate the programs. The quickest way to cut your time in half is to invest in training.

We can tell you how much time we spend. Matt spends an average of 30 minutes a day total—posting, following, unfollowing, messaging, retweeting, validating, friending, liking, and reading others' posts. Crystal spends approximately an hour or two throughout the day, but her entire business is social media and it is also her main method of client acquisition, so it makes sense that she spends much more time than the average person.

Matt conducts his social media activity in increments of 15 minutes, two times a day. When he gets up in the morning he will check his pages over breakfast and that is also when he does his daily post. He posts on average one time per day. This keeps traffic up on each of his pages; activity is key. Frequency is key. He will scan each of his sites to see if there is anyone he needs to follow back and respond to comments on each of his sites. All social media sites have tools to track your activity. This is like Google Analytics built in to each of the sites. There are also tools that are outside of the sites themselves that can help track your efficacy all the way down to time of day, keywords that are in common, and demographics of those reading your posts.

Crystal conducts her social media in a couple of time blocks and then with mini-checks throughout the day. She spends about a half hour in the morning checking her social network activity for comments and posts that require a response. She also checks her news feed, dashboard monitoring tools, and groups for opportunities to engage. Finally, she uses her dashboard to immediately send or schedule new status updates/posts. She repeats this at lunchtime for about 30 minutes and at the end of the day for 15 minutes. Throughout the day, about once an hour or when she has dead time waiting for a meeting to start, she will skim through her LinkedIn news feed (the social network that has the highest priority) using her computer or smart phone for quick opportunities to interact with her network based on what they are posting.

Matt hears from his advisors all the time that they are already bogged down with email and that adding another "thing" to their lists is just overwhelming. We understand and have seen how much stuff you all get in your inboxes on a daily basis. However, by taking advantage of some of Matt's email management tips, it can free up time that can be dedicated to your social media activities. Here are some of his tips:

Tip No. 1. Not everything that comes into your email inbox is vitally important. You can usually tell with a quick glance what is needed and what is not. If you have others in your office, quickly forward those messages to them and have them deal with responding.

Tip No. 2. Unsubscribe from everything you can. When you go to meetings, presentations, or you just had that wholesaler who had that one thing that you could not live without, unsubscribe! You do not need 400 reports on the market. Whittle it down to less than five. You get so much trash and you know it. Take a week and unsubscribe to as much as you can.

Tip No. 3. Turn off your computers auto-notification sounds for email. You do not need to respond immediately to everything that comes into your email inbox. This will get even worse if you have those notifications on your social media sites. Block off three times a day to check email and voicemail: (1) morning, (2) when you return from lunch, and (3) before you leave for the day. In two of these times, incorporate your social media time.

Bonus Tip. Guess what? All of the above apply to social media, too. If you are reading your Twitter feed and see that there is someone who is just posting like crazy and you do not think it is valuable, you can unfollow them or block their posts. Social media sites want to see who you block or ignore. They use this to fight spammers. The power of social media is it is not corporate or government media; it is your media and we need to help police it. Those few clicks that take seconds can make a huge long-term difference for you and your brothers and sisters on social media.

We know these tips sound too simple, but most advisors are not doing them. Be someone who does. Matt's top advisors, who are using these techniques, say things like, "I thought I had control over email; I did those three things and now feel I control it." Initially, Matt got a lot of resistance with those tips, but once his advisors realized he was right, things changed.

We know advisors are control freaks. This is a good tendency that most advisors *should* have. We all want our advisor to be controlling of our portfolios and hyper sensitive to detail. Take control of your computer before you add more to what you are going to do on it. It will change your relationship with the computer to something you hate to fire up in the morning, to a welcome friend and tool that allows you to communicate with people in a way you control.

Here is one last big picture tip to make this effective and a part of your daily routine. Set a timer. When you get on social media, especially at the beginning, you should set a timer. Use your phone or an egg timer. Matt really likes egg timers because they are really loud and annoying when they go off. Your phone is also a good timer but the relationship you have with your phone is different than an egg timer. Buy and/or bring that old school timer that you have to turn the dial to start into your office; you know, the one that you have to turn past 60 and then back to the number you originally set.

Set it for 15 minutes at a time. Keep it in your line of site. Work as fast as you can for that short burst of time. When you see that you are close to the timer going off, get prepared to exit and close out of your social media sites. You have to be accountable to yourself here. If you have an assistant, when that timer goes off, have them come in and remind you ever so politely to get back to getting ready for prospecting or for that next client meeting.

As for timing, there are optimal times for you to be posting your content and it does differ between the three social networks. There are industry standards based on when there is the highest activity, but it also comes down to knowing your audience.

A prime example of why it's important to be aware of both is with Facebook. If your audience/target market are small business owners, then you want to be posting when they are more likely to be using social media. Since they are fully in control of their situation, that could very well be during the business day. However, if most of your clients and prospects are employed professionals working for large companies, then chances are that Facebook is blocked at work. Therefore, if you want your Facebook posts to be seen, you need to do that in the evening and on the weekends when they aren't at work.

Since LinkedIn is the "professional" social network, most companies allow access to it at work. Therefore, posting during the business day will get the most activity because working professionals use it at work and not as much at home in the evening. First thing in the morning is high activity time as people tend to use LinkedIn while they're having their first cup of coffee and getting started. Over lunch is another popular time. You'll notice the news feed really slowing down after 5:00 P.M. We've also found that Saturday mornings are an active time for people to engage in LinkedIn groups. Since that activity takes more time, some people do save it for home.

Activity for Twitter tends to be more situational. Yes, people tweet general messages all throughout the day, but you will see high activity and people watching around events, happenings, and Twitter activities like Follow Friday (#FF). 4:00 P.M. to 5:00 P.M. on Fridays are one of the busiest hours for Twitter. The World Cup almost broke Twitter. Twitter was just gaining traction for the 2008 Summer Olympics, who knows what will happen for the 2012 Summer Olympics. Are you going to plan to get visibility on Twitter during that time? Don't need that big of an audience with your target market? What conferences, TV shows, and events are important to your market? Tweeting and engaging during those times gets you seen by people you couldn't reach otherwise.

So, if you're doing LinkedIn during the business day, Facebook in the evenings and weekends, and Twitter mixed in throughout, you have to be doing social media 24/7, right?

Social Media Dashboards

One way to save a lot of time and really be in control of your social media strategy is through the use of a social media dashboard. Essentially, a social media dashboard is a software program that allows you to manage all of your social media activity from one place instead of going into each social network and doing duplicate work or worrying about having the updates feed from one to the other. Additionally, they allow you to schedule your status updates to happen at specific times without you being around to do it manually—thereby letting you do social media 24/7 in very small amounts of time. Further, they also allow you to have other staff people or consultants manage your social media without logging directly into your personal accounts.

Some of the social media archiving programs like Actiance, Hearsay Social, and SocialWare have companion social media (or marketing) dashboards that your company can purchase to go along with the necessary archiving program. There are other archiving systems that only deal with the practical side of the need (like Erado and Arkovi) and don't offer the marketing tools because they stay focused on what they do best.

If you're using a system that doesn't provide a companion marketing dashboard, you can consider using some of the other social media dashboards that are created for individuals, small companies, and even small marketing agencies. One thing to keep in mind when picking a dashboard separate from your archiving platform is to test and make certain that the dashboard and archiving platform work together. There are two different types of technology employed with the archiving software—proxy and API. Without getting very technical, we have heard that if your archiving platform is proxy-based, status updates sent by social media dashboards have been and can be missed by the archiving system. Bottom line is to talk to the providers you're using to see if there are known conflicts, or test it well before committing 100%.

Every significant premium social media dashboard available offers a free trial to test it out. They all have different features that combine the ability to post and message, monitor, and measure to some degree or another. Some of the tools are focused mostly on one specific social network (predominantly Twitter) so their features may be limited for the other social networks. This is where it's important for you to know what you want to do most with these social media dashboards. Is posting to all three social networks at the same time what's most important? Or pre-scheduling? Or using auto-posting of RSS feeds? Or watching keywords? Knowing which features are most important to you will help you compare and decide which dashboard to use.

Some of the most popular dashboards are TweetDeck, Seesmic, Social Oomph and HootSuite. TweetDeck and Seesmic are currently free and both offer desktop and web based programs. HootSuite and Social Oomph have limited free levels as well as affordable premium levels with more advanced features. While widely used, these dashboards are limited in their capabilities. However, they do have scheduled posting and monitoring tools.

For more comprehensive social media dashboards, you can look at tools like Send Social Media, Sprout Social, and HubSpot. These are not free tools and some are more affordable than others, though their capabilities are very powerful. Hubspot is a comprehensive "inbound marketing" platform that extends far beyond simple posting. Sprout Social is a comprehensive dashboard that appears to be built with small business owners in mind and provides most integrations and features needed for coordinating posting and monitoring.

Personally, Crystal uses Send Social Media. It's the only dashboard that allows her to have full control of her posting in LinkedIn and is the only affordable dashboard with this level of control in LinkedIn. Not only can she schedule and post status updates, but she can post directly into her groups and specify which tab in the group her item will post to (this will make more sense after you read the chapter on LinkedIn groups). For less than $50 a month, it saves her time and keeps her consistent and fast in getting valuable content out to her network and groups.

In the last chapter, we discussed a content service from Advisor Products Inc. that provides quality ghostwritten articles for your website. It also includes a dashboard that allows you to schedule status updates to all three social networks that are tied to the articles they provide and you can even use it to schedule status updates in general. So, if you want content and social media scheduling, then this tool handles both affordably.

We highly recommend looking into tools like these. Matt talks about some additional tools in the Twitter and Facebook sections that do similar things on a much narrower scale. The dashboards described above can often handle all of those tasks from the smaller programs in one place in addition to other management, measurement, and monitoring functions. Some of the big benefits are the ability to enter your status updates months or weeks in advance and specify exactly when they will go out. Additionally, if there are trusted sources of information and news, you can use RSS feeds to automatically post the articles taking you completely out of the equation. Of course, if you were to set something like that up, you need to make certain it is a source that is safe for distribution to the general public.

The world of social media dashboards and tools is ever changing. The smaller function tools are often gobbled up by the larger dashboards. For this reason, we decided against fully outlining all of the options available and their features. We will, however, have a companion website that is discussed in the final chapter as a place to list, describe, and link to such tools that can be easily changed and updated. For more information about social media dashboard options, go to http://socialmediahandbookfor financialadvisors.com.

Final Thoughts

We wanted to write this chapter with strong language to try to get you to understand how easy it is to lose yourself in social media.

Matt first started using social media about eight years ago, both Facebook and LinkedIn. He was a therapist at the time and had extra time between appointments. Instead of prospecting, which he should have done more vigorously, he just jumped on his Facebook or LinkedIn page to see what was going on.

The next thing he knew, he was watching YouTube videos and listening to music a friend recommended and found a whole hour was gone. He would have to scramble for the file for his next client and prep in minutes. *This can happen to you!* He had not yet thought of the egg timer idea; boy, he wish he had. He would have been a much more successful therapist.

Social media has a way of sucking you in. Limit yourself. Like everything in life, things are good if you do them in moderation. Moderate your social media time; if you don't, it will moderate you. When possible, take advantage of tools to streamline and plan ahead so that you aren't stuck managing all of your social media in real time.

PART II

Twitter

CHAPTER 6

Why Twitter?

Matthew Halloran

WHAT IS TWITTER?

A microblogging social media tool that limits its users to communicating in 140 characters or less.

I first heard about Twitter about three years ago. I was listening to National Public Radio's (NPR) marketplace and they were talking about this new kind of social media that limited its users to 140 characters or less. As an aspiring writer, it seemed interesting to me; what can a person communicate effectively in 140 characters or less? I wanted to give it a try. I was already on LinkedIn and had just started Facebook; how different could this be?

I found out it was very different. This was microbursts of news, quotes, and information. I could scan hundreds of tweets in a matter of minutes. If there was something or someone I wanted to explore, it was only a click away. I thought it was amazing. For anyone who has a short attention span, whether it is from mild or not so mild forms of ADD or ADHD or just because you are busy, Twitter is a great tool for consumption of information.

I want you to keep that last statement in mind. Twitter is to be used to consume information in a timely and efficient manner. There are a lot of websites and Twitter tools that will tell you that you can make copious amounts of money directly off Twitter. I do not agree. They are multilevel marketing companies preying off people who need money. Stay *away*! Buying followers and selling your tweets is, as my grandmother used to say, too good to be true.

Social media, especially Twitter, can be indirectly used to make money and a lot of it by getting your message in front of the right potential clients—teasing them so they want to find out more.

Your state of mind when working on Twitter should be that you are using this social media tool as a means of communicating a message to your clients, prospects, and centers of influence. In today's world of web-based everything, you as a financial services professional need to meet your clients where they want to be when it comes to how they digest communication.

> **READ IN A CLICK!**
>
> Twitter is like a weekly newsletter that just takes a click to read more.

Texting and Tweeting

Why does Twitter allow only 140 characters or less? The founders of Twitter wanted tweeting to be like text messaging, which they believed was going to change the way we communicated. Boy, were they right with that one! Texting has changed an entire generation's way of communicating. Text speak has found its way into so much of our daily communication. My wife, who is a high school science teacher, texts me with this new form of speaking; I usually need to ask her to tell me what different capital letters signify. You need to be open to this new speak; it does not replace what you actually say, verbally, to people, but it will change the way you tweet.

With that said, to truly interact on Twitter you will need to familiarize yourself with basic text speak. It is used widely in most tweets. There are great references online about translating text speak. I would bookmark the website www.lingo2word.com and reference it regularly, especially if you know a teenager. This site will help you shorten your tweets, too. I have used this tool many times and find it user friendly and helpful. You can choose a program to manage Twitter after you have gotten it set up, but it is not necessary. If you do decide to use one, you can click one button and it will find words that it can turn into text speak for you.

WHAT IS BITLY?

Bitly is a great tool to shorten long web addresses so you can tweet them.

Twitter continues to grow in users and tweets exponentially. It sometimes crashes due to high traffic (too many tweets). This is called a *failed whale*—why, I have no idea, but that is what they call it. A whale with birds carrying it will show up on your screen when Twitter servers cannot handle the number of tweets. I think this is going to be a new normal.

WHAT'S A WHALE?

If you get a whale showing up on your screen when you are using Twitter, just wait a second and refresh the screen. Twitter got overwhelmed.

Setting Up Your Account

Reliance upon outside facilitated means of communication rescinds a lot of control from its users. With all of that said, you want to use it. I will show you step-by-step how to set up your account, what to say on your bio page, who to connect with, how to gain more followers, what following and unfollowing mean, where to get your account listed after it is set up, what to say with your tweets, and how to prospect using Twitter. Following are the steps required to set up your Twitter account.

Step 1: Registration

Type www.twitter.com into your web browser.

Figure 6.1 shows the screen you should see, but this changes often due to Twitter updating their home page.

FIGURE 6.1 Twitter Home Page

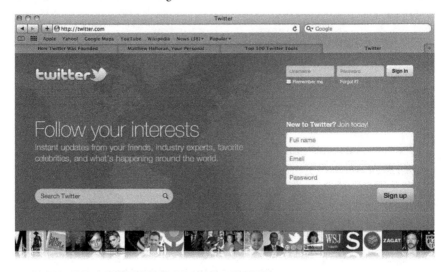

FIGURE 6.2 Registration Page

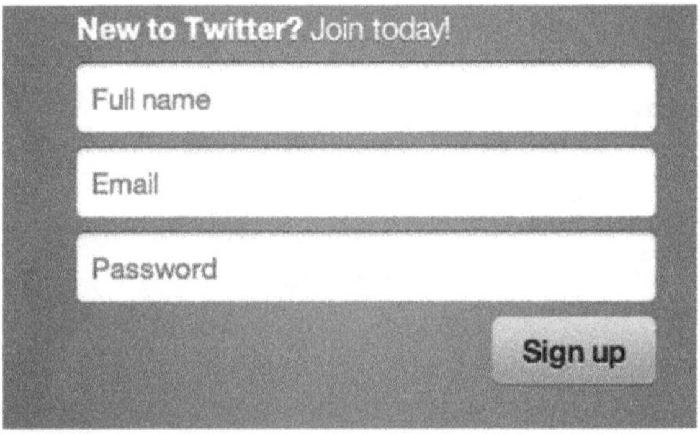

The important thing to look for is the registration page, as shown in Figure 6.2. This is where you start the whole process of getting signed up and starting your life as a twitterer today!

After you finish registration, you will need to create a Twitter *handle*. This can be the name of your company, your name, or your process.

FIGURE 6.3 Twitter's Completed Registration Page

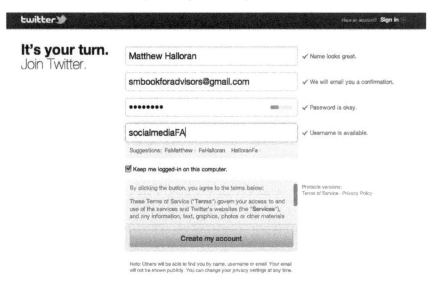

So many handles are already taken that you may have to try a few different ones before you find one you are comfortable using. This is branding 101. Think about what you want to be known as. We will refer back to this name when we discuss Facebook and LinkedIn. Twitter will tell you immediately if the handle you chose is available. Do not pick names that are personal jokes or terms that people will not understand. It needs to be clear to your followers that this term refers to you or your company.

For example, if your company name is also your name and you see that your name is taken, you can put an *LLC* at the end. There are few people who do that on Twitter and this will allow your followers to identify you as a business, not just a person on Twitter.

After all of the prompts on the right-hand side of the registration page (all those check marks go from red to green), you can click on the *Create my account* button, which is yellow and at the bottom of the screen, and your account will be live! (See Figure 6.3.)

After you click on that yellow button, you are now officially on social media. You are a tweep, a twitterer, a hip cool person who will gain more friends, and be liked by more people than ever before. Once registered, you will be taken to a screen; this is your home screen.

FIGURE 6.4 Twitter Search

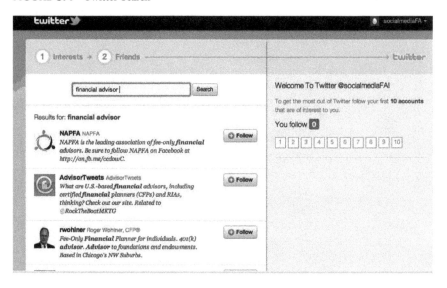

Step 2: Choosing Tweeps to Follow

The screens shown in Figures 6.4 and 6.5 are important for your greater understanding of Twitter and how it works. You will want to search topics using the search bar to learn what tweets are all about in your area of interest. I assume you will want to search for tweets related to financial advising. Type in *financial advisor* in the search bar, and then click on *search*.

This is your first opportunity to see who is listed, generally by number of followers, and who is already using Twitter under the guise of a financial advisor. You can follow any of these people with a quick click of the follow button. I recommend you follow organizations that you already belong to and not other advisors. Who you follow is very important because it says a lot to your followers about your brand. The last thing you want to do as an advisor is follow someone questionable in our industry. This can backfire quickly.

FOLLOWING ORGANIZATIONS

Follow organizations you are a member of on Twitter. Use the search function to find CFP, NAPFA, MDRT, and your BD.

FIGURE 6.5 Twitter Profile Page

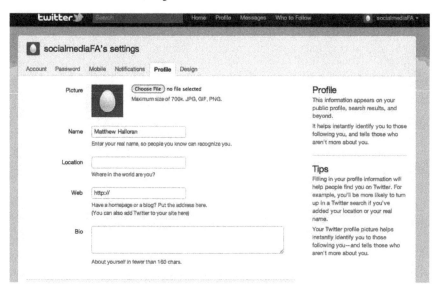

Now that you have started following some tweeps (Twitter participants—by the way, you are a tweep now), you have to understand that they might not follow you back right away, or in some cases ever. I do not think this is a good practice for people not to follow you back, but that is just my opinion. Many businesses do not follow you back, but if you find their tweets informative and beneficial, keep following them. I suggest you follow back everyone that follows you. Unless you are a celebrity, you will always follow more people than follow you.

I would suggest you follow your broker-dealer or the person who you clear through if you are a registered investment advisor (RIA). If there are products or services that you use and believe in, follow them, too. You can always unfollow them later if their product or service is discontinued.

Step 3: Setting Up Your ProfileTwitter

Twitter wants you to follow at least 10 people to start. Find 10 people to follow and then go to the email sent to you after you signed up at Twitter to confirm who you are. After you click on the confirm link, a screen will pop up asking you to set up your Twitter profile. You will be prompted to write your first tweet, and access your Twitter account on your phone or other mobile device.

I do not want you to write your first tweet yet. First, I want you to set up your profile and upload a profile picture as shown in Figure 6.5. You cannot keep your Twitter profile as an egg, which is the default image. This does not bode well for you. You have to have a custom picture. I recommend if you are a solo practitioner to use a professional headshot of yourself. If you own a branded (which means having a logo) company, use the company's logo. Choose that professional picture or your company's logo and then upload it.

Next, you will be taken to your profile page. Here you will include basic information that will help communicate your brand and also help people to find you for what you do.

Use your professional name. If you have a professional website, please put the URL in the box titled *Web*.

This all seems simple enough and self-explanatory. The *Bio* section, which allows only 160 characters, may be a different and difficult animal to wrestle.

Your bio needs to have keywords about what services you provide and what makes you different. It needs to be in narrative form. Here are a few examples:

- I am a certified financial planner who specializes in helping mid-size business owners plan for the present and their long-term business growth. (144 characters)
- With 20 years of personal financial services experience, I have helped hundreds of people retire. Are you ready for retirement? If yes, follow me and I will help *you*. (162 characters)
- As a stockbroker, I live, eat, and breathe the stock market. Sure you can do it on your own, but shouldn't you have a pro in your corner just in case? (150 characters)
- As a professional risk manager, I help remove the worry surrounding unexpected life events. Let me help you help your family. (126 characters)

RESTRICTIONS

All social media restricts the number of characters you can use to identify yourself. Keep this in mind and be succinct.

You do not need to use up all 160 characters here. Your description needs to be a powerful and compelling statement. It also needs to be approved by your compliance department. If you have an approved bio that is used on your company's website, you might have to use that. Compliance will start loosening the reigns soon so you can create something that is more *you* without making ridiculous claims that you know will get you in trouble.

Step 4: Twitter Tools

Now that you have your account set up it is time for you to learn how to use a few of the available tools to help you focus your Twitter efforts to get your brand in front of the right people.

Ask yourself the following questions.

1. What is the scale and reach of my company? How big of a geographic area do I want to cover? Am I going to be a local, regional, or nationally marketed company?
2. Do I want to gain a mass amount of followers or do I want to keep my Twitter account mainly to my clients, CIOs, and prospects?

WHAT IS YOUR REACH?

Advisors need to think of their scope and reach with social media; do you want to be local, regional, or national?

The first question in very important because it will change how and who you follow. Using tools like www.tweetbig.com and www.tweepi.com can help you find the right people to follow, auto-follow them for you, and unfollow those who do not follow you back. I will address these tools more in the next chapter.

Piggybacking is one of the best things any advisor can do to make sure that those tweeps that are following him or her are worth the follow. You can do this manually by finding an advisor in your area that is currently on Twitter or looking at people in your area you want to prospect.

So let's say you find a local advisor who is on Twitter and that advisor has 400 followers and is following 250 people. Go to that advisor's Twitter page by clicking on his Twitter name, look on the right-hand side of the screen toward the top of the page and you will see links to *following* and *followers*.

After you click on *following*, you will be able to see everyone that advisor is following. This is a much more appropriate count of who that advisor values because he is following them. That is a deliberate action. *Followers*, on the other hand, are not deliberate; they are passive, and you have little control over who follows you. Many people have a lot of followers who are not of value because they are spammers or people just trying to increase numbers.

WHO TO FOLLOW?

Find an advisor/company in your area whose followers you want to prospect. Click on their profile and then click on *followers*. Start following the people they follow! You will start using Twitter in a powerful way!

On Twitter you want quality followers and people you follow because it does help you brand. It is not just your picture or the short explanation of who you are or what you do that tells people who you are. People can tell a lot about you by who you are following.

It would be wise to follow any professional publications you read, blogs, magazines, your broker-dealer (BD), products you use, associations such as Certified Financial Planner Board, or Financial Planning Association (FPA), and if you are interested in social organizations such as Relay for Life or the American Red Cross, you should include them, too. You can get bite-sized pieces of information from these tweeps and it can keep you up to speed on what is going on with them. Remember, memberships can round out your brand, but if you are an active member of a questionable group, do not follow them unless you want others to know you are a member or support them.

I was working with an advisor and helping him brand. He was from the deep south and was having issues with some of the questions I posed. They were kind of touchy feely questions, but they were important to answer because it revealed who he was and how he did business. I asked him about social organizations or movements he believed in so strongly that he would volunteer or donate money to their causes, and assured him there would be no consequences to his answers, no one would find out, and he would not get in trouble. He got really quiet. This is usually a good sign as a coach, because the other person is either thinking hard or checking his email. The latter was not the case in this interaction. He said, "I have never said anything about this before." I reassured him he was in a safe and confidential place and that I was not there to judge. He continued, "Have you ever heard of the United Front?" I replied in the affirmative. The United Front, which I had thought disbanded years ago, was a right-wing neo-Nazi group much like the KKK but more heavily armed. He said, "I am a member and have been for years." I asked him why he was a member and he gave the standard response I expected: "A well rehearsed call to action," in other words, it was something he memorized to say to get people motivated and on his side.

You should not follow people like this on Twitter. Remember, who you follow is part of your brand.

This is a great example of what can lie underneath the surface that should not be used publicly as part of your brand. I am sure there are things you believe in or that interest you, but that does not mean you need to broadcast all of them to the twitterverse. Twitter is very public and what you post can go viral quickly. The last thing you need is your face all over the net as a morally questionable financial advisor. You will probably get attention that you do not want.

The second question is one of prestige. There is a certain prestige with those who have over 5,000 followers. This number is going up, but it can make you look quite important if you have many followers. This again is coupled with your reach. You can be a small boutique firm that only caters to a specific niche or you can be a company that helps anyone who needs financial advice.

Figure 6.6 shows my personal Twitter account page. It shows how many people at the time were following me and how many people I was following. It also shows how many tweets I have tweeted.

I created the @FAmediabuilder's page in Figure 6.7 to show you how to set up your account. Like many professionals, I have more than one account. @The_Life_Coach is my personal account.

Direct Messages

You need to familiarize yourself with the following term: *DM*. DM (direct message) is a message that is sent directly to one of your followers. This tweet is only seen by the tweep you want to talk to. I use DM with a standard greeting to all those who follow me. So when I get new followers,

FIGURE 6.6   Personal Twitter Account Page

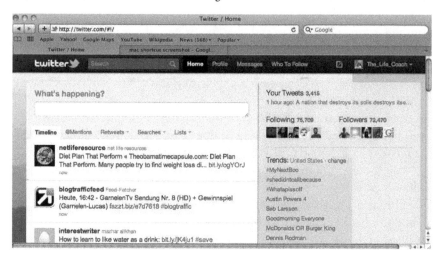

FIGURE 6.7   @FAMediabuilder

Socialoomph.com (one of the tools I will talk more about in the next chapter) sends them a DM thanking them for the follow and directs them to my Facebook page to see if they will *like* me there. I am making my web of connection stronger and stickier by having my followers connect with me in more than one place.

If someone DMs you and it does not seem like it comes from a live person, do not respond; they are spammers. If they use your name or make a comment about your page or your message, please take the time to respond to them. They will realize you are real and an active Twitter user. It will make the connection deeper and stickier. In the following, I present a few examples of a real person DMing me, as well as a spammer. I will usually unfollow spammers if they DM me more than once with a spam message.

WHAT'S A DM?

DM = Direct message; it is a message sent only to the person you are messaging, it does not end up in your Twitter feed or timeline.

There are many places you can direct people to in your direct message; for instance, you can direct them to your website if you would like.

Following are some examples of DMs that advisors can use to contact followers. Remember, you only have 140 characters:

- Thank you for following me! I provide comprehensive financial advice. If there is anything I can help you with, please DM me!
- I help families plan for unexpected life events. I hope you find my tweets helpful and informative. (Enter link to your website here.)
- Thanks for following me! I will look at your profile and check out your tweets.
- As a financial planner who loves helping others, I will tweet planning tips to help you plan for your financial future.
- It is great to connect here. If you want to know more about who we are and what we do please check out our website at [insert URL here].

Retweets

Now that you are starting to get followers, what's next? This is a question I get all the time from advisors. You have to keep in mind the nature of Twitter here. You might get as many clients or prospects from Twitter as you have from advertising in the Yellow Pages. This is a communication tool with latent prospecting abilities. You want to use your Twitter account to drive prospects and clients to another page—for instance, your website, Facebook page, or LinkedIn profile. Twitter should never be the final destination for your following.

WHAT'S AN RT?

RT = a retweet—posting a tweet that someone you are following tweeted. This will go into your timeline with credit to the original tweeter.

One of the best things you can do to make your Twitter followers stick and continue to follow you is RT. RT = retweeting. This means that you are going to post what they posted on their Twitter page on your Twitter page, thereby giving credit to their Twitter account.

Tweeps love this. It is free exposure for them to a whole other set of people they have never been introduced to on Twitter. If you get RTed make sure you reply to that tweet and thank them.

Hashtags

There are so many other things that you can do with Twitter that there is no way to cover them all considering how quickly things change. I am sure that since this book has published there have been great advancements. I will leave you with one great organizational tool that can help your followers follow everything you say and find you very quickly. It is called the hashtag (#). This is an underused tool for organization and marketing.

WHAT'S A HASHTAG?

= hashtag—a way for people on Twitter to organize their tweets and allow them to be searchable by that hashtag keyword.

Advisors I work with have used many hashtags. You can use the name of your company, your first name, your process, or a word that is short, meaningful, and memorable. You do need to make it distinct so that others are not using it to muddy up your organizational waters.

Examples: #advsiorzen, #financialplanning, #defensefirst, #planningadvice, #finance, #retirement.

By using hashtags you can filter only the tweets that have that hashtag. Type the hashtag into the search bar at the top of your Twitter screen and you will see how many tweets have been tweeted with that hashtag.

Final Thoughts

Twitter is one of the easiest social media networks to use. It has kept itself simple for one reason—everybody can use it. If you know how to text message, then you can tweet. Following are a few simple reminders of what you should know about Twitter.

1. Use a good picture (professional) of yourself or use your company logo.
2. Your description should be your mission statement or tag line that has been approved by compliance.
3. Tweet things that are of value to your clients and prospects. Do not tell them unimportant things about your day.
4. Use Twitter tools to make your life easier on Twitter. Auto-DM and auto-follow programs are great.
5. Respond personally to personal DMs. This way the tweep will know you are real and not a spammer.
6. Find the right followers and check who you are following. You can find the right followers by piggybacking on another advisor and following the people they follow.
7. If someone RTs you, thank them for the RT by replying to their tweet and saying something nice.
8. Use hashtags to track the conversations you are having on Twitter; this is great for organization and can be used for marketing purposes.

In the next chapter, we will continue on our journey with Twitter as our companion. We will start looking at effective use of this wonderful social media tool!

CHAPTER 7

Marketing on Twitter

Matthew Halloran

Twitter was going to change everything for everyone in every way. In 140 characters or less you were going to be able to change the way people looked at your business and the world.

Well, the second one came true. Due to Twitter, governments have been overthrown, political winds have changed, and news reporters are almost obsolete. However, the first part about business did not.

Regulations and Restrictions

You need to have a presence on Twitter. You should gain followers, follow people back, retweet often, and thank those who retweet you. Is this enough to gain new clients? I for one do not think so, at least not directly.

If you sell widgets and have followers that want your widgets or are in the widget buying business, then Twitter can be a good tool. If you are an author trying to get people to buy your book or read your article, Twitter is great. If you are a musician and just want people to listen to your music, Twitter has changed lives. But as an advice giver, a professional that is heavily regulated by the Financial Industry Regulatory Authority (FINRA), it is tough for you to add value without getting in trouble.

It seems interesting that doctors who are on Twitter can provide medical advice to their followers. Now, their tweets may not be specific to you as a patient, but there are some interesting posts out there. There are no disclosures from the American Medical Association (AMA). They give plain advice, some of which is questionable. I have read about how to cure the common cold and just about every other ailment through Twitter. Do these suggestions work? Well, I would not bet my health on it.

So why is it that you can give advice that can kill someone, but you cannot tweet about what to do when the market gets all screwy? Or that you are watching the foreign markets to see if there are indications of a trend? Or that you just came back from a conference and got a great new product idea that you believe could help your retiring clients? As of this writing, these are regulated by compliance, mostly out of ignorance and fear.

With all that said, Twitter is a great way to drive people to your Facebook fan page or your LinkedIn account. You can mass follow people on Twitter and get your number of followers up fast. This is the power of using Twitter as a marketing tool—*numbers*.

TWITTER IS A MARKETING DRIVER.

It takes your prospects by the hand and leads them to the information you really want them to see.

Twellow

There are some great tools you can use to get Twitter working for you quickly.

First, include your Twitter handle on the signature line on your business cards, letterhead, website, and whatever else you can put it on.

Second, list your account on the Twitter yellow pages and directories at www.twellow.com. Twellow (see Figure 7.1) is the biggest and most widely used directory. It is indexed by the number of followers and sorted into categories using keywords from your profile. The more followers you have the closer to the first page you will be.

Twellow is a great tool that can help you find out who in your professional area is on Twitter. Sign up for Twellow by clicking on the *Join Twellow* link (the yellow button).

FIGURE 7.1   Twellow

As with all social media, it will ask you to fill out some basic information and use that *captcha* code again. But once you are in, you can start poking around and get your Twitter account listed in the correct categories. Twellow will automatically categorize you by your Twitter profile information, but you are allowed up to 10 categories. You can add yourself to other categories manually. There are a lot of them so use the following steps to narrow them down:

- Using the search function, find the category you want to add yourself to such as:
  - Business Services: Business Planning and/or Business Trusts (if that is your area of business)
  - Financial Advisors—choose from the following:
    - Financial Advisors
    - Personal Finance
    - Money Coaches
    - Financial Counselors
    - Wealth Management
    - Financial Planners
  - Insurance: Risk Management

- Investing—choose from the following:
  - Investors
  - Responsible Investing
  - Investment Opportunities
  - Stock Trading
- Personal Finance—choose Wealth
- Small Business—choose Small Business Owner

CAPTCHA CODE

The captcha code is a security screening device that stops computer spamming bots from opening up dummy accounts. It also helps stop spam.

You will want to list yourself under each of these major categories. If you are passionate about a hobby, list yourself there, too. Be careful because at the beginning, you can only list yourself in 10 categories. Be specific and targeted, as you should with all marketing.

WHAT DO YOU CALL YOURSELF?

Whatever you call yourself, see if there is a Twellow category for that name. If it is not there, you should reconsider how you refer to yourself professionally.

Twellow is constantly changing their categories so check back and log in often.

Now, how can you use Twellow to help you market? Since you have listed yourself in many categories, see who else is listed in those categories. You can directly follow your competition or you can click on their Twitter profile and see who they are following, and then follow the same people. This is how you can gain followers and prospect your local competition!

Before you leave Twellow, do some more searching for people in your geographical area who are financial advisors and write down on a separate piece of paper their Twitter handles. You will use this information to your advantage with another tool I'll cover later in this chapter.

FIGURE 7.2   Bitly

Formulists and Bitly

Formulists (www.formulists.com) is another Twitter tool that will help you to organize your followers into categories. Chief information officers (CIOs), clients, prospects, networkers, referrers, and top clients are just a few lists you need to create to keep yourself organized. These lists allow you to sort the tweets within each group so that you can take the pulse of these followers quickly and see what they are doing.

Another tool I want to highlight is bitly (http://bitly.com; see Figure 7.2).

This tool shortens your URLs and also tracks the number of clicks on each one. Remember, Twitter only allows 140 characters or less. URLs can be very long. If you want to redirect your tweeps to an article or a featured part of your site, or invite them to an event, shortening the URL can leave you enough characters to write a post that will entice the tweep to click on the link to find out more.

WHAT'S A URL?

URL = Uniform Resource Locator. This is your web address.

The best thing about bitly is that it lets you customize your shortened URL. This can help you with brand consistency and help you get your brand out there. Name recognition is really powerful with a customized URL.

Two Recommended Tools

I discussed auto follow, piggybacking, and unfollowing in the previous chapter. You can decide to do these things yourself or you can pay a company a small fee to do these things for you. As a coach who has worked with hundreds of advisors, I always recommend delegating this work, especially if it is to someone you can trust. You will be told about Twitter tools often while you are on the site but most of them do roughly the same things. Some tools have features that will resonate with you more than others. Since I have vetted many tools, following are the two I will discuss and recommend for you to use.

These two tools are quite different than Twellow or Bitly. These are tools that will both increase and maintain your Twitter base.

SocialOomph (www.socialoomph.com) is the first tool I recommend (see Figure 7.3). With SocialOomph, when someone follows you, you can send that person an automatic *direct message* (DM). This is a great tool to

FIGURE 7.3   SocialOomph

FIGURE 7.4   Direct Message

connect with someone quickly by sending him an automatic thank-you message. You can use this tool for free. I use it just for managing my direct messages.

Figure 7.3 shows what the page looks like. You need to click on the *Register* link at the top right-hand side of the page. Make sure you check out all the free things you get just for signing up.

After you successfully register, click on the *Direct Messages* link and next on *Edit Welcome DM* (see Figure 7.4).

WHAT'S A DM?

DM = direct message. A message you can send to an individual tweep directly without it showing up in your timeline.

In the previous chapter, I gave some DM guidelines and examples. You should change your DM at least one time per quarter just to keep it fresh and up to date. Your DM needs to be 140 characters or less so think about what you want your first piece of communication to be when someone connects with you. It needs to be thankful, intriguing, and personalized.

FIGURE 7.5   TweetBig

Following is my DM:

If you would like to see the commentary on the quotes each date, like my page on http://www.facebook.com/personaltelescope. Thank you!

I have checked two boxes on this page—one to say I want this message sent automatically to new followers and another to say that I choose to automatically follow people who follow me from this point forward. At the bottom of this page is the *Optional @ Replies Digest Email* option. For compliance reasons you should always check this box so that all @ communication that mentions you on Twitter is sent to your formal compliance-archiving email address. Remember, you should have every piece of communication sent to your compliance department in order to cover yourself.

The second tool I use to increase my followers and to maintain my account is TweetBig (www.tweetbig.com), shown in Figure 7.5. I really like this tool because it is quite inexpensive (there is not a free version) and very robust. I use this tool to find people to follow, unfollow people who do not follow me back within a specific time that I set, and to allow me to follow people by keywords.

If you are going to effectively use Twitter without it taking up hours from your day, you need a tool like this.

FIGURE 7.6 TweetBig Piggyback Tool

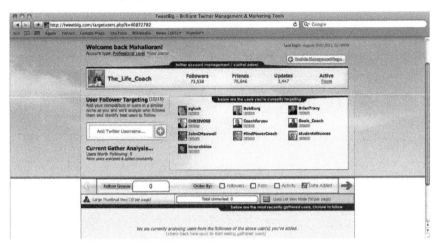

TweetBig includes six different categories (see Figure 7.6). They are easy to use and make sense intuitively. The first one I want you to look at is the *piggyback* tool.

Since you have just been on Twellow, you can put the Twitter usernames in this tool and start to automatically follow their followers. You wrote them down on that separate piece of paper, right? This tool will analyze their followers and find ones that you should follow.

So you add those tweeps from your paper in the box and click the + button. Next, the program will give you lists of people that you should follow based on who they follow or who follow them. This can allow you to be very targeted in who you choose to follow!

The second tool on TweetBig that is great for gaining followers is the *Keyword Gathering* tool. It is called *TwitHawk*. This is another way to focus on what people are saying right now.

You can create up to 15 keywords to focus on (see Figure 7.7). This is very powerful for advisors. What this tool does is go through all tweets in the twitterverse and look for the keywords you selected. Now, my keywords may be different than what you would want, so the following are some keywords that will help you focus on and follow the right people. Remember, these are words you want potential clients to use, not words that are focused on you as an advisor.

FIGURE 7.7 TwitHawk

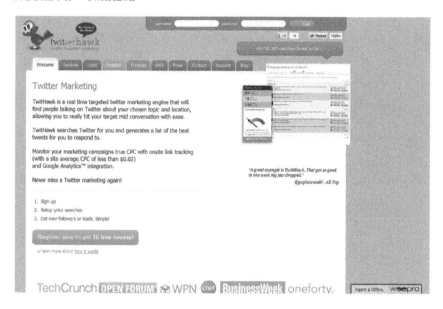

retiring, roll over, investments, financial planner, "can't retire," economy, stock market, loss, safety, guarantee, recession, double dip, jobs, unemployment, fed, Ben Bernanke, government, stimulus, bailout, Tim Geithner, Obama, unemployment checks, rollover, 401(k), 403(b), 457, deferred compensation (or *comp*), pension, defined benefit, defined contribution, savings, withdrawals, annuity, CD, structured note, real estate, commodity (commodities), futures, or mutual funds.

Since you are probably frugal, as most advisors are, you most likely did not pay for TwitHawk. These tools let you accomplish the same thing without paying for it. If you find a person who has tweeted about something that you can help them with, you can reply to their tweet using @reply (the @symbol and their name) and "talk" to him or her.

There is a website called Social Mention (www.socialmention.com) that can check the effectiveness, sentiment, reach, and top users of these keywords (see Figure 7.8). You can also check the effectiveness and use of # (hashtags). After you type in the keyword, you can see who posted it and how long ago.

FIGURE 7.8 Social Mention

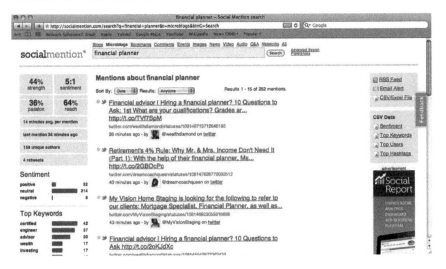

Unfollowing and Blocking

Unfollowing people is important because it removes spammers and people who are not actively following your account(s). It is also helpful in keeping your follower-to-following ratio in line. As a social rule, you should always follow more people than are following you. This applies only if you are not a celebrity, which we already covered.

There is something called an API limit in Twitter. This limit stops spammers from following too many people or Tweeting too often. Do not get on their radar; you do not want to get marked as a spammer.

People who are not active on Twitter are not the followers you want. We want to communicate with people who like communicating on Twitter. So if they are not very active, Twitter is not their preferred means of social media communication. Some people like Twitter because of its short bursts of information. If they are not paying attention to the tweets, you do not want to follow them. They could be spammers.

If you are following a person that you find never sends tweets, click on her picture and see when the last time she tweeted was. If it has been over two months, consider her off Twitter for all intents and purposes.

If there is someone getting through your filters and filling up your Twitter timeline with stuff you don't care about, or if someone is trying to sell you something, you have recourse. You can block that person and report the account as a spammer. Please take the time to do this if you see it happening. Twitter has its own police, but the most effective police person is you and your fellow tweeps.

IS IT SPAM?

Twitter is a system that is best when it polices itself; if you are getting dehumanized tweets selling you some random thing, report that account as a spammer to Twitter.

Here is an example of how I blocked and reported someone as a spammer. There has been a serious spam issue with something called the Trump Network. It is a multilevel marketing program that seems quite shady, as most of those multilevel things are.

First, I clicked on his name and found his profile. There was a person icon to the far right next to the button shown in Figure 7.9. You will click on that to see a drop-down menu, which lists:

Mention
Add to List

FIGURE 7.9 Block and Report Spam

Block

Report

You want to click on *report* for spam. This will unfollow, block, and report for spam all in one click. Please help your fellow tweeps report spam on Twitter. It makes Twitter a better place for all.

Tweet Scheduler and TweetDeck

Ever wondered how people tweet when they should be sleeping? Well, I am sure you don't, but in case you want to set up tweets while you are on vacation, you can with the *Tweet Scheduler* tool (see Figure 7.10).

This is a great tool to help you prepare for upcoming events such as seminar advertisements, holiday greetings, an anniversary of your firm, or attendance at a workshop or conference.

TWITTER AND COMPLIANCE

Compliance wants to know what you are tweeting; use a tweet scheduling tool to give compliance time to approve your tweets.

Since compliance does not want you to tweet impulsively or in an untimely manner, this can be a great way to pacify them. Tell them that the tweet is scheduled for a certain time on a certain day to be repeated *x* number of times. Boy, you will make great friends with compliance using this tool.

The last tool I would like to recommend is the most popular marketing and management tool that exists at the time of this writing. *TweetDeck* is a great tool to manage all of your social media posts in one place. TweetDeck has applications (apps) for all types of phones and computers so you can monitor your accounts while on the go and post to multiple accounts with one click. There are other apps that are available on all types of phones and computers, but this is the most popular and user friendly in my opinion. You can see all your tweets as well as the activity you have on keywords, DMs, and @ replys—all on one screen. This allows you to take one glance and see all the inner workings of your Twitter account. It gives you the

FIGURE 7.10   Tweet Scheduler Tool

chance to easily reply to comments and messages from one screen. It is the easiest tool I have found if you're a visual person. It is the icing on the marketing cake. Marketing only works if you know what your potential clients are doing, saying, and what they want. TweetDeck gives you that in one glance.

Self-Marketing Tweets

Lastly, we need to address what you should tweet to market yourself. It is about activity and persistence of message. If you use a weekly market commentary or newsletter, hold conference calls and seminars, or however you currently market yourself as an advisor, Twitter can help.

When you send out that email about an event, seminar, or commentary, inform compliance that you are going to tweet it, too! People love free information. You can invite and direct people to attend an event or start reading your commentary. You can gain numbers easily on Twitter. This can gain more attention for your logo, name, brand, and message.

Final Thoughts

To close out this chapter on marketing on Twitter, I want you to remember a few things. Twitter is a communication tool that can be used to get the attention of prospects and communicate with existing clients. I have not seen it used well for direct business. Twitter is indirect. LinkedIn and Facebook can be used for direct marketing, and we will cover this aspect of them in the next few chapters.

> **COMMUNICATE!**
>
> Twitter is a communication tool that can be used to get the attention of prospects and communicate with existing clients.

This does not mean you should rule out Twitter as a social media tool! In fact, it is a great way to create another fiber of the web you are creating. You want as many threads out there under your control, with the same message, brand, and logo, as you can. Having people see the same message in different places helps you permeate and get your message out amongst the noise on the web. It is also a way to get very quick feedback through mentions and RTs (retweets).

Tweeting messages that have hot links to Facebook, LinkedIn, or your web page can increase your traffic. We want to make our World Wide Web as sticky as possible, going where the people are and trying to engage them in conversation where they are. Marketing has changed. People do not want to be talked at; they want to participate in a conversation. Start that conversation, enjoy the conversations, meet new people, make new friends, and get into the twitterverse. You will never be the same, in a good way.

CHAPTER 8

Getting Leads from Twitter

Matthew Halloran

Getting in front of hundreds or even thousands of people is great for your ego. Having people retweet your posts can make you feel like you are making a difference. But, you want leads and qualified ones at that. Well, I have good and bad news for you.

If you only want to use this section of the book, the Twitter section, I do not feel that you will be overwhelmingly successful. You will have some success, you will meet people in need of your services, but in order for you to find the greatest success, it seems in all of my research that Twitter needs to be a tool that is used in conjunction with many other social media tools and approaches.

A POWERFUL TOOL!

Twitter is a powerful tool, and its power can be magnified if used in conjunction with other social media outlets.

Twitter: A Driving Force

I think you can have success using Twitter to drive people to more robust social media tools, like your LinkedIn page, your Facebook fan page, or your

81

website. Having a great *landing page*, the page or pages you redirect people to, can really improve your effectiveness on Twitter.

Remember, people will get tired of clicking. When they leave your Twitter feed, there should be no more than two clicks to get to something meaningful. One is even better. The first click takes people from your Twitter page to some other link. Show them what you want them to see from that link! Do not make it hard for them to find the content you want them to read, or your bio, or the event you want them to attend. Get them to some place with substance and they will value your posts and come back to see you again and again.

MAKE YOURSELF SEEN!

Make it easy for people to see what you want them to see about you; they should not have to click more than two times to get to your information.

TwitHawk people are having success with lead generation on Twitter. Here is how you, too, can get the most out of Twitter. It is by means of another tool that I have used and researched. And it is quite effective. By using the keywords I referred to in Chapter 7, search Twitter using TwitHawk (www.twithawk.com). This company was acquired by Twitter, so with that, I decided to look into it more.

What I have found is if Twitter buys a company that has created a tool that uses Twitter API (application programming interface—a set of instructions and rules a site creates to limit spam), it is worth a serious look. I also referred to TweetDeck in Chapter 7. This is another independent company that Twitter paid a lot of money for a few years ago.

When you sign up for TwitHawk, you are given 10 free tweets. Let me explain how this works. Someone in the geographical area you service posts something like, "My finances are out of control, I need some help," or, "I do not know what to do with my 401(k) since I lost my job." TwitHawk has a search function for keywords in your area of expertise or geographical area. After that tweet is posted, TwitHawk sends out a message to them with an @ reply. For example: @jolly411 tweets, "Anyone have any advice what annuity is consumer friendly instead of advisor friendly?"

TwitHawk will send a message from your account that says, "@jolly411, we can help you with your annuity questions. Please call ###-###-####."

Because they are in your area of expertise or geographical area and the tweet is specific, you will get attention from that person who is, as far as you know, in need of your help.

This may sound ridiculous to a financial advisor, but you need to allocate a budget for this type of marketing. Since TwitHawk has been acquired by Twitter, it will only let you send out one response tweet to your keywords every hour. If you have 20 active campaigns going at a time, you can send out 20 responses per hour at an average rate of $0.02 per send. That is only $0.40 per hour, but in one 12-hour day, that's $4.80, and if you ran it for 30 days, that is $288.00! It adds up quickly.

Let's look at that $288. Think about how direct this type of marketing is. It is a timely response to a current need or a question someone has on Twitter. That is quite powerful. As I stated in the beginning of the book, social media marketing is very powerful because your audience can see that you are listening to what they need—rather than talking *at* them.

TwitHawk is the best tool I have researched since I have been using Twitter for the last two years. Its capacity for specificity is pretty amazing. You can specify the search parameters if there is a question like the one above. Figure 8.1 shows how to construct searches.

So as you can see, this is a really powerful way to weed through the noise and thousands of spambots on Twitter.

FIGURE 8.1 TwitHawk Searches

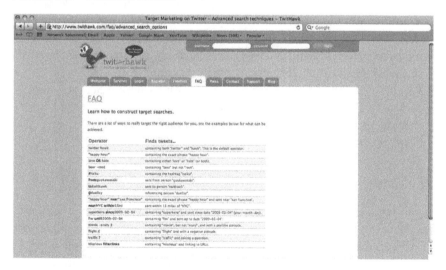

I am a big fan of tools because as a coach and consultant for many years I know how pressed for time many of you are. I also know that a lot of you are really cheap, frugal, responsible with money, or whatever you want to call it.

If you do not want to pay for this tool, you can do what this tool does for you on your own. However, the site helps reduce the amount of time you will need to spend on searching Twitter for these keywords.

If you are stubborn and have a lot of time on your hands, you *can* do it yourself. But no matter how much time you have, you cannot and should not monitor Twitter or any other social media tool all the time. The site is designed to help you! It notifies you when something comes up. If you do it on your own, you will only see the people you need to respond to during your dedicated social media time and not in real time. And regardless of the many business benefits of social media, face-to-face time remains powerful.

You will also need to have your compliance department approve the response tweets, so do not start using TwitHawk until you get their approval. Following are the steps that you (or your assistant) can follow if you are not going to use TwitHawk:

- At the top of the Twitter page after you log in is a search bar. You can type in the keywords you want to search for in that search bar.
- Scroll through all of the other people who are providing advice or are your competition. This takes a lot of time! There are so many people talking about finance. Most of them are okay, but many of them are regurgitating stuff they know nothing about. I found out that Dr. Phil was actually trying to provide financial advice. If he is doing it, there is a lot of noise you will need to filter through to get to the good stuff.
- When you see a tweet that seems to be in your wheelhouse, you need to click on the tweet itself. You will see that you can respond to that tweet. Fashion your preapproved response to the tweet and then click send.
- Now, repeat these steps hundreds of times!

More on Lead Generation

If you want to use Twitter for lead generation, use a tool. Spend the money and let the tool do the work for you. These tools are more effective than you at finding the keywords you should use to target the people you want to reach. I do not rightfully feel that Twitter alone can get you great leads.

I think it is an excellent service you can use to create buzz and redirect people to your main page, site, or article. Twitter creates traffic. Do not expect too much from Twitter when it comes to getting you direct leads.

Some of you may already be well off and sitting on a huge pile of cash. If you are one of these fortunate people, you can get increased traffic and followers if you spend some real money and advertise directly on Twitter. But realize this will be very costly. I want to be honest with you here—I have not done this myself. I have not seen any real reason to spend this kind of cash. I have been quite successful on Twitter by working with the auto-follow function and using it to create traffic to my other sites. Promoting accounts, promoting tweets, and promoting a trend is a great way for you to get a lot of attention quickly. If you want to be *the* number one financial advisor in your region on Twitter, using these tools is the way to do it quickly.

Figure 8.2 shows what a Twitter advertising page looks like and how much you can expect to pay for each of the three advertising services Twitter offers:

1. *Promoted Tweets.* This allows you to get your tweets in a person's time-line, even if he or she does not follow you. There is a targeting system you are able to use to make sure your tweets are in front of those you want. Cost to begin: $5,000 per month.

FIGURE 8.2   Twitter Advertising

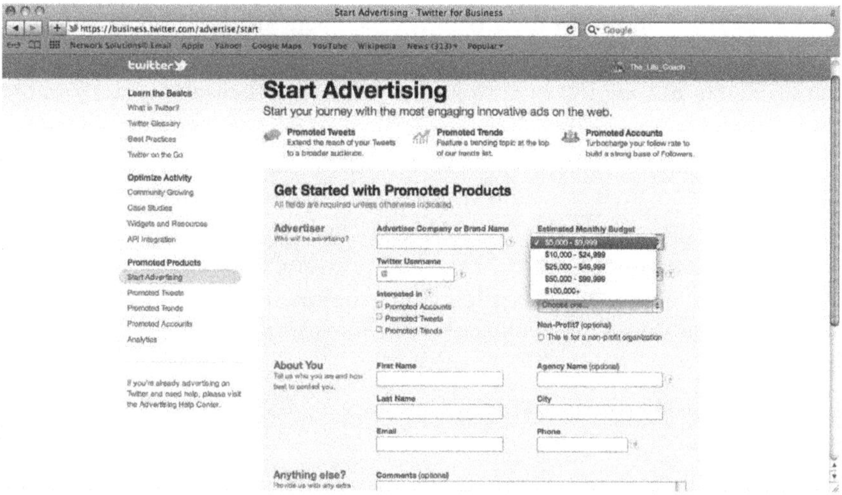

2. *Promoted Trends.* On the right-hand side of your Twitter page, you will see *Trends.* Well, if you pay, your hashtag or trend can show up on your targeted prospects' pages. Cost to begin: $5,000 per month. Note: This is not open to the general public yet. They are beta testing it.

3. *Promoted Accounts.* Your smiling face can show up in the "Who to follow" portion of your prospects' pages. This is available to the general public now at a low monthly fee, beginning again at $5,000.

There is competition out there for these promotions. You get what you pay for here. If you are the lowest bidder, your tweet, trend, or account will not show up often. Advertising this way is for large companies or offices that have a huge advertising budget. I do not recommend trying this as an advisor. It is too costly. I wanted to cover it to show you the difference in reach and price each of the social media tools has to offer.

Final Thoughts

There are some big players saying that promoted tweets, accounts, or trends have made a huge difference in their sales. These are larger companies, such as Virgin and Red Bull, but if it works for them, can't it also work for you? If you have the money, it sure can. Promoted presence, no matter which one you choose, is said to result in a huge increase in advertisement engagement rates. There are huge numbers of retweets when something is being promoted. Do you want to know why? Because when something is becoming a trend, people use that hashtag to gain attention to their account. If something is trending, whether it is an account, tweet, or trend, tweeps who want attention put that trend or account or tweet in their own tweets. Then, when someone does a search on that account, trend, or tweet, their accounts show up. This is a really powerful viral aspect of Twitter.

Twitter can be your friend. It can be a powerful tool on its own, but it is so much more powerful when you use it in conjunction with the other forms of social media. Use tools like TwitHawk and you can maximize your use of Twitter!

CHAPTER 9

Public Relations on Twitter

Matthew Halloran

Now that you know how to use Twitter, you have followers, good tweets going on a regular basis, people are retweeting (RTing) you, and you have made some good connections, what's next? Is there more? Can you use this tool for something else? Yes you can!

I will show you how to use Twitter for public relations (PR) to help promote yourself in your local newspaper or on your local news.

I have worked with one of the best PR/marketing companies in the world. I took the opportunity to learn as much from them as I could. Boy, I learned a lot. The greatest piece of information I got from them is: News means new content; writers and editors want what is new before anyone else has it. They want your content; don't be afraid of getting it to them.

> **NEWS MEANS NEW CONTENT.**
>
> Writers and editors want what is new before anyone else has it. They want your content; don't be afraid of getting it to them.

News has to be new. If you have old news, it will not get in front of the right people. What is happening right now that you need to tell someone about? Did you hear a speech from a speaker at a conference that gave you a new way to do something? I bet the local press was not at that event and might just want to know about it. If it is impactful to you or your clients, it is worth a try. Trust me on this one, what qualifies as news is a lot less than you are thinking.

Caution! Compliance alert! News needs to be timely, but still approved!

Okay, so I have this great idea or story; now how in the heck do I get it to the right person? Twitter is a great tool for this!

Tweet Grader

There are some great tools available with Twitter that will help you to find writers, editors, or other PR types. The first one is *Tweet Grader*. Tweet Grader (www.tweetgrader.com) is a tool you can use not only to see how well your own tweets are received but more importantly, to find out who in your region are the authorities on specific subjects. (It also tells you who your competition is on Twitter so that you can see how active they are, and you can start piggyback following their followers as well as those they follow.)

Here is how Tweet Grader works. You go to the site and search, using one of your keywords, to see who is tweeting about that specific word. You can use hashtags (#) or just simple search terms. The results will list the tweep's name, Twitter handle, tweet, bio, influence grade, number of followers, number of updates, and location.

It is important for you to find out what others are tweeting about in your location or in your field and to find out what the buzz is all about. You need to know what the top tweeps are tweeting. You can also use this information to show your local editors how up to date you are on stuff in the industry.

Muck Rack

Muck Rack (www.muckrack.com) is an amazing site geared toward journalists. This site takes a little work, but if you are located close to a major city you can find all the reporters that are covering your area on Muck Rack. I believe this site is great because you can target exactly who you want to target.

Let's say you find someone located in your area that is on Muck Rack. Follow them immediately. Next, look through their Tweets and find something you want to RT (retweet). Retweet it with a positive comment like: What a great article. I learned a lot from this and my clients need to read this. Thank you for this post!

Your best bet is to not only find people who are well known locally, but also those who are freelance writers or journalists. They are always looking for stories! They are good writers who have great connections. I really like having a few freelance journalists close by. You can direct message them on a weekly basis with story ideas, or as frequently as you would like, but no less than once a month. Keep yourself top of mind.

If you do not find anyone that is close to your vicinity or if you are from a smaller town, follow someone from the largest city closest to you. Send them an @ reply with a question to see if they can direct you to someone in your local area. Most people on Twitter are kind and want to help you out.

Making News through Twitter

One of the best things you can do outside of Muck Rack is search Twitter for a local press, local leads, or young professionals group. Type in your local television stations' call letters, the name of the local newspaper, or the local chamber of commerce to find leads.

Connect with people who are locally influential. Twitter is still new enough that it is cool to find someone well known who lives or works near you and to then connect with that person. I have had great luck connecting with local TV personalities. They have followed back quickly and usually send a personal DM to me. They will do it for you, too!

Check your accounts twice a day and look for tweets about editorial opportunities. Reporters will tweet asking for information on a story. If you see such a tweet, DM them as soon as possible and give them the information they are searching for or offer your time for an interview.

Lastly, if you are going to go out and try to pitch a story to a person like a reporter or journalist, check up on him first through Twitter to see when his last post was since this may tell you a lot about him. Maybe he is working really hard to meet a deadline and does not want to be bothered. Maybe he is sick. Or even better, maybe he is working on a story that you can help him with!

Twitter is a great way to communicate to reporters. It offers short and concise blasts of information. A reporter or journalist can get through copious amounts of information on Twitter quickly. Make your communication stand out. DMs are very personal and most tweeps read them. If you take the time to DM someone, that person should read your DM. This is one of the unwritten rules of the twitterverse.

Final Thoughts

Twitter can be a very powerful way to connect with the public relations universe or twitterverse. If you follow the simple and manageable techniques in this chapter, you will be able to use Twitter to its full potential.

Now that we have covered Twitter, we will move to Facebook. Facebook is a more complex tool that has more things to offer the financial advisor. Get ready: You are about to join your teenage kids! You, too, will be on Facebook!

PART III

Facebook

CHAPTER 10

Why Facebook?

Matthew Halloran

If you had to choose the one thing over the past 10 years that had the greatest impact on the way people communicate, it would have to be Facebook. Cell phones and texting aside, Facebook has changed communication. Many people believe that Facebook has not changed the world for the better. I disagree. I think it has connected us in ways that are very beneficial.

Statistics

Following are some statistics on the use of Facebook taken from digitalbuzzblog.com:

- There are 500 million users on Facebook.
- 1 in 13 people on Earth use Facebook.
- 50 percent of users log in at least once a day.
- 700 billion minutes a month are spent on Facebook.
- 206.2 million Americans (71.2 percent) are on Facebook.
- 27.5 percent of Facebook users are over age 35.

Let's put all of this into a visual perspective. Table 10.1 shows that people in your key demographic group, those between the ages of 55 to 64, are on Facebook. Grandparents are using Facebook to connect with their

TABLE 10.1 Facebook Demographic

Age(s)	Total Users	Male	Female
13–17	14,402,580	6,646,820	7,719,380
18–25	50,679,700	23,004,960	27,048,020
26–34	29,703,340	13,588,320	15,577,380
35–44	23,596,860	10,216,440	12,775,140
45–54	17,425,520	6,915,900	10,176,980
55–64	10,459,580	3,982,340	6,301,480

Source: insidefacebook.com.

children and grandchildren who live far away. They are enamored by this medium and are ripe for targeted communication and advertising.

This is what this table tells me—Facebook is huge. It is larger than most of us can comprehend, and it is growing.

I am sure you have heard those stats before and for some reason you are still staying away from Facebook. Let's now look at the business applications. Since you are probably math inclined, here are some more statistics:

- More than half of business-to-business (B2B) marketers agree that Facebook is an effective marketing tool.[1]
- More than half of small businesses agree that Facebook is beneficial to their business.[2]
- More than one-third of marketers say Facebook is "critical" or "important" to their business.[3]
- The number of marketers who say Facebook is critical or important to their business has increased 83 percent in two years.[4]
- 67 percent of business-to-consumer (B2C) and 41 percent of B2B companies that use Facebook for marketing have acquired a customer through this channel.[5]

---

[1] Outsell, December 2009.
[2] Ad-ology, November 2010.
[3] *HubSpot State of Inbound Marketing Report 2011.*
[4] *HubSpot State of Inbound Marketing Report 2011.*
[5] *HubSpot State of Inbound Marketing Report 2011.*

These are some compelling reasons why you should be using Facebook. It is easier to set up a page on Facebook than it is to create your own website. And, Facebook is free. Facebook is a simple face for your company and you need to have a presence there as soon as you finish reading this chapter. Almost every legitimate business has a Facebook page. The financial services industry has always struggled with legitimacy. This is a great way to show that you are throwing your proverbial hat into the ring of legitimacy. Marketing is changing, and clients and prospects want you to meet them where they are with a message that is tailored to them. This is what Facebook can do for you and your business; get your message to the people who want to hear it, in a medium they feel comfortable using.

Building Your Page

Facebook compliance regulations are spotty at best. Due to the Financial Industry Regulatory Authority (FINRA) and broker-dealers' lack of knowledge on how social media works, Facebook compliance memorandums have not been very complete. They are vague guidelines that leave much to interpretation and mistake. We began this book with a discussion on compliance. Compliance is ever changing, and you need to keep up to date on what is the latest and greatest.

I recommend that you create your own personal Facebook page before creating your business Facebook page. This will help you to get comfortable using Facebook and will also let you connect with some friends you may have lost touch with over the years. You will find that Facebook is quite intuitive and easy to use. That there, folks, is the draw of this tool. It is easy and intuitive.

After we discuss setting up your personal and Facebook fan (business) pages we will discuss how to market your business using Facebook's wealth of information.

Facebook page = your personal page that shares personal information. You connect with friends and family with this page.

Facebook fan page = your business presence on Facebook. You will do business and communicate business ideas through this page.

Let's begin. www.facebook.com is where it all starts. First, you must sign up by entering your full name, a non-business email (this is for your personal

FIGURE 10.1 Facebook Sign-Up Screen

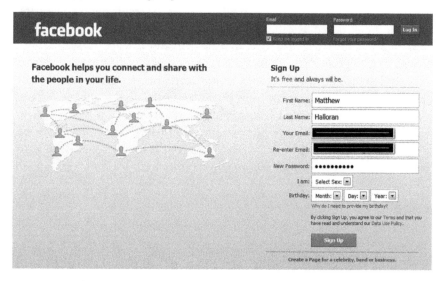

page), and a password that you will remember (see Figure 10.1). Next, you will click on the green *sign up* button. If you do not have a personal email account, you will need to create one. I recommend using Google (gmail) or Yahoo!. This is your personal account. You do not want personal messages being sent to your business email account because that could get you into some trouble with compliance.

On the next screen, you might see a *captcha* box similar to the one shown in Figure 10.2. This is one level of security. Type in the box the exact letters and numbers displayed and click on the green button. Captcha is a system that is used to reduce the spambots that auto sign up for accounts, which are actually dummy accounts. Computer programs currently cannot read these letters so they cannot bypass this page. Since we (well most of us) can read the letters, it is a level of protection for you!

Now, let's go step by step through each of the screens that you will see on Facebook to make sure you are maximizing it for your personal use.

Step 1: Friends

The Friends page lets you find and connect with people. In Step 1, you can import your personal contacts directly into Facebook. You can do this using

FIGURE 10.2 Captcha Box

your personal email contacts from Google, Windows Live Mail, Yahoo!, and others. By allowing Facebook to access this information directly from your email, they can connect you with your contacts and save you a lot of time. You will get messages from the people you connect with telling you it is about time you are on Facebook. It happened to me and I have been using Facebook for years.

Facebook will search its database to find and connect you with people you already know (see Figure 10.3). You can bypass any of the following screens by clicking on *Skip this step* in the lower right-hand corner of the screen. *Reminder!* Do not import your professional contacts here! We are setting up your personal account, so you should not have used your BDs (broker-dealers) or GA (general agency) official email account.

Step 2: Profile Information

This step is another approach to help you find connections and groups you might want to join. Enter your high school name, where you went to

FIGURE 10.3 Friends Page, Step 1

college, and your current BD or GA as shown in Figure 10.4. Facebook will store this information and help you connect with people who want to connect with you!

There is another reason I want you to fill this information out. This information is vital to marketers and you, too, will be a Facebook marketer soon. You will need this information to target your messages. You can only be successful at reaching your targets by using this shared information. So share it. Facebook lets you use this information to tailor your messages and you, in turn, will receive the messages that you want to receive. Remember, we want people to share information; it will increase the power of your message when you advertise.

Remember, Facebook is all about connections. It will help you find people. It helped me to connect with my first girlfriend. Let me explain.

Remember those youthful days when you first met someone who you thought of as *the one*. It was that special girl or guy who made you feel, well, special. Mine was a redheaded waif who just drove me nuts. She was my first

FIGURE 10.4 Friends Page, Step 2

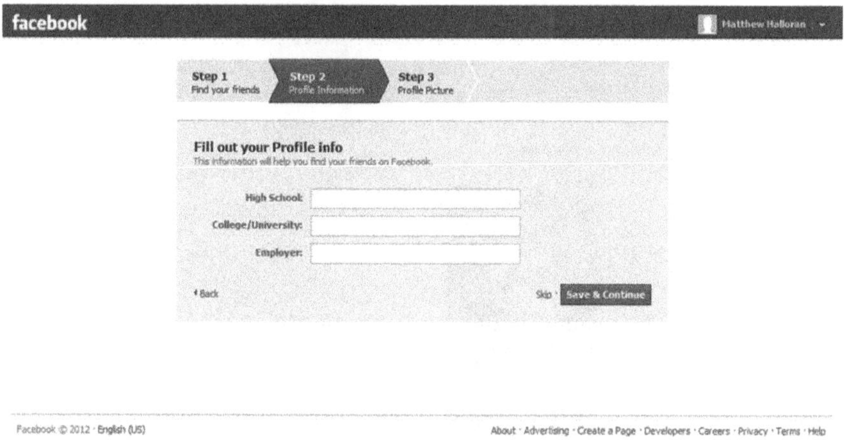

kiss, crush, and someone I thought of as a girlfriend. She, of course, did not think we were dating, which was only uncomfortable for me.

We had lost touch over the years because we had both moved. I ran into her once when I was home on leave from the Navy, but after many years I wondered what had happened to her. Being older, married, and with two sons, I was not trying to reconnect with my old high school flame; I actually wanted to see if she was still alive. She was kind of wild and since many years had passed, it was possible—people die.

During the first six months on Facebook, I had connected with many of my high school friends. I inquired to one if she had heard from her or knew where she was. She told me to look through her friends list because (at the time I was quite a novice on Facebook) she was listed as one of her friends. I clicked on her picture and she looked exactly the same. I have not aged well (bald and gray) compared to many of my high school classmates. I sent her a friend request and she connected with me. It was great getting caught up and seeing how successful she had become.

Facebook can allow you to reconnect or communicate with family who are not in your general proximity. We are all incredibly busy these days, and Facebook for personal use can help you connect and communicate with the people you need and want to remain in your life.

Now, back to setting up your Facebook profile.

FIGURE 10.5   Profile Picture, Step 3

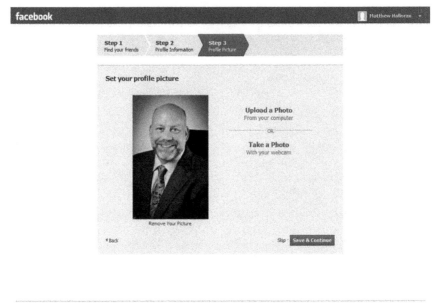

Step 3: Profile Picture

I suggest that you get a good headshot, one where you look nice, and one where you smile (see Figure 10.5). This is a step I do not want you to skip. Your account should have a face on it. Hence the name Facebook! I know some people do not want their pictures on Facebook or out there on the web because they think it will be used against them in some way, shape, or form. Trust me, if someone wants to see who you are, it is not hard to find you online. Your face conveys so much; I have used my kids, dogs, and my mug as my Facebook image. If you get negative feedback about your appearance, then use a picture of something else. However, your face is a wonderful thing, so put it on Facebook.

After you choose which picture file to upload, click on the blue *Save & Continue* button. Facebook supports many file types. You can use *jpg*, *png*, and *tif* files. Facebook will automatically resize and reformat the pictures upon upload.

After you you upload your picture, you will receive a confirmation email from Facebook. Go to your email account and click on the link Facebook provides for you. You might want to write down the code it provides, just in case it asks for it. The email completes your registration and makes it possible for you to access your page.

Working with Your Home Page

It is vital for you to understand what features Facebook offers to its users and how you can control your personal information.

Your home page will looks something similar to the screen in Figure 10.6. Let's look at this page and what all this stuff you have never seen before means.

This is going to be where the Facebook magic happens. The list on the left-hand side under your picture shows your navigation controls. Using this list will allow you to control what is seen on your personal Facebook page. Up at the top of the list, you will see your search tool. This is a great way to find out who is on Facebook, who you want to connect with, and a great way

FIGURE 10.6 Facebook Home Page

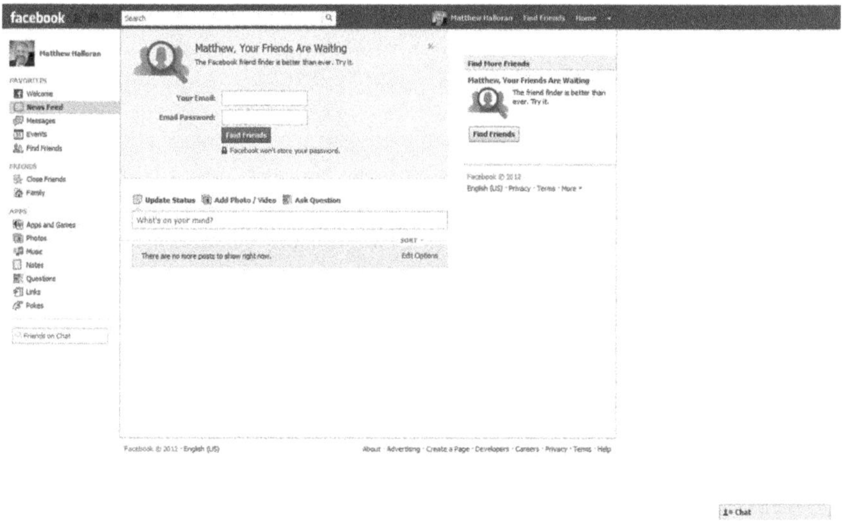

to find out who is saying what. You will also see, in the blue bar at the top, tabs labeled *Home, Profile, Find Friends*, and *Account.* Let's break each of these tabs down.

> *Home*: This will be your one click back to see what is going on in your Facebook feed. If you ever need to refresh your feed, you can just hit this button.
>
> *Profile*: This is where you will gain access to edit your profile information, settings, and general stuff you are willing to share to the powers that be on Facebook.
>
> *Find Friends*: This means just what it says; this button or tab helps you find people to connect with on Facebook. The more meaningful people Facebook helps you connect with, the more time you will spend on their site.
>
> *Account*: This is where you will find your master controls for your permissions, as well as the option to delete your account if you ever decide to do so.

Click around and get familiar with each of the tabs on this page. Look at where each of the links from your list on the left-hand side of the page brings you and see what you can do with the search tool. Clicking around will not hurt anything; it will just get you more comfortable with this medium.

Controls

As you click on the page links, you will begin to see redundancies. Facebook will consistently ask you if you want to make connections using your email contacts. You can also activate your mobile phone so it will notify you when specific things happen, but I would not do this now. Facebook can become addictive. If you remember from the discipline section of the book, you do not want social media to take control of your life.

Let's talk about controls, what they are, and why they are needed. As an advisor, you like control. People pay you money to control very important aspects of their life such as their finances. Facebook gives you a lot of control over what information is shared and what people can see about you.

You need to set controls to your comfort level. If you are still quite paranoid about social media, I would reduce the permissions you allow

Facebook to access. Facebook wants you to be happy and they want you to use their site. They want you to let them use and share your information, if you will let them. This whole control section was expanded to give you more options because people told Facebook they wanted more control. Because they are a good, socially responsible company and one that's whole existence is to serve people, they made huge changes. See Fig. 10.7.

Control settings allow you to restrict access to your personal information. This is where you will say who can view your information.

Setting Controls: Step by Step

First, click on the down arrow on the right hand side of your page. You should see your name, find friends, home, and then the arrow. A drop down box should show up and you will see privacy settings. Click on privacy settings.

FIGURE 10.7 Control What Information You Share Page

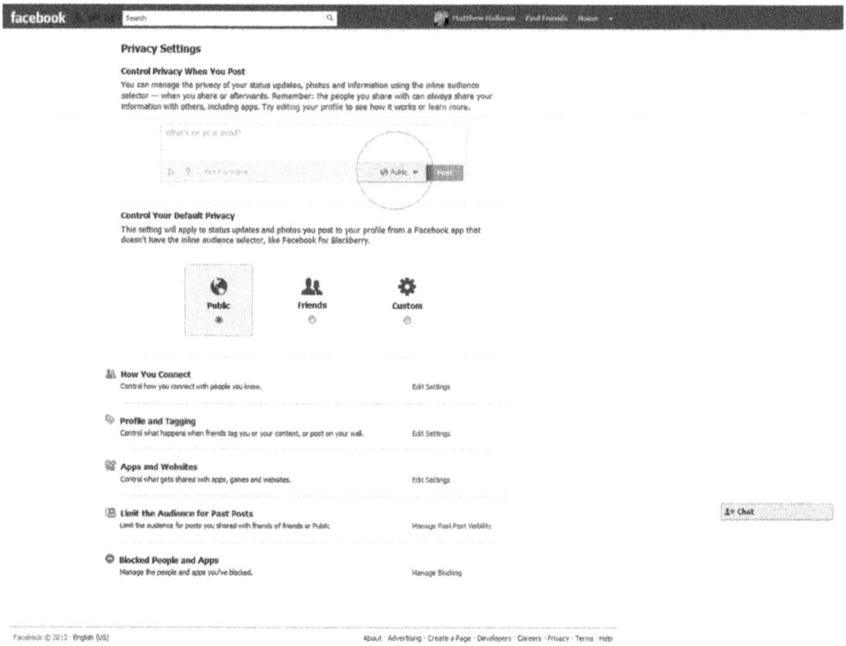

Due to privacy lawsuits and feedback from the user base, Facebook has had to give you as the consumer more options to protect your privacy. This screen changes all of the time! I will provide the most up to date settings recommendations we have at the time the book was published. You may want to limit the information other people have access to since this is only a start up account. Here are my recommendations:

1. Do not give Facebook your phone number. There really is not a need for them to have that information, and it will be posted on your Facebook page.
2. Only grant access to your posts to your friends and family whose requests for friendship you have accepted on Facebook.
3. Only accept friend requests from people you actually know and know well. There are a lot of people on Facebook who will want to be your friend, but unless you know them, do not accept their friend request.

If you follow these three easy rules, your safety and your information's safety will be increased exponentially. This has nothing to do with FINRA (Financial Industry Regulatory Authority), but it will limit the amount of information shared and what you will receive from others.

At this point, you are probably wondering, *What is this guy telling me to do?* I wanted to use Facebook to market my business, and he wants me to do all these personal things. Well, we are going to get to the marketing aspect, I promise. It will be covered after you have set up your personal Facebook page and your fan page; then we will get into how marketing on Facebook works. I am trying to force you to get familiar with Facebook in general. The better you learn where things are and how it works, the better you will be at using this powerful tool for marketing. If you know what information is defaulted on each of your potential prospects, you can tailor your marketing efforts and really get a lot out of Facebook. Now, get back to clicking!

How Control Settings Help Your Marketing Plan

Facebook is a marketer's dream! People share their information with others voluntarily! You can focus your advertising on birthdays, religious and political views, location, places visited, and interests. As with all legal battles, as Facebook found, the level of control you have now is quite powerful.

FIGURE 10.8 Control Settings

We will start from the top. As you can see in Figure 10.8, you can choose Public, Friends, or Custom. I recommend you click Friends.

If you do not want to share anything and you only want to focus on business, click on custom and where it says, "Make this visible to," click the drop down and select *only me*.

Here are my recommendations for each of the options:

1. How you connect:
   a. Who can look you up using the email address or phone number you provided? *Select friends of friends*
   b. Who can send you friend requests? *Select friends of friends*
   c. Who can send you Facebook messages? *Select friends*
2. Profile and tagging:
   a. Who can post on your wall? *Friends*. This means that friends of yours can post things that will show up in your timeline. If you are

concerned that an old college roomate will post pictures of you on your wall of that party you vaguely remember, select, *No One.*

b. Who can see what others post on your profile? *Friends.*

c. Review posts friends tag you in before they appear on your profile? *Select enable.* This will take you to another screen, click on *enable*, and it will show up as on.

d. Who can see posts you've been tagged in on your profile? *Select friends.*

e. Review tags friends add to your own posts on Facebook. Again when you click on the *off* button it will take you to a screen, *Select enable* and it will show up as on.

f. Who sees tag suggestions when photos that look like you are uploaded? Leave that as friends.

We should pause here to explain what "f" means to you. Since you uploaded a picture, Facebook will remember your face. When a friend takes a picture of you, Facebook scans that image to see if "it" recognizes that face. Yes, it is a little spooky, but the software has been around for many years.

Now you can click on done and move to the next privacy setting, Apps and Websites.

3. Apps and Websites:

a. Apps you use: You do not currently have any apps. You do not need to adjust these settings.

b. How people bring your info to apps they use: I recommend you de-select all of the checked boxes here. I am not a big fan of my friends being able to "bring" my information to the apps they use. You will thank me for this down the road.

c. Instant personalization: Watch the video but do not let it pursuade you too much! Unless you plan on being a Facebook junkie, click the box that says *Enable instant personalization on partner websites.* Facebook really wants you to allow them to use the instant partner function. When you click on the check mark to disable it a pop up will again try to convince you to keep it. Click confirm. Then click "Back to Apps" at the upper right part of the page.

I would like to explain myself here. As a marketer, I want my potential clients to put as much information on Facebook as they can. But, I do not want too much of my information out there, and most advisors I consult agree. It is better to err on the side of caution. I am recommending you be cautious, not paranoid. So, let's continue.

d. Public Search: You need to ask yourself, do you want your personal Facebook page to show up when someone types in your name into a search engine? Since many of you have your name as your practice identity or name, I recommend you click that check mark to un-select it. Facebook will deliver another pop-up here, read it, but still click *confirm*. Then click "Back to Apps".

Well, we are halfway done with your privacy settings. Only two more to cover.

4. Limit the Audience for Past Posts: This is a very simple change Facebook has made recently. It is really good for high school and college aged kids. They post some stupid things on their walls that will most likely bite them in the tail someday. Since you are an older, much wiser sort of person, I know you will not ever regret anything you ever post personally. Just kidding. Please click on *Manage Past Post Visibility,* click on *Limit Old Posts,* and then click *Confirm.*

5. Blocked People and Apps: You do not need to Block People and Apps now, because you have not really experienced what your Facebook friends are posting. It is good to know it is here.

If you follow my recommendations, and if everyone did, Facebook would not be as powerful of a marketing tool as we want it to be. Since you are new and compliance is going to potentially look at your page, I would lock it down; that is what I just showed you how to do.

The Power of Advertisements!

Advertisements, such as those shown in Figure 10.9, are tailored to your posts, preferences, interests, and the pages you follow. You, too, can have access to this powerful tool! Let's talk about this for a moment. You will get to experience Facebook marketing on your own page. Facebook will look at your posts and your friends' posts and likes, and create a tailored advertisement section on your page every time you visit. Remember, I told you that the power of Facebook marketing is that it gets pertinent advertisements to the right people. What better way to advertise? The more you post, follow, and like things on Facebook, the more tailored your advertisements will be. You will see how advertisers do this when we advertise your fan page, which

FIGURE 10.9 Advertisements

we have not built yet. We will do this in the next chapter, but I want you to start noticing the power of this new type of marketing. This is a screen shot from my personal Facebook page so you can see the advertising.

Now that you are officially on Facebook and you have set up your page, we will talk about how to set up a compliance-approved (well, at least they *should* approve it) fan page for your business.

The Facebook Fan Page

The Facebook fan page is one of the best free marketing tools you can imagine!

Before we discuss this in depth, I want to give another compliance heads-up. Different compliance departments have very different opinions on this topic. Some understand how fan pages work, but most don't. My opinion is that social media is another form of communication. If the information has been approved for you to relay to clients and prospects, it should be able to be used here. If you have a market commentary or newsletter you send out weekly, monthly, or quarterly, it should be posted on your fan page wall. Invitations to seminars and educational events should also be posted here. There is even an application on Facebook that allows you to invite and track attendees' RSVPs.

Since you are still reading, I am going to make the assumption you are planning to build your fan page. If you are going to take this leap, you need to understand that you will want to communicate with the people following you and liking your page. Compliance will most likely not let you do this because if you do, you will need to archive every piece of communication on your fan page. All of my research says that you are to have two-way communications with your followers on Facebook. There have been a few forward thinking broker-dealers and companies that have started providing this service. TAKE ADVANTAGE of these services!

This is why compliance departments like the website idea so much. It is considered one-way communication, with no feedback at all, especially immediate feedback. Websites are like billboards; you cannot talk to a billboard and expect it to talk back. People cannot post comments on your website, but they can and will want to post comments on your fan page. Compliance looks at comments on your fan page as testimonials. And they *hate them.* Financial advisors are immersed in one of the only industries where clients cannot tell others in writing how much we have helped them. Quite backwards, but people (the legislators) are concerned about the one unethical advisor out of 10,000 ethical advisors who does something wrong; and that is not necessarily in the client's best interest.

Moving along, once you have set up your profile page, you can create your fan page. At the very bottom of the home page, you will find the *Create a Page* link (see Figure 10.10).

Click on that link and do the following:

1. Create a page as a *Local Business* or *Place* (see Figure 10.11).
2. Click on *Choose a Category.* You will need to choose *Bank/Financial Services* because that is the only category that compliance will allow you to choose. The list is not that comprehensive.
3. Input your physical address and include your phone number.
4. Agree to the terms after reading them. (Specific terms are not included here.)
5. You should now be on the page creation screen. I know some people are quite creative and others are not. It is easy to set up a functional page that

FIGURE 10.10 Create a Page

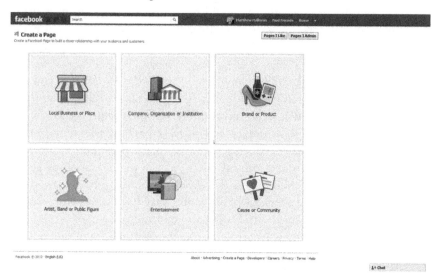

FIGURE 10.11 Local Business or Place Page

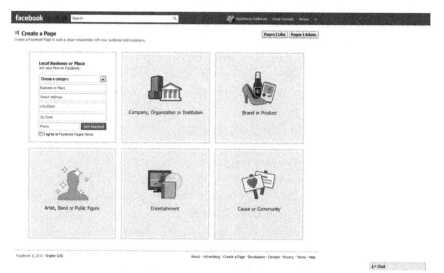

will work. The more creative you are, the more you might want to do to make it look even better. Here I will only discuss the basic setup.

The Company Page

Figure 10.12 shows the *Create Your Page* screen.

Please use your approved company logo for your image. Your Facebook fan page is there to continue to get your brand noticed.

Set up for My Financial Services Company is Figure 10.13.

It is asking for you to put in information about your company here. Please use compliance approved company information here. If you have information on your website or brochure, use that exact same information here. Also if you have a website already, copy and paste the URL in the *Add Another Site* box.

Now, do you see how and why businesses are flocking to this? Do you see how easy it is to set this up? Let's break down the setup into manageable steps.

FIGURE 10.12 Page Creation Screen

FIGURE 10.13   Page Creation Screen

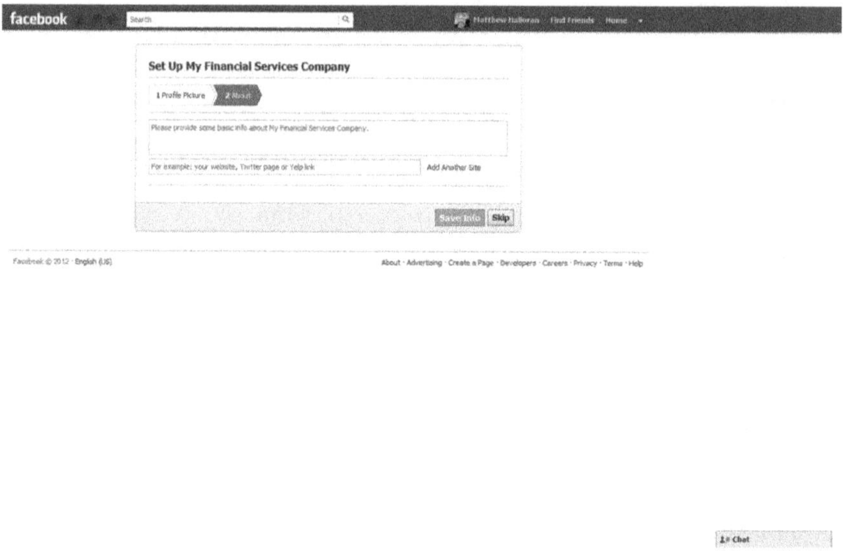

The page will ask you to "like" the page you have just created. Do not click "Like" yet. We need to do some other steps first. So click *Skip*.

Another pop up will show up to ask you to invite your friends. Again, we need to do some more work before you advertise your page, even to people you know and trust. COMPLIANCE PEOPLE! We will need to get everything approved before you really launch this page. Click *Next*. Same thing with the Invite your Email Contacts, please just click *Next*.

You might get a little frustrated because Facebook wants you to use this page and start posting right away. DO NOT POST ANYTHING, yet. I know I am using a lot of capital letters here, but please, do this right. Slow down and follow the steps. Click *Skip*.

You should stop getting prompts now. Your page should look somewhat like Figure 10.14.

Your first step is to go to the upper right-hand corner and click on *Account* (see Figure 10.15), and then *Account Settings*.

After clicking on Account Settings, click on *email* (Figure 10.16). You will need to change your primary email address to the official business account that your compliance department sees. This way, all notifications that come in to your fan page will go to your compliance department for

FIGURE 10.14 Your Fan Page

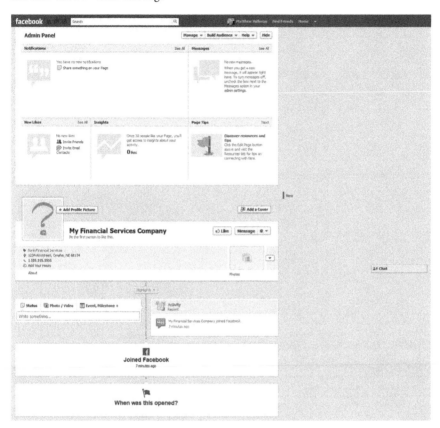

screening and archiving. There are companies out there that are offering archiving solutions, but that is company specific.

When you get to the notifications section (see Figure 10.17), you need to switch all the notifications to go to your business email. Everything needs to be sent to your official compliance-reviewed email address; click on *edit* in each of these categories and check all the boxes for everything!

You cannot be too careful here. Even if you don't know or understand what it is that you are giving permission to have sent to your compliance-approved

FIGURE 10.15 Account Settings

FIGURE 10.16 Account Settings—Primary Email

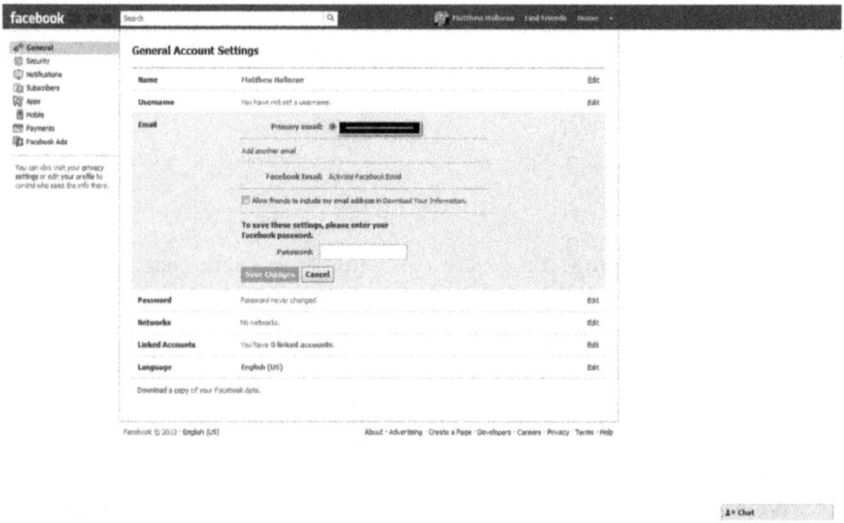

FIGURE 10.17 Notifications Section

email, don't worry. It is better to have them be overcommunicated with than to miss having something important sent to them. Save everything and then click on the Home button at the top of the Facebook page (the blue bar at the top that has Your Name, Find Friends, Home, and the Drop Down Arrow).

There is one more step for security and to make your compliance department happy. In the upper right-hand corner, you will see the search area. This is where you will type the name of your broker-dealer (BD) or GA followed by the word *compliance*, such as: Raymond James Compliance (see Figure 10.18). If your BD has a page, *like* the page and then send them a

FIGURE 10.18 Message to Compliance

message. On the right-hand side of the page, first find, then send a message, and in the text box you can enter something like, "Please add my page."

Timeline

Starting March 30, 2012, Timeline changed the visual aspects of your Facebook pages. We will discuss some advanced Facebook Fan Page techniques that I feel are a great opportunity to expand your brand and see what you can really do with Facebook Fan Page branding.

As you can see there is so much going on here. The top panel will tell you everyone who has interacted with your page, and whether they have liked it, posted on it, commented on a post, or messaged you directly. This is a huge improvement Facebook implemented to increase the ease of managing your page.

As your page grows in interaction with the world, this panel gets very informative. But before it becomes an information center for you and your business we need to get some more branding in place.

FIGURE 10.19 Admin Panel of your Fan Page

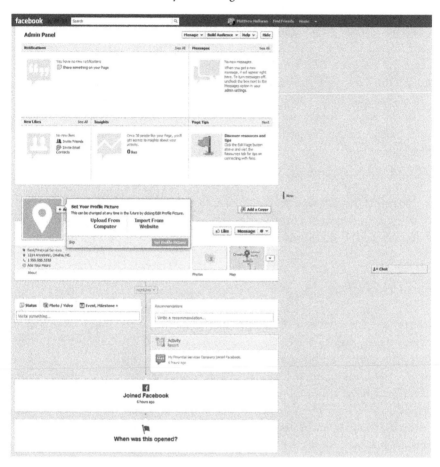

As you can see in Figure 10.19 you can upload a Profile Picture and off to the left you will see *Add a Cover*. You should have used your company logo as your profile picture, but now you can add an eye-catching cover to your page. Click on *Add a Cover*. It will prompt you with an explanation, then click on upload photo.

I have had the best results working with advisors who have a strong connection with their location. I feel that one of the best "covers" you can use on your Facebook Fan Page is a skyline of your city. Take one yourself or check with your local Chamber of Commerce. They should have one that you can use. Upload this photo and it will show your affinity for your local.

If you scroll down under your newly placed great cover, you will see another new feature that can give your company immediate history and depth of the page. Click on *Event, Milestone+*. You want to put any milestone your company has had over its lifetime. This is where you will put when your company was founded, when you were awarded your first recognition award from your broker-dealer, when you were featured in your local paper. Take time with these milestones. It will give your page history that most others do not have. People will be able to, at a glance, see your growth and development as a company. This is one of my favorite new Timeline offerings.

Timeline has allowed you as the small business owner to create a functional web presence that tracks all activity on that page. Bravo Facebook for empowering the small business person!

Final Thoughts

I have taken a strict stance in this chapter based on the many compliance departments' notes I've seen on Facebook fan pages. I am asking you to do more than your compliance department might want you do to. It is better to be overcautious than to leave something out that they feel is important. Once you have appeased the compliance watchdogs, you can focus your attention on ways to make your page more appealing so that when you advertise your business, you can give people a good understanding of who you are and why they clicked on your link.

CHAPTER 11

How to Advertise on Facebook

Matthew Halloran

Facebook does a great job gathering data for you on your page, especially now with Timeline. You and, if applicable, your assistant should be the only administrators on the page. Now, I am going to switch from the made up page to the fan page I have been using for a number of years.

Facebook Insights

As I said before, I use my fan page to track both the traffic and the effectiveness of my Twitter relationships. I post motivational sayings with commentary on those sayings. My page is pretty simple. But, even with a limited amount of content, I get a lot of daily traffic. Just think: You are going to be able to post meaningful information people really need. Can you imagine how sticky your Facebook fan page relationships will be?

Let's look at the fan page insights on my page shown in Figure 11.1.

What does this tell you? Well it shows how often people return to your page. Wouldn't it be great to have a hundred or more people looking at your page each week or every day? That would be a great chance for you to keep at the very top of your mind with clients, prospects, and centers of influence.

119

FIGURE 11.1   Fan Page Insights

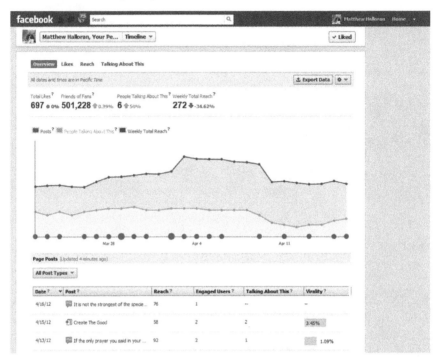

Now, this is just data. You will not have anywhere near this many views or likes on your page to start unless you aggressively go after potential clients. You can use the Twitter tools I referred to in the previous chapter to drive people to the fan page by piggybacking on the followers of your competition, but that will only get you so far. You will want to advertise. And after you see how robust and specific Facebook advertising is, you will want to do it even more!

Advertising on Facebook

I suggest you mentally prepare yourself for the power of Facebook advertising. With Facebook, you are able to target *exactly* who you want to get your page in front of.

Let's take a look at how you get to the advertising section. Click on the button at the left that has your name and the name of your page. Then you will

FIGURE 11.2 Advertise on Facebook

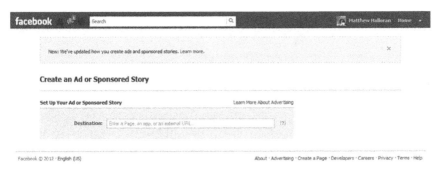

see Manage, Build Audience, Help, and Hide. Click on *Build an Audience* then *Create an Ad*. Start by clicking on that button (see Figure 11.2).

You can change the destination of your advertisement/sponsored story to go to your website, Twitter account, or your Facebook fan page. Since you are going to try to drive people to your fan page, then you should have that be the destination. Just to be clear, the destination is the site at which the person who clicks on the ad will arrive upon clicking it.

You can use your fan page to send people to view your communication feed (Timeline), information about your location or the contact information of your company (info), and your friend activity (not recommended). The video section is effective because you can direct people to view a commercially recorded video or a videotaped speech. (I will show you how to upload a video later.) This is also a great opportunity for you to create a short video (professionally shot) to welcome people and introduce yourself. People like to see who you are and it creates the beginning of a relationship because they will feel like you are talking to them.

Here is a sample script:

Hello and welcome to Johannson Financial Services fan page. My name is Omar Johannson, I am the founder and lead advisor and wanted to thank you for taking time to click on our page. On this page you will find out a lot about our service, team members, and be able to keep up on all the wonderful things that are happening in the market and with our clients. You can see, on the left side, all the upcoming educational events and a few events we are sponsoring around town. From all of us here at Johannson Financial Services, welcome.

It is short—around 30 seconds. Make it your own. Make it warm and personal.

After you choose your fan page as the destination, it will ask you what you want to promote. Do you want to promote the page or a post? If you have posted an event on your wall and that is what you want to drive people to, use that specific post. If you want to get them to come and check out your whole page, choose your page.

If you do educational workshops or seminars, the Events tab is what you will want the responders to the ads to land on. It is a great way to drive traffic to the page and also let people sign up for the event. (We will talk about that soon, too.)

It will then ask you what you want people to see. You cannot choose, "Stories about their friends liking (your page)!" Compliance will explode if you try to use a testimonial to drive business to your fan page. Choose, "A new ad about . . .". This will create a cascade of options.

With Timeline you will have a headline. This is fixed and you cannot change it. Not sure why Facebook would not allow you to edit something like this. I am sure they will fix it in the future.

You can change the body of the advertisement. You will want to be ready to try different things. Since I am going to recommend having people land on an event you have planned, we will discuss how you can position it in a short and succinct manner to get their attention.

Remember, this has to be approved by your compliance department; do not think that I have already done that for you because I have not.

You only have 90 characters, so you have even less space than you do when you are tweeting. Following are some samples:

Markets confusing? Come and learn how to interpret the markets and make educated decisions. (88 characters)

Can I retire? Asked that question over and over? Find out how to decide when you can. (85 characters)

Lost your job? Wondering what to do with your 401k? Come see a transition specialist. (85 characters)

Now, let's say you don't do workshops but you want to scale the effectiveness of your ad. Maybe you are sponsoring a local golf outing or Relay for Life. You can use the Facebook ad to drive attendance to your booth and advertise for the event you are sponsoring. If you look directly below the text box we are working on, you will see that you can add an image. This is a great way to do co-advertising with the event itself or another business. For example:

> Playing in the OCC Golf Outing? Get a free sleeve of balls; you might need them. (81 characters)
> 24 hours of walking/running in Relay for Life is a good kind of tired. Stop by our booth. (89 characters)

You can choose an image for your ad. I recommend you use your company logo. This will help with overall brand awareness and recognition. It will ask you where you want those who click on your add to land. I recommend you have them land on the Timeline itself so they can get a good feel for your company.

You might be asking, why would I advertise implying I know these people are coming to that event? Well, this is the cool and kind of spooky thing about Facebook advertising. *Facebook knows what you are doing!* How, you might ask? Well, people are very free telling their friends what they are doing. You can put in keywords to search specific profiles and in specific locations so you can target the right people (see Figure 11.3).

First, you can be location-specific all the way down to zip codes. We want to be as specific as we can be; if there is a more affluent zip code or codes in your area, make sure you put that in. If you do not know what those zip codes are, Google Maps will help you. All you have to do is go on Google Maps, find the rich areas near your town, zoom in, and you will be able to see a house number and zip code.

Demographics

I am assuming you want to target a specific age group; baby boomers, I assume. Well, you can also put in a specific age range. If you only work with women, this is a great way to target them directly.

Now, I want you to notice that the box on the right-hand side, as shown in Figure 11.4, started out with a really large number. As you get more specific, the number will go down. Watch that number. You do not want it to be too big, because it will be expensive and you would not be using Facebook marketing efficiently. This is meant to be very specific. Use the tool to get that number down to a manageable number. You will be targeting exactly who you want to reach. Now, we will get more specific.

FIGURE 11.3 Targeting the Right People

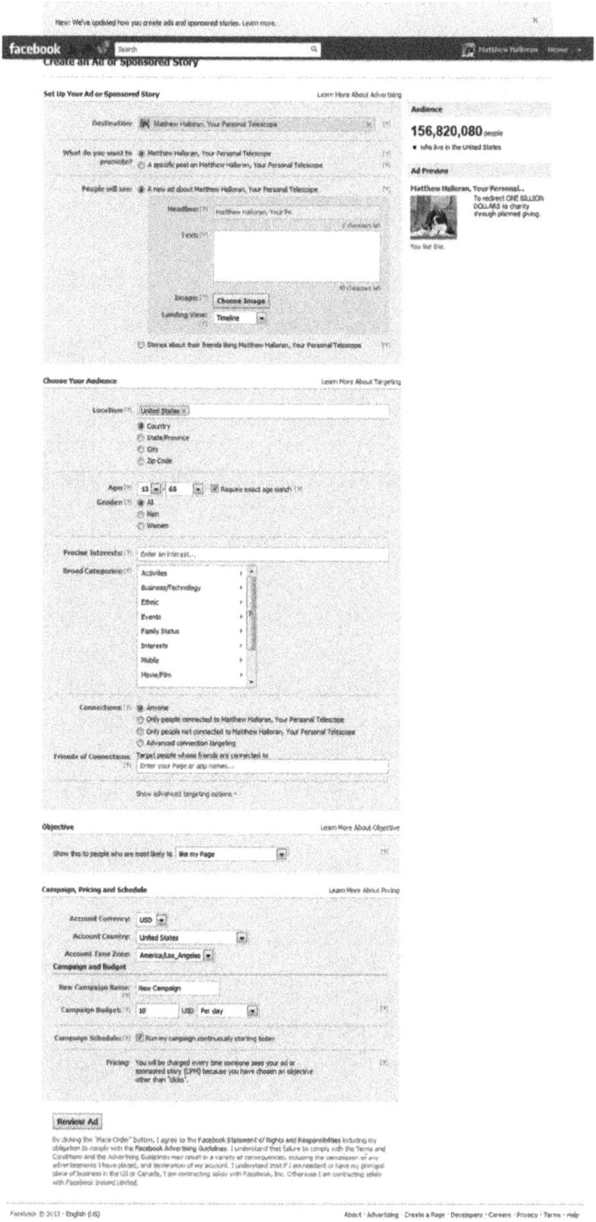

FIGURE 11.4 Targeting

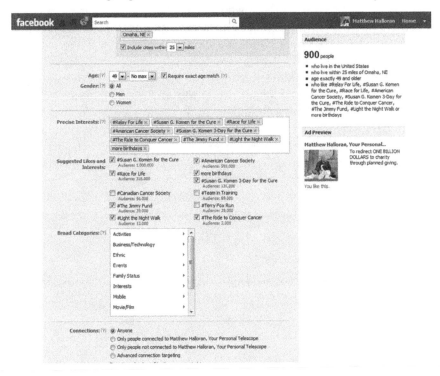

As shown in Figure 11.4, I input Omaha, NE, as my location because it is a mid-size city, checking the box to include cities within 25 miles; I chose age 49 and older, both men and women; and then targeted precise interests. Since I used the Relay for Life as an example, I selected all of the organizations that were like Relay for Life to increase my target audience.

I went from 158 million down to 900. This is how powerful Facebook advertising is. Let me explain further what this means. There are 900 people in the greater Omaha area who are age 49 and older who have already *liked* those five specific interests. I know they like them because they took the time to click on *like* for those pages. When your ad shows up on their page on the right-hand side, it will speak to them and their interests.

But wait, there's more!

- Connections on Facebook:

  You can advertise to those who are not fans of your page and those who are fans, and to get even more advanced, you can connect with friends of friends, or anyone. I recommend *anyone* since we are trying to drive traffic (see Figure 11.5).

- Advanced Targeting options:

  As you can see from Figure 11.5, you can click on *Show advanced targeting options*. Let's say you only focus on single women. You can target them here. Maybe you only want to work with people who are about to get married or who are married. Again, you can get that specific. In bigger cities, I would recommend you get really specific; in smaller towns, be less specific.

- Education and Work:

  Are you an advisor who wants to get in the door with a specific company locally but you have had an impossible time getting past their

FIGURE 11.5   Connections on Facebook

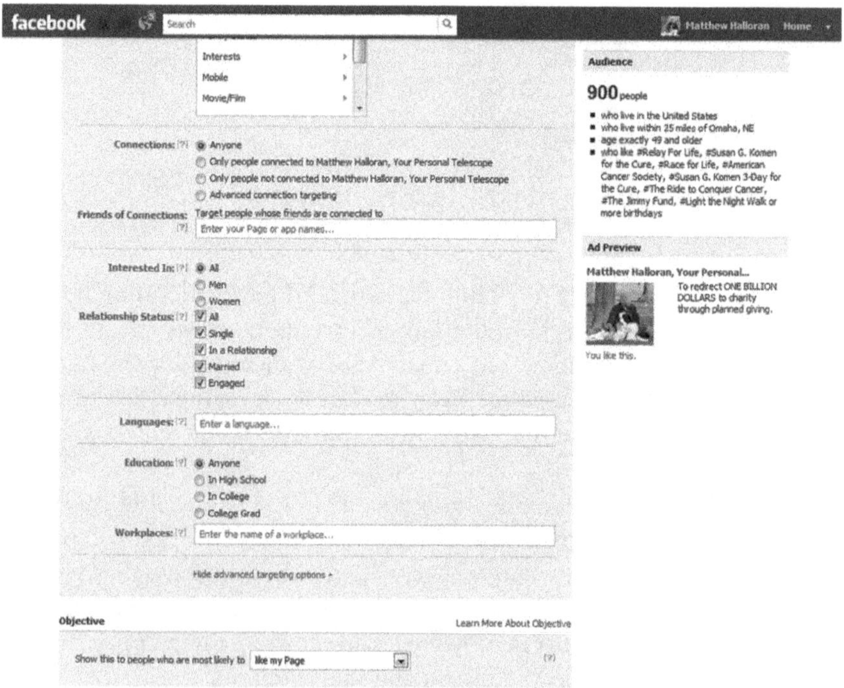

human resources gatekeeper? Well, Facebook can help! Let's explore this quickly.

You have a national headquarters for, let's say, Verizon in your hometown. You have a few Verizon employees, but not enough. You can change this advertisement to focus only on them.

Attention Verizon employees, are you taking the planned buyout? Attend a free workshop. (87 characters)

You can then get specific again with your targeting. You can assume those who will be taking the buyout are over age 53, live within 50 miles of your town, have Verizon as one of their interests, and currently work at Verizon.

There are no limits to how and who you can target on Facebook. Even if you are an advisor who only wants to work with people who do live-action role-playing of Civil War battles, you can target those people. You can run multiple ads at a time and see each one's effectiveness. Maybe one wording works better and gains more attention than another. With Facebook, you will be able to track this information.

Pricing and Scheduling

Let's finish the ad. We will use the Relay for Life example to finish this out (see Figure 11.6).

We need to talk about money. Yes, you will need money. This is how Facebook makes its money. Do you remember how much that magazine article was going to run you? Well, I promise Facebook will be less and with the specificity available, it is worth it.

You need to modify your time zone at the top of the page if you are anywhere outside of the Pacific time zone. I am not sure why, but it always seems to default there.

I have worked with so many advisors who are really cheap. Being financially responsible with your own money is a great trait to have—and one all advisors should have. But please do not be too frugal here. Just because you say you want to have a $500 budget for the lifetime of the ad does not mean you will always spend that amount. It depends on the activity the ad creates. I always recommend setting a lifetime budget. That way, if you suddenly get a huge response and a lot of people liking your ad and

FIGURE 11.6 Campaigns, Pricing, and Scheduling

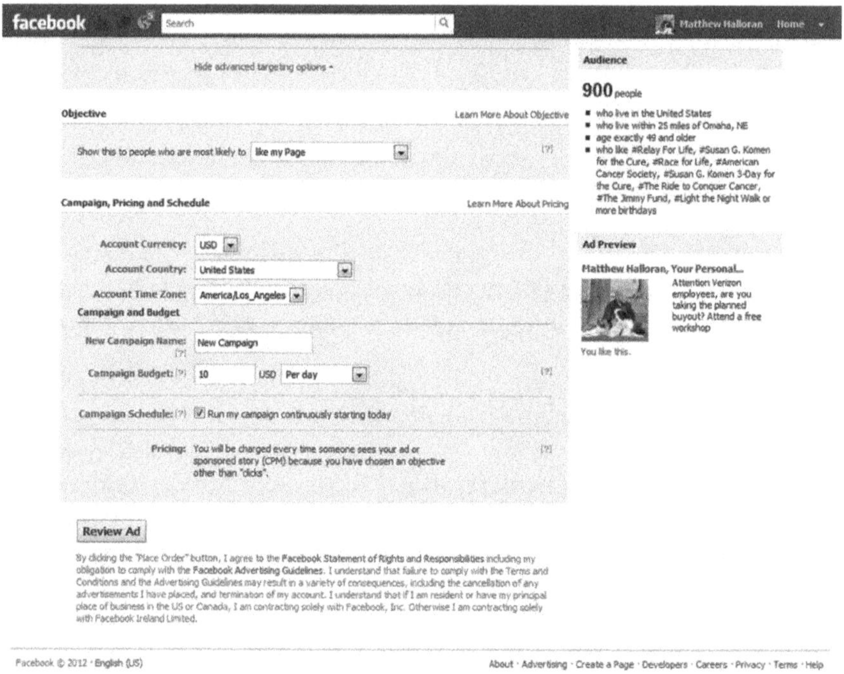

visiting your page, well, you know the ad worked and it was money well spent. You should put more money on the advertisement. Making a lifetime budget is also good for your overall budget and tracking.

Now, let's take some time to talk about pricing. According to the Facebook Help Center, the cost per click or cost per impression does influence the placement of your ad and the amount of exposure it will receive.

> For any available ad inventory, Facebook selects the best ad to run based on the cost per click or cost per one thousand impressions and ad performance. All Facebook ads compete with each other to show for each impression, regardless of their bid model.

This means you should not be the cheapest and you need not be the most expensive bid. There is a good amount of competition. Think about it this way: If MasterCard is paying $10 per click and you are paying $5 per click, yours will get shown, just not as much as MasterCard. At the bottom of the page, you will see a suggested bid. I do not believe Facebook is trying to influence you; this is most likely what you should pay. Just pay it and see what happens.

Now, put a timeframe on the advertisement. Start it today and run it for a month.

Remember to use the CPC (cost per click) so you will only pay if a person clicks on the ad itself. And make sure you review the ad (see Figure 11.7) to make sure it looks the way you want it to before it goes live.

This is your invoice. Click on *place order* only after you submit this sheet to compliance. This is the document you need to submit along with your compliance approval form. After they approve it, you can place the order.

Facebook will track the effectiveness of your advertisement. Very few print marketing sources, if any, can provide you with the real-time data Facebook can when it comes to advertising. There are countless companies who have stopped using wildly expensive television and radio advertising

FIGURE 11.7   Review Ad

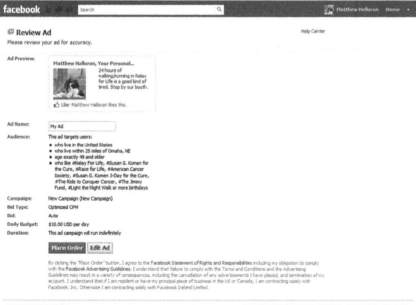

and have just started focusing on Facebook advertising. This is the wave of the future.

Television and radio can give you some rough information about who your ad will get in front of, but you tell Facebook exactly who you want to target.

I want to show some personal examples. These are companies who advertise to me. I also want to show you what the consumer of your advertisements can do to give you better feedback.

Figure 11.8 shows advertising on my fan page. Again, it is nothing special—just a hobby that gets a lot of traffic. I have posted a lot of quotes, commentaries, and other posts on here for a while now. Some time ago, I posted that I was going to do the P90X workout to get back into shape. I communicated this because I thought if I was going to do speeches on success and goal setting, it would be hard to pull off if I was overweight. So I would post updates on my progress, how sore I was, and then how many inches off my waist I lost. I said I was not sure what I was training for, and then these ads started to show up.

These advertisements are specifically targeted to me because of what I posted on my wall. This is both the unsettling part and the genius of Facebook. The keywords *exercise, P90X, training, workout,* and *race* are all

FIGURE 11.8 Fan Page Advertising

things I posted on my wall. Now the ads are speaking right to what I have talked about. Your ads can do this, too.

There is another layer of power the consumer and you have with these advertisements.

Feedback

So many times, we think we know what to say to whom. Most of the time, we are wrong. Should there be an alcohol commercial at every break during a hockey game? Well, maybe on some level it makes sense, but they are casting such a wide net. Kids see those commercials. With Facebook, you can control the ages of the people who will see your ads. Television and radio cannot do that, and neither can magazines or newspapers.

Here is what the viewers of your ad can do: If they hover their mouses over the ad, in the upper right-hand corner a little (very small) X will show up. When they click on the X, a box, as shown in Figure 11.9, will replace the ad.

The person viewing your ad can give feedback, some of it quite pointed. By clicking that X, they are removing your ad from their page. On the other hand, if they click *Like*, they register that they like your page or ad. If they really like the ad, they can click on the ad itself and see where it takes them.

FIGURE 11.9 Feedback

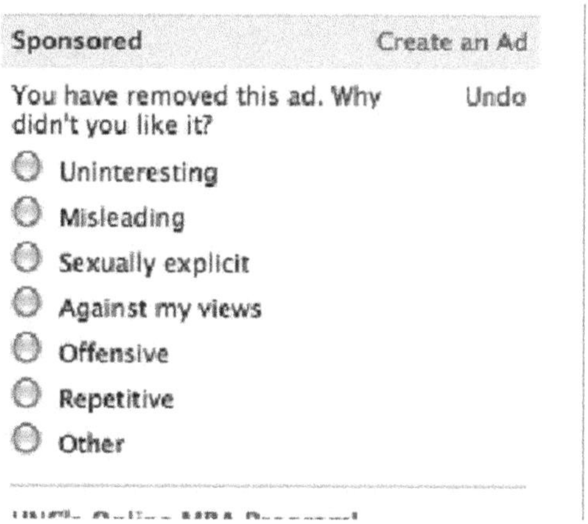

Sponsored   Create an Ad

You have removed this ad. Why   Undo
didn't you like it?

○ Uninteresting
○ Misleading
○ Sexually explicit
○ Against my views
○ Offensive
○ Repetitive
○ Other

I cannot impress on you enough how powerful these advertisements are. I have learned about races I want to compete in, ways to support my fellow veterans, kept up to date on my favorite present day philosophers, and learned new and important information pertaining to issues I care about, because Facebook does such a good job targeting me. If I do not like the ad, I tell the advertiser about it. I have bought many products from these ads. In fact, I am going to run in two races because of such ads.

Final Thoughts

A final thought before we get to some of the tools that can make your Facebook experience even better. Advertising, if done well, does work in the financial services industry. I know many of your mentors have told you that advertising is just throwing away good money you could spend somewhere else. That thinking has sailed. Those old timers (no offense to my fellow gray-haired folks) need to update their thinking. Even though the rest of the world has embraced this type of advertising and advisors are a little late to the dance, there is still a dance going on. It is a huge dance party where people want you to be dancing. People who are on Facebook like the tailored advertising; they want it, and it is becoming the new normal. Welcome aboard to a new way to get your message to those who want to hear it. It is about time.

In the next chapter, I will show you how to add videos and schedule events using your Facebook fan page!

CHAPTER 12

Facebook Applications and Tools

Matthew Halloran

There are a lot of options on Facebook, just like there are on Twitter, when it comes to applications. Applications are tools that help you maximize your use of the social media tool. On Facebook specifically, I will recommend a few applications that will increase the professionalism of your fan page as well as give you the flexibility to offer more on the page itself.

Advanced Facebook Applications

Since you are the administrator of the page, you have many options available to specialize your types of communication. As with most advisors, you will have clients from all over the country. Some of you have clients that speak different languages. With geotagging, you can focus on, for example, your Spanish-speaking clients.

Geotagging works by specifying in what location or geographic areas you want your media to post. It also specifies what language your followers or prospects speak. I believe Facebook will eventually allow you to be more specific on location, but now you can only specify a country, not a specific geographic location within a country.

For example, say you want to target those clients who speak Spanish and Swedish. Perhaps you are having the first Spanish/Swedish potluck. I am sure those two types of food will match really well. I highly recommend someone out there try this event! I would love to hear how well tamales and salted herring mix together on one's palate.

First, you create the invitation to this event and you specifically invite people who speak those two languages:

> Johannson Financial Management would like to invite all of our Spanish and Swedish clients to our first Double S potluck. Bring your favorite dish that represents your country! It will be June 19, at 5:00 p.m., in our main conference room.

You have the opportunity to click on *Public* and access a drop-down menu (see Figure 12.1). Public means that everyone can see your post. You can customize who sees your posts if you want. I do not recommend customizing; you want to post things that everyone can read. That is how you will get compliance approval anyway, for the general public.

FIGURE 12.1   Choose Your Audience

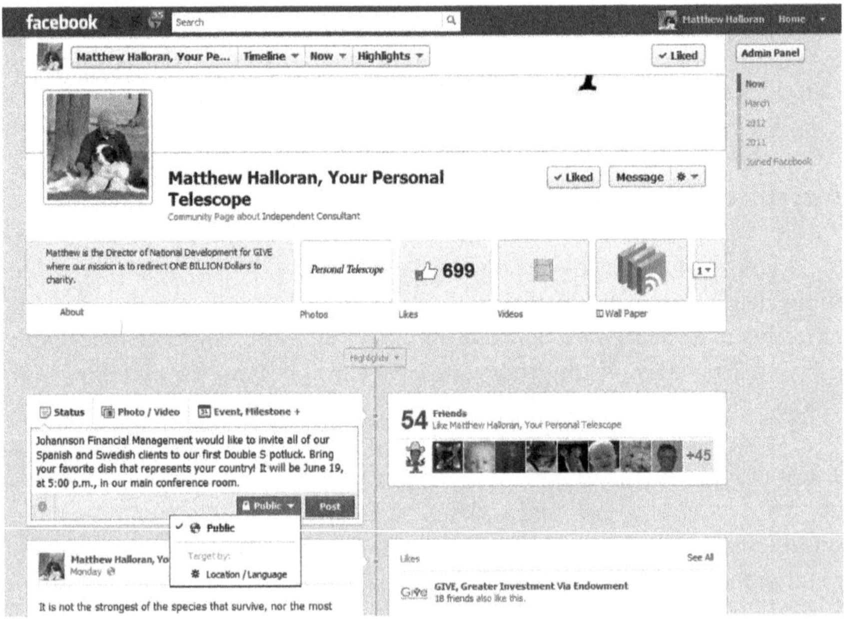

FIGURE 12.2 Customize Options

Next you will click on *Location/Language*. This screen will show the country and language options you want to choose, as shown in Figure 12.2. Start typing languages into the languages section. It will allow you to select from a drop-down menu (see Figure 12.3) of specifically spelled and tagged languages. You must choose the suggested ones that appear in order to get the results you want.

As Facebook continues to make improvements to geotagging, this will be a great tool to focus your communication to specific groups. I do not think Facebook is too far off from this, and that is why it is included here.

Video Apps

Let's say you are a speaker who does public workshops in addition to giving speeches in your community. Facebook is a great place to advertise these workshops and announce when those events are happening. Before we

FIGURE 12.3 Audience Drop-Down Menu Options

discuss events, however, let's first get a video of you on your page so you can show off a little.

The best way to find applications on Facebook is to use the search bar that is at the top of your page. But with Timeline you have a Video button right in the middle of your page (see Figure 12.4).

Note: You can upload both videos and photos. I highly recommend you also upload professional photos here such as pictures of your office, staff, you, events, and local landmarks. Your fan page is a great way for you to round out your brand; it is a way for people to feel connected to you in the privacy of their own homes. You should have action shots of you meeting with clients and pictures of you smiling and enjoying yourself. Fake it if you have to.

Now, back to videos. If you have done workshops before, I hope you had someone record it. If you have not, make sure you get a high quality camera and videotape your next workshop.

FIGURE 12.4 Video Search

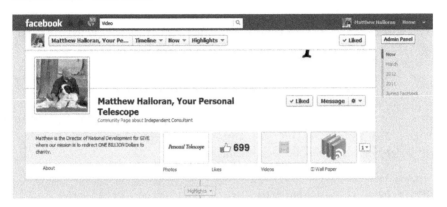

A word of caution: Do not post poor quality videos! This is a professional page and everything should look and sound professional. You should spell check every post and you should make sure you check your videos for quality.

I would like to ask for all advisors to budget a small amount—$2,500, depending on your area—and get a local studio to videotape and edit it for you. If you are in Los Angeles, this will be more expensive. If you are in a small town in the Midwest, well, it could be less.

After the video is shot and it looks great, you will post it. For those out there who are trying to save money and do this on your webcam, *don't do it!* I can feel that some of you are looking at your computer right now and are saying to yourself, "Hey I have a camera right here on my computer so why can't I make something more intimate and just shoot it here in my office?" Some of you are thinking that; I know because I have been asked that same question many times by the advisors I have worked with.

Spend the money; it will put a much better face on your company than a cheap webcam with a terrible background, with you looking at the computer screen instead of the camera. Get someone to shoot it for you!

Okay, I am done with my rant.

The video should be saved in a normal format: .mov, .mp4, .avi, .mpeg, or .wmv. Facebook should convert it to a standard user-friendly video format. For instance, if you have it saved as a .wmv, Mac users cannot view the video. After you pay someone to shoot and edit the video, ask them to save it in an .mpeg format. This will be the most user-friendly format; you can even see those types of video files on tablets and phones.

Click on the *Add Video* button at the top of the page. (See Figure 12.5.) Find where that video is saved on your hard drive (or wherever it is saved). All you have to do is click on that file location and it will start uploading the video to your fan page as shown in Figure 12.6!

You can also tag people in the video. You should only have people in this video who are on your team. If there are clients in the video, then you need to get releases from them for compliance and it gets somewhat complicated. So tag yourself and any team member in the video. Tagging notifies that person that they have been identified in a video or a picture and can authorize their name to be used in that post.

FIGURE 12.5   +Upload Video Button

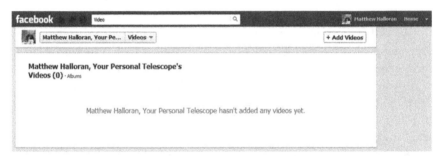

FIGURE 12.6   Uploading Video Screen

Come up with a good title. I would recommend you use the title of your talk. Create a complete description with keywords. What are you talking about? Explain what the video is and where it was taken.

After you have the video(s) posted, you will see a still shot of the video show up in the middle of your page right by the number of *Likes you have.*

You can share these videos in posts as often as you would like. Since the video we are working with here is one of your workshop, you will want to post this along with your event invitations (advertisements) so people can preview what they will be attending.

Creating Events

This leads us to events. I love this part of Facebook. It is a robust, free application that lets you market your events to all your friends or to people who like your page on Facebook. You can get some traction here with your events; so let's create one.

You heard that other advisors have had great success with a shredding party after April 15th every year (some do, by the way; there is a free and proven-successful event idea). Clients and their friends bring their documents and you sit down with them to advise them on what to shred. Advisors I have worked with get one or two new clients from the event every year. Your clients will thank you and you will enjoy it. So let's get some more people to attend!

Begin by looking in the status box. Select *Event/Milestone* (Figure 12.7.) Now, click on *Event*, as shown in Figure 12.8.

There are a lot of pieces to this event puzzle. I want to take them one section at time (see Figure 12.9).

On the left of the screen, you will see that you can add a photo. This should be the cover of your compliance-approved invitation. We are working on overall brand recognition. The cover of your invitation should explain the event and also brand your company.

After you have uploaded either your logo or the complete invitation, you need to input the start date of the event. Here is some basic event advice: Do not hold an event two weeks out and then wonder why people don't show. It is proper etiquette to give at least four weeks' notice on an event. That also depends on the time of year. The closer it is to the holidays, the more time you need to give.

FIGURE 12.7   Events App Menu

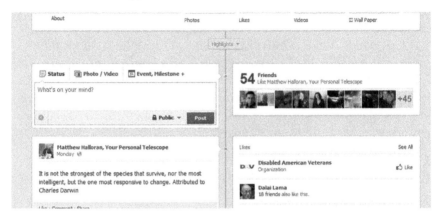

FIGURE 12.8   Create an Event Screen

So, since you are doing a shredding event, the date should be as close to April 15th as possible. We will look at April 16th to hold the event.

You will select it from a calendar that appears on screen. The arrows will advance the months. After you add the date, you can put in a time. Since we are going to have a definitive start time and end time, you will want to click on the add end time button next to the time box.

The event starts at 10 a.m. and ends at 1:30 p.m. Since you will be serving lunch, we want to give them time to sit down, enjoy a meal, and get their shreddables shredded.

FIGURE 12.9   Create an Event

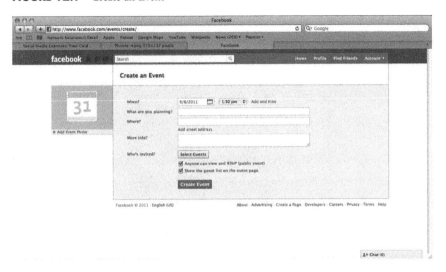

FIGURE 12.10   Johannson Financial Services Create an Event Page

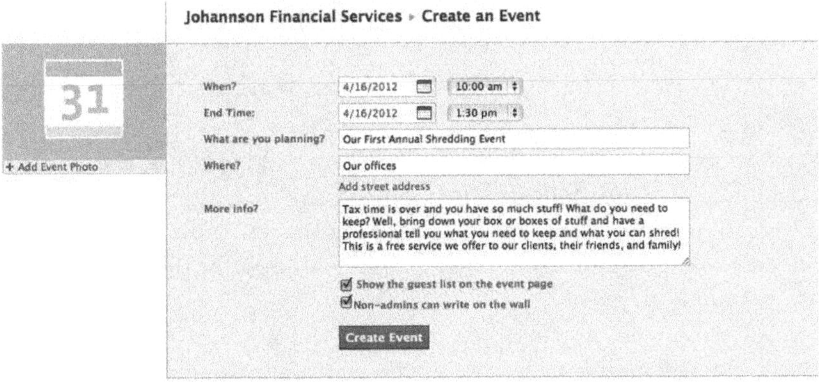

You should also make sure to put down the exact address of your location. Use a snappy title and a complete description of the event itself (see Figure 12.10).

You will see at the bottom of this page that there is a way to select guests and send them a formal Facebook invitation. I would recommend if you

FIGURE 12.11   Our First Annual Shredding Event Page

have people who like this page, select them to send them something on the event. I would also uncheck the *Non-admins can write on the wall,* just to be safe with compliance, or leave checked if compliance will allow you to do this. Your compliance department might allow you to have attendees write on your wall saying they are attenting an event. Some will and some won't. Some compliance departments will look at the *Show guest list on the event page* as a testimonial. You and I know this is not true, but beware.

We want people to view this event and RSVP. When you are ready, click on *Create Event* to make it active.

You can share this event on your wall by clicking *Share,* and writing a post informing your followers that you posted an event as seen in Figure 12.11. Inform all of your fans that you are having this event and then post it on your wall. Make sure you click the *Join* button to be the first to say you are attending the event.

All those who are attending the event will say they are attending the event. You will be able to get a good idea who is attending and who is not. If they are fans of your page, the event will show up on the right-hand side near the top. It will ask them if they are going to attend the event, maybe attend, or not attend.

This is a great way to use your fan page for business. I really like the event application. I have had friends and business partners use this for years and it has given them some great feedback on their events. It can do the same for you.

More Facebook Apps

Now that we have looked at the video app and the event app, what else can you do on your fan page? Well, the possibilities are limitless. New applications are created for Facebook every day. I want to highlight a few more.

Polls

If you want to engage your fans, polls are a great way to do it. You can also use the information you gain from polling your fans to get your face on the local news or in the local press. Ask good questions such as, "Do you see the current political climate as something that will change the market?" or "How concerned are you as a client about the troubles the European Union is facing?"

Again, these polls have to be compliance approved. As per the regulations I have reviewed, polls are not even mentioned. Some advisors think they need to show their clients that they know everything and will not want to use polls. I find that polling is a great way to keep your finger on the pulse of what concerns your clients have right now! This can help you create presentations or hold a conference call.

For instance, you can say: "I wanted to hold this conference call because we did a poll on our Facebook fan page and a number of clients are quite concerned how the European Union debt issues will affect their retirement income. So we will take about a half an hour today to talk about what we feel is going to impact you and what we are doing about it."

This is a great way to connect and communicate with your clients. It also will inform the clients who are on the call that there is a fan page out there they need to like. Having a poll can help you create another event on your page. It is all intertwined.

Extended Info

This application allows you to expand or extend the amount of text you were and are able to write in a specific space. Let's say you wanted to elaborate on what your company does or who you are. The extended info application allows you to elaborate to your heart's content. Please be careful; short and sweet is the best way people digest social media posts. Do not get too verbose!

Final Thoughts

Now you have the ability to create a Facebook fan page, post updates, link your account to your Twitter account, post images and videos, create events, advertise, and get some snappy applications that can help your fan page to be everything you want.

As I said in the beginning of the Facebook section, your fan page will become your main web presence. You, for the time being, will still need a web page, but the days of web pages are not long for the twenty-first-century technological reality. Why would anyone pay huge sums of money to a web developer when they can build an interactive page that can look as good and function as a web page for *free*?

There are companies out there now who can and will create and maintain your Facebook pages. There are very few that exist in the advisor market. I would highly recommend that you try to do all this yourself. You need to know how this stuff works. You need to have a presence. You need to be able to post, upload, and create events. Even if you are a good advisor and delegate this to a twenty-something person in your office, you need to have procedures in place to make this still happen when your twenty-something taps into his true calling as a MMA fighter.

Facebook has changed everything just as much as the telephone once did. This is the way people are communicating. If you do not exist on Facebook, then there is a growing demographic of people who will not think you exist at all. That demographic is getting older and is becoming the demographic you want to reach with your advertisements.

CHAPTER 13

Public Relations on Facebook

Matthew Halloran

As with Twitter, Facebook can be a great tool for your public relations. With Twitter, you only got a glimpse of how to work with reporters to promote yourself. With Facebook, you can do so much more.

Research has shown that over 70 percent of journalists use social media for research and story content. How do they do this? They use the search functions available through social media!

Making Use of the Groups Platform

Do you see the search bar at the top of your Facebook page? That is a search engine. Let's say you want to find people who are experts in retirement income. Well, why not type that in to your search?

What you hope is that there is not a group or a company with that name because if there is, you will link directly to that specific company's Facebook page. If there is not a group that focuses on retirement income, well, create it! Again, make sure your compliance department knows that you are creating a group on Facebook specifically for educational reasons.

How do you create a group? On the left-hand side of your Facebook page (not your fan page)(see Figure 13.1), you should see *groups*. Since you are not following or involved with any groups yet, there should not be anything under it.

145

FIGURE 13.1 Facebook Groups

If you do not see *groups* on the sidebar, type *groups* into your search bar at the top of the page. You will probably see many things; look for the Groups App. Click on that, and you will be able to create a group.

Next, click on the *Create Group* link, as shown in Figure 13.2.

Type in the name of the group you are creating, such as *retirement income information*, or whatever field it is that you specialize in. Next, click on the privacy button and make it open for all to see. You have to add at least one member to create the group. If the name of your group is already taken, get creative but not too creative. We want people to be able to find and identify your group as you. The best way to specify and to create a group name is use the name you came up with and put your location at the end. For instance, you could use *Retirement Income Information, Cleveland, Ohio*.

Creating a group is a good way to draw attention to you in relation to a specific topic. Your fan page may include keywords, but for someone to find you in relation to a specific topic, the group function is the way to go.

Once the group is established, you can post specific information to that group. What I recommend is when you post something to your fan page that is specific to the group, post it on the groups page, too.

You need to know what your standard talking points are going to be when you are communicating here. This is because you created a group that

FIGURE 13.2   Create Group Screen

might be pulled up in a search but that won't get noticed by journalists. You want to take advantage of messaging and learn how to post the sort of message that will effectively get you noticed.

I would like for you to go to your local news station's website and see if they have a finance section. If they do not have a page dedicated to consumer finance, search their site for finance topics. Do this in order to find out what information the general public is learning from the news. You can also post links to good stories in your area on your fan page or your group from your local news station. If the news organization has any social media savvy, they will see that traffic is coming from your page and might pay attention to you.

Spend more time using Facebook for public relations (PR) research. Seeing what your colleagues are talking about can give you a great opening on topics to talk about with an editor! Ask your followers open-ended questions about current events. Facebook also has polls you can create and use to your advantage! Create a poll (again, by searching *polls*, in the search bar) and poll your followers. When you speak with the editors at your local news station, you can tell them you created a poll on Facebook and received feedback from over 100 people (or whatever number); the results could shock you and get you attention from your local press.

More Ways to Get Noticed

There are other lead-ins you can use when talking to editors or with newspapers, blogs, radios, and television stations.

> Wall Street is getting raked over the coals as you know; would you be interested in talking to a person who has to ride the line between Wall Street and the average investor?

There is much information available dedicated to teach journalists how to use Facebook search tools to find stories! There is also a Facebook page dedicated to information on the search functions (see Figure 13.3). If you want to find more information on any topic, all you have to do is conduct a search with your favorite search engine.

Keywords are important to use in the information section (info) on your fan page. If you want people to find you, include all of the related search words in your profile!

Be Proactive

Okay, so we know the media is out there looking for us. Do we wait until they find us? Do we stand idly by waiting for CNN to call us or friend us on Facebook? Heck no! Let's find them! Who should you connect with in your community that is in media? Who is your favorite local news anchor? Who is your favorite radio host? What is your favorite program? Is there a writer at your local paper whose articles you just can't pass up reading?

If you have been a financial advisor for more than 10 years, research shows that you have mastered this profession. So that also means you are an expert! Experts do not know everything; they know a lot. You know a lot. It is your duty as a professional to tell people what you know. I used to talk to my consulting clients about this all the time.

I was consulting an advisor in New Haven, Connecticut, who really wanted to have a presence on the local TV station. He started researching the local talent and found out who he needed to get his face in front of in order to get himself on television. I advised him to use LinkedIn and Facebook to

FIGURE 13.3 Facebook Search

More than a billion pieces of content are posted to Facebook everyday. Facebook Search enables journalists to filter through that content to find sources and story ideas on the platform.

For journalists, Facebook is a rolodex of more than 500 million potential sources. Using tools like the People Search and Group Search, journalists can find relevant sources for a story they are working on.

Similarly, during breaking news situations, journalists can use Facebook's Open Search to find out how people are reacting to the news on Facebook. Here's an outline of how you can use Facebook Search as a journalist:

1. **Open Search:** Use Facebook Search to find public "posts by everyone" that are relevant to a news story you are covering. Use key words from your story to filter results. You can put quotation marks around words (i.e. "word here") for exact phrase searches.
2. **People Search:** The people search enables you to find sources that you're looking to contact on Facebook. You can filter by location, education and workplace. If you find someone who you may want to use as a source, you can go to their profile and message them privately through Facebook Messages without being their friend.
3. **Facebook Groups:** You can also search Facebook Groups to find sources who are members of specific groups. This can be useful for finding sources affiliated with political organizations, local organizations, etc.
4. **Events:** The Events search enables you to search through open Events being posted by people or organizations. If you're covering an event, you can usually find the event organizers based on who created the event on Facebook.
5. **Pages:** Similarly to Groups, Pages are often used for organizational and distribution purposes and can garner useful information around an organization or event. You can search for Pages by keywords.

find out who exactly those people were. He contacted them, messaging them on Facebook and LinkedIn and calling them the old-fashioned way. He was very persistent. It paid off exponentially. He is currently on the local television Saturday morning news once a month being interviewed about the economy! He has solidified those relationships by following them on Twitter, friending them on Facebook, and connecting with them on LinkedIn. This is not an isolated example of one advisor. You, too, can be as successful as that advisor. The press loves social media and it is a free way for them to get leads, story ideas, and contacts.

Being on Facebook lets you connect with other people on Facebook. To get good public relations contacts, you should type in the name of your local news reporter or editor and request them to become friends with you. Search the web to see if they have a blog. If they do, subscribe to it, and like that blog (there is a Facebook *Like* button on just about every blog). Comment on the blogs when you see something you like (again, inform compliance you are doing this). Post links to the blogs on your fan page. The new compliance regulations allow you to post links so that people will know you did not write the content yourself. Just make sure the blogs you are linking to do not contain inflammatory content.

Final Thoughts

I love Facebook, and after you get more comfortable with this medium, I know you will, too. It is such a great way to communicate with your clients, prospects, and centers of influence. Facebook is the way younger people communicate with each other. If you do not learn this medium, you will be losing market share. Instead of spending thousands of dollars on a website that is static, you can create a free fan page and interact with your clients at your convenience and theirs, in the comfort of your own homes.

PART IV

LinkedIn

CHAPTER 14

Why LinkedIn?

Crystal Thies

After going through detailed descriptions of using Twitter and Facebook, you may now be asking yourself, "Why LinkedIn?" Isn't it essentially the same thing? Not really. LinkedIn is known as a business social network. Meaning that the goal and purpose are not to connect to have fun and make friends, but to connect to strengthen your business, career, and professional life.

You Can Control Referrals

A general rule of thumb for trying to sell using social networks is that if you're selling *business to consumer* (B2C), then Facebook and Twitter are the tools you need to use. If you're selling *business to business* (B2B), then LinkedIn and Twitter are the tools you should use. For the vast majority of financial advisors, your businesses would be considered as B2C and not B2B (except for those who focus on the small business owner niche). So again, you're likely asking, "Why bother with LinkedIn?"

Financial services belong to a very small subset of B2C companies with visible prospecting opportunities for a service or product that is more personal in nature. Because the LinkedIn profile is oriented toward professional and career experience and expertise, it would be difficult to determine if a person needed a chiropractor. However, since many people often engage a financial services professional during a time of transition in their lives—marriage, children, divorce, *and* job change, it is often possible to tell when someone is in transition and may have a need. It is particularly evident when someone is in job transition. As financial advisors, what gets us all excited when we hear job change? 401(k) rollover! LinkedIn is a gold mine for 401(k) rollover opportunities; we'll learn how this works in a later chapter.

401(k) rollover opportunities are not the only reason why LinkedIn is potentially the first social network in which you should invest your time and energy. Actually, they are part of the main reason to use LinkedIn—referrals! If you want to get to that 401(k) rollover opportunity you see or that small business owner or powerful corporate executive you'd love to have as a client, then you're going to have to be referred by someone who knows you and who knows them.

The true power of LinkedIn is that you can see who connects you to the people you want to get to. LinkedIn is the *only* social network that lets you do more than simply browse your 2nd degree connections (Facebook friends, Twitter followers). You can run highly targeted, advanced searches that will show you how you're connected with perfect prospects to the 3rd degree of your LinkedIn network. You've likely heard of a party game known as the *Six Degrees of Kevin Bacon*. Well, think of LinkedIn as your own personal version of *Six Degrees of Kevin Bacon*! Except in this case, you can only see three degrees, and instead of movie stars, the degrees span business connections and prospects.

If you've mastered the techniques taught by referral masters like Bill Cates (I first read his "Unlimited Referrals" as a financial advisor in the late 1990s when it was pretty much hot off the press), then using LinkedIn takes away a lot of the hard work and all of the mystery, except the ultimate answer because you pick the *who*. Additionally, you're not as dependent on your clients having to carry the weight of the activity to connect you. The frustration of trying to get your clients to follow through and actually contact the people they've agreed to refer you to and connect you with can make you want to beat your head against the wall! With LinkedIn, there is no more waiting because you initiate the introduction and the client simply forwards this with his or her own note attached. Even better is that since you're writing the original message to your client—which the referral will see—you control the actual message that the referral gets. We'll get more into that later.

LinkedIn Members Are More Affluent

LinkedIn is essentially an enormous database that you can mine to cherry-pick prospects. With a couple of clicks of a mouse, you can get all of the information about the person's professional accomplishments, which will save you a lot of time. It allows you to more easily prequalify them based on assumptions that can be made as a result of their career history. It can make the prospect more willing to meet with you because they can see all of the connections you may have in common so that you're no longer seen as a stranger. Think about how much this type of data could change your practice! No more wasted introductory meetings with prospects that clearly are not qualified or part of your target market. This means more time for strategic activity focused at getting in front of those prospects you really want.

Another reason why I believe LinkedIn is a *must use* social media for financial advisors is that I think it's easier to establish yourself as an expert within your professional network with the tools available on LinkedIn. Even though an individual's personal financial plan is technically a personal interest, because it's financially related, I think most people prefer to deal with the subject matter during business hours and not think about it once they get home. Most companies block access to Facebook and Twitter in the office, but many don't block LinkedIn. Therefore, if you want to be sharing content and have it seen during the business day, it's more likely to be seen on LinkedIn.

The final reason why you should be using LinkedIn is the demographic makeup of most of the people using LinkedIn. LinkedIn reached 100 million users shortly before its IPO, or initial public offering (as of this writing, less than a year later there are more than 150 million). Just following the 100 million milestone, www.OnlineMBA.com released an infographic with some very interesting demographic data:

- 45 million of the 100 million users are in the United States.
- 69 percent of users earn $60,000 per year or more.
- 39 percent of users earn $100,000 per year or more.
- 68 percent of users are older than 35 years.
- 74 percent of users have a bachelor's degree or higher.
- 26 percent of users have a graduate degree.

Are you salivating yet? You should be! If that's not enough, let's look at a more recent and direct comparison between LinkedIn and Facebook demographics of financial services customers. These statistics, shown in Figure 14.1, come from comScore Data Mine and are *true* statistics and not self-reported data. (www.comscoredatamine.com/2012/01/linkedin-financial-customers-more-affluent-than-facebook-users). Not only are the incomes higher, but so are their savings and checking accounts, suggesting that they have more disposable income available for investment or purchase of insurance products.

FIGURE 14.1 LinkedIn Financial Customers More Affluent than Facebook Users

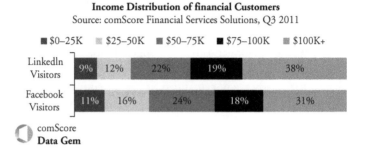

Income Distribution of financial customers
Source: comScore Financial Services Solutions, Q3 2011

■ $0–25K   ■ $25–50K   ■ $50–75K   ■ $75–100K   ■ $100K+

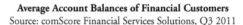

Average Account Balances of Financial Customers
Source: comScore Financial Services Solutions, Q3 2011

■ LinkedIn   ■ Facebook

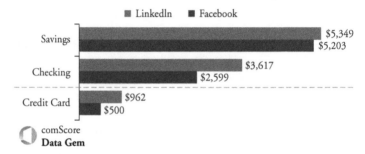

Financial Advisors Are Having Success With LinkedIn

At final review of this book, LinkedIn released the results or two important studies that I wanted to share with you.

The first study was a study of affluent investors using social media and was done in partnership with Cogent Research. They found that:

- There are 5 million "affluent investors" with $100,000 or more in investable assets and 73% of them use LinkedIn to research investment decisions.
- The "ultra affluent investors" with $5 million or more in investable assets are 157% more likely to trust articles shared on LinkedIn and 37% more likely to trust information shared by their LinkedIn network.
- Finally, 52% of affluent investors say that they would interact with financial advisors via social media, but only 4% currently are being engaged by financial advisors online.

The second study was a study of financial advisors using LinkedIn and was done in partnership with FTI Consulting. They found that:

- 62% of financial advisors actively prospecting on LinkedIn over the past year converted new clients from that process.
- 32% of the financial advisors who converted new clients from LinkedIn had $1 million or more in new assets under management from new clients.

The implications when you combine those two studies are resoundingly clear. The one place in social media where financial advisors have a great chance at successful development of new clients is LinkedIn.

Final Thoughts

So basically, in my opinion, if you were to only pick one social network to use as a financial advisor, I believe that LinkedIn is that social network. It's an amazing data source, prospecting tool, self-referral machine, and it has the most affluent users of any other public social network in the world.

Let's get started!

CHAPTER 15

Setting Up Your LinkedIn Account

Crystal Thies

If you have never set up a LinkedIn account, we're going to walk you through it in this chapter. If you have set up your account already, then you can skip to Chapter 16, where we'll talk about building an effective LinkedIn profile. Yes, you may technically have a completed profile, but that doesn't mean that it is completed in the best way or is an effective LinkedIn profile, so you definitely won't want to skip that chapter.

Joining LinkedIn

For those of you who haven't been on LinkedIn before, I'm going to include some screen shots of what you can expect to see as you set up your account. Depending on when you're reading this, what you see may be very different. To be honest, LinkedIn makes changes to its layout and user interface much more frequently than either Facebook or Twitter. LinkedIn is always changing. Additionally, they only apply new changes to small parts of the member base at a time until all the bugs are worked out and they are committed to the change for everyone. So I have literally been looking at two different LinkedIn accounts at exactly the same time, which look different and even have different functionalities. However, for the most part all of the important parts should still be there.

Step number one is to go to www.linkedin.com and click *Join LinkedIn*, as shown in Figure 15.1. Each LinkedIn account is tied to an email address. The same email address cannot be associated with more than one LinkedIn account. Actually, this is how people end up with duplicate LinkedIn profiles. They start using a new email address and forget that they already created a LinkedIn profile using the old email address. By the way, I don't recommend using the Facebook connect to sign up. First, as of this writing, there is little integration with Facebook. Second, if you've been using Facebook for personal use, LinkedIn is going to grab that personal email address as the main email address for your LinkedIn account, and you don't want that if you're using LinkedIn for business.

Remember what we talked about back in Chapter 1? In regard to compliance, if you're using LinkedIn for business purposes and you're all signed up with your social media archiving program, then the email address you *must* use is you official FINRA email address. If your broker-dealer isn't allowing use of social media for business purposes yet and you are planning on using LinkedIn for personal use only, then use a personal email address.

LinkedIn will forward notifications and messages from connections to your primary email address (you can have more than one email address affiliated with your account). If you're using your FINRA email address, this means that all of these notifications and messages will be captured by your

FIGURE 15.1   Join LinkedIn

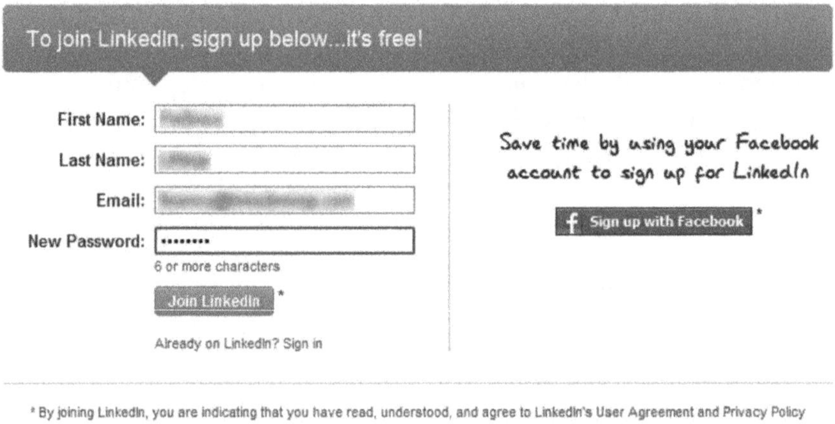

To join LinkedIn, sign up below...it's free!

First Name:

Last Name:

Email:

New Password:
6 or more characters

Save time by using your Facebook account to sign up for LinkedIn

f Sign up with Facebook *

Join LinkedIn *

Already on LinkedIn? Sign in

* By joining LinkedIn, you are indicating that you have read, understood, and agree to LinkedIn's User Agreement and Privacy Policy

email archiving system and reviewed by your compliance department. Therefore, if you're using it on a purely personal basis and you use your FINRA email address, your broker-dealer will know that you're using LinkedIn and will see the personal messages.

WHY EMAIL ADDRESSES ARE SO IMPORTANT

You can have multiple email addresses affiliated with your LinkedIn account, but only one email address is designated as your primary address, which appears on your profile to your connections and is used by LinkedIn for sending notifications and log-in purposes. You should add every email address you actively use to your LinkedIn account. Additionally, if you leave a company or stop using an email address that is on your LinkedIn account and that has been confirmed, you should *not* remove that email address from your account. The reason for this is that when people want to connect with you, they may be required to use your email address, depending on their relationship with you or if their LinkedIn account gets restricted. If the email address they use is not affiliated with your account, then LinkedIn won't see that invitation to connect as intended for you and consequently, you'll never get it.

LinkedIn will walk you through a wizard to gather some basic information. This information can and will be easily changed once we go into the profile editing process, so I wouldn't be too concerned about it right now. We'll talk more in detail about how these fields should be completed in Chapter 16. When I set up a new test account to use for the purpose of writing this book, what I entered in the first setup step shown in Figure 15.2 wasn't even saved to my new profile and I had to add it again. So, enter something in this field because LinkedIn requires you to, but know that you'll likely change it after you confirm your account. I can only assume that it didn't save my information because of some sort of glitch in the program. LinkedIn is an extremely large and complex program that is always changing. So don't be surprised or concerned by little issues like this.

In the second step, LinkedIn wants to invite people in your address book to connect (see Figure 15.3). I highly recommend skipping this step at this time. We're going to want to do this when we can be more strategic and have greater control.

That's as far as you can go until you check your email and click on the confirmation link that LinkedIn sent you (see Figure 15.4).

FIGURE 15.2 Setup Screen

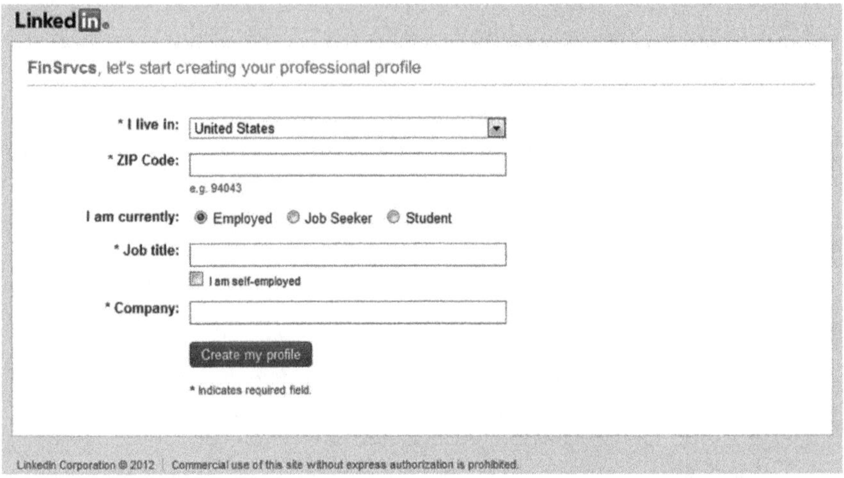

FIGURE 15.3 LinkedIn Contacts

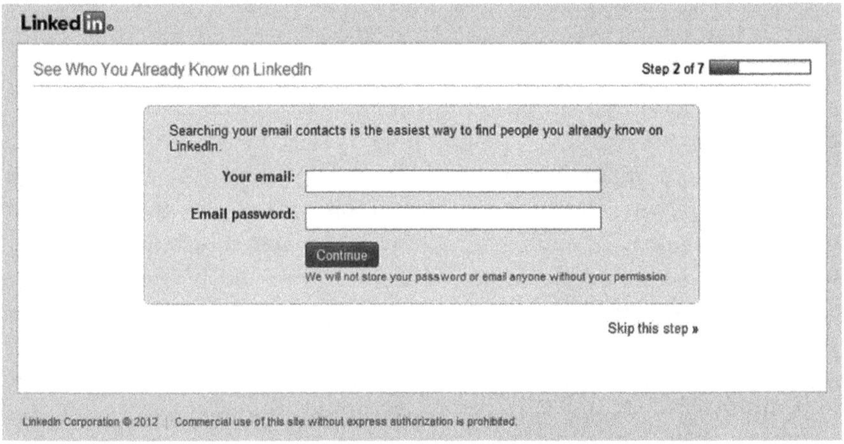

Next, LinkedIn will try to convince you to share on Twitter or Facebook. Personally, since you don't have your profile built out yet, I think it's a waste of opportunity to broadcast that you're on LinkedIn until your profile is finished (see Figure 15.5), so I recommend skipping this step.

Next, LinkedIn will ask you if you want to stick to a Basic or Premium account (see Figure 15.6). For now, just click on *Skip* or *Basic*.

FIGURE 15.4 Confirmation Email

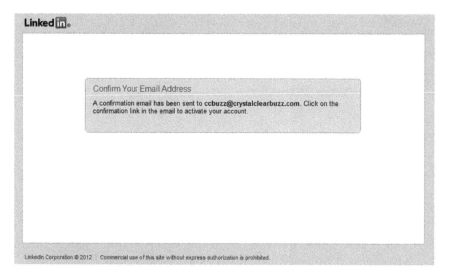

FIGURE 15.5 Confirmation and Congratulations

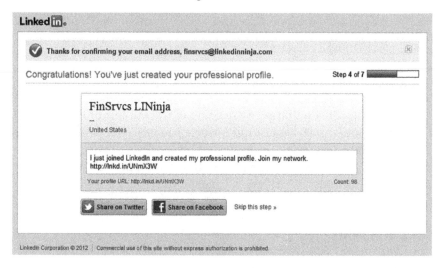

I'm a big believer in the Premium account, but we've got some work to do before you'll be ready to take advantage of its benefits, so why start paying now?

Finally, LinkedIn will put you in a profile-building wizard that will walk you through step by step as shown in Figure 15.7. To be honest, I think this wizard takes longer than just going into the *Edit Profile* section of your

FIGURE 15.6 Account Set Up

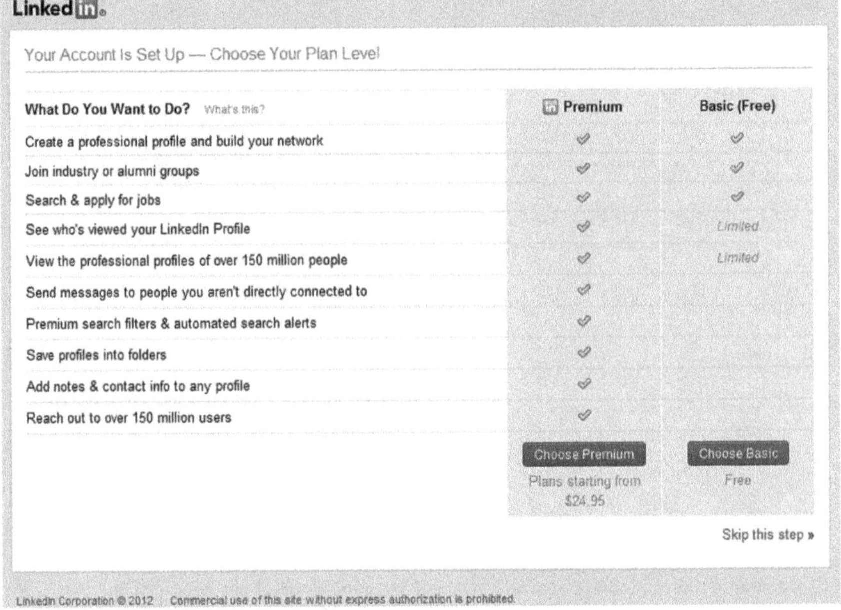

account. However, you may want to use it if you want or need the step-by-step help.

For instructional purposes, we're going to use the edit profile function to build out your profile because this is where you'll be going in the future to make profile changes. Additionally, it's where those who have had accounts will need to be to improve their profile. Instructions on how to access the edit profile function will kick off in Chapter 16.

Final Thoughts

So, you're finally on LinkedIn! Time for some champagne, right? Not yet! You still have a lot of work to do. I'm going to be honest; a well-developed LinkedIn profile takes a lot of time and effort. As you'll see, it's much more involved than just creating a resume. I'm not trying to scare you, because I think it's extremely important that you finish what you've started, but

FIGURE 15.7 Profile-Building Wizard

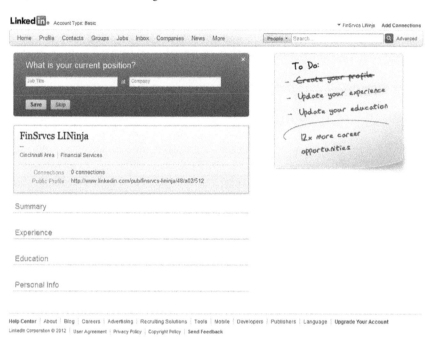

by comparison, writing a resume is a piece of cake. The number of moving parts can be mind-boggling. I do recommend reading through Chapter 16 completely before trying to get started. If you're entirely new to LinkedIn, you're really going to want to get the big picture first. Once you have the big picture, you'll better understand the true potential that is a LinkedIn profile and you'll likely want to spend more time strategizing and gathering the content you'll need to complete your profile.

Building an Effective LinkedIn Profile

Crystal Thies

A complete LinkedIn profile and an effective LinkedIn profile are far from synonymous. This chapter is for everyone, whether you just started your LinkedIn account in the previous chapter or if you've been on LinkedIn for years. However, these instructions and guidelines are for those who are using LinkedIn openly for business purposes within the compliance guidelines.

Before you get started, you'll want to gather some information, starting with your social media compliance policy. Although the suggestions that I will be making in this chapter are in line with what is allowable by FINRA/SEC (at this time, but we are anticipating significant clarification from both organizations over the coming year that could change the applicability of this guidance), your compliance policy may have more stringent guidelines. First and foremost, you want to follow your compliance policy. So if your governing organization has decided that you cannot use a particular section, then you won't be able to use that section. One specific section I have seen forbidden in compliance policies is the specialties section. Since some areas of specialization require additional certifications and licenses, I'm assuming they see it as easier to just forbid than to monitor. Ultimately, you're responsible for following your compliance policy.

Here's a checklist of information you'll want to gather. One method that I know has been used successfully with clients in the past is to create a

Word document and copy and paste the information you gather from your checklist into it before composing your profile. I've never used this method, but I can see where it could come in handy.

You'll need the following:

- Resume
- Digital photo file—JPG, GIF or PNG file (file size limit is 4 MB)
- Three website links
- License and certification numbers and dates
- Titles and links to articles and books authored by you or about you
- Honors and awards with dates received and organization
- Volunteer organizations and community services leadership positions

To get started, log in to your LinkedIn account and go to the Edit Profile function, as shown in Figure 16.1.

FIGURE 16.1   Edit Profile

If you just opened your LinkedIn account, then you'll see a blank profile with lots of edit links. Before we do anything else, we're going to want to turn off public visibility of your profile. If you've had a LinkedIn profile already and it hasn't been approved by your compliance department, or you have an approved profile but you plan on making changes to it, you'll also want to turn off the public profile until your profile has been approved by compliance.

To hide the public profile, look at the bottom of the box where you'll see *Public Profile*, as shown in Figure 16.2, and click on the edit link next to it.

In the right-hand column, you'll see the option to hide the public profile (see Figure 16.3). Click on the button next to the sentence *Make my profile visible to no one*. Then go back into the Edit Profile function.

FIGURE 16.2 Edit Public Profile Link

Search Engine Optimization (SEO)

One last thing before you start building your profile is to make an important decision: What phrase will you use as your primary search optimization phrase? People are turning to LinkedIn to search for providers of services and products that they or their company need. People who need financial advisors are searching in LinkedIn for financial advisors. How you build your profile will determine your likelihood of being listed in those search results, being seen, and hopefully being contacted and hired as a financial advisor by someone motivated enough to go looking on their own.

Financial advisors use many different titles to discriminate themselves from the competition and identify area of focus or target market. Financial advisor,

FIGURE 16.3 Public Profile Visibility

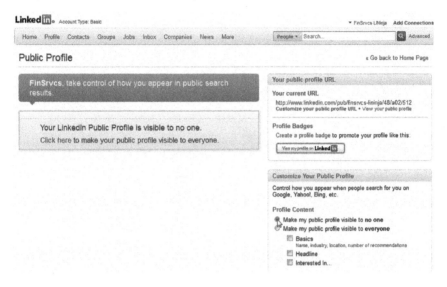

financial planner, investment advisor, investment manager, wealth advisor, wealth planner, wealth manager—so many different titles! Yes, not each of the people who identify themselves in these different ways provides the same financial services. However, other than a small minority of other people, we're pretty much the only people who understand what the differences usually are.

As of February 2012, the total number of people in the United States on LinkedIn who are using the following titles are:

Financial Advisor	62,562
Financial Planner	10,127
Investment Advisor	7,285
Investment Manager	2,296
Wealth Advisor	3,345
Wealth Manager	1,491
Wealth Planner	148

Now, you may be thinking that because there are so many more people using the title *financial advisor*, then that's not the one you want to be using. Basic algebra tells us that our odds of ranking higher increase when we use one of the less competitive titles. And typically, that is true. However, it's only one part of the equation.

According to the Google Adwords keyword tool, the numbers of people who search on these phrases in Google each month are:

Financial Advisor	673,000
Financial Planner	823,000
Investment Advisor	165,000
Investment Manager	110,000
Wealth Advisor	33,100
Wealth Manager	49,500
Wealth Planner	9,900

Unfortunately, there's no place to get statistics on the search terms that are actually being used in LinkedIn, but I think that Google usage is a good predictor of what may be happening. I was actually surprised by some of these results. I was expecting *financial advisor* to be the most searched term, but *financial planner* is. Combined with the lower numbers of competition in LinkedIn for that title, financial planner appears to be the best technical choice for your title on LinkedIn.

You really need to think this decision through. Being found in a search is important, but your title is also a big part of your brand, so you need to find a balance. If the title that you are currently using isn't optimal for being found in a search, you can pick a secondary title or phrase and work it into other places of your profile than just your title field so that you will hopefully be listed for both phrases.

In order to affect the search results, the title or phrase needs to be used many times throughout your profile. You want to use it as many times as possible without going to the point of simply repeating it over and over again. (I've seen people who do this and I think their profiles look ridiculous.) You need to balance the search optimization with copy that is compelling, makes sense to the reader, and adequately conveys your message. A profile of nothing but repeated keywords does not do that!

Additionally, your primary search phrase needs to be used in some very specific places. LinkedIn's search algorithm does weigh the results based on where in the profile the words are located. We will go into more depth as we work through the full profile, but here's a quick listing of the main parts of the profile that have greater weight for keywords.

- Headline
- Summary (use multiple times)
- Specialties
- Titles (This is the most heavily weighted and having the terms in multiple titles has the biggest effect on your ranking.)
- Job descriptions

Experience

If your career has included more than your current position as a financial advisor, you want to include all of the significant past positions on your profile—even if they have nothing to do with the financial services industry. As I'm sure you know, people pick their financial advisors because of their expertise *and* how much they like them as a person. Your past experience tells people more about you as a person. Additionally, people who currently work in your past industries may be more comfortable with you because you have something in common.

The fastest way to add all of your past experience into your LinkedIn profile is to use the *import résumé* function—if it works! I've really had hit or miss success with this function and when trying to use it for the example in this book, I tried at least three times and still couldn't get it to work. If you have a résumé, give it a try because if it works, it will save a lot of time. If it doesn't work, then open the résumé and simply copy and paste the content into the correct fields when adding an experience manually (see Figure 16.4).

To add an experience manually, you can click on any of the multiple links to *Add a position* or add experience (see Figure 16.5).

If you are affiliated with one of the larger financial services providers, then start typing the name of your firm in the *Company Name* field, as shown in Figure 16.6. You'll see a drop-down menu with existing company names. These are also the companies that have existing LinkedIn company pages. It's important that you pick the correct company or subsidiary of that

FIGURE 16.4 Import Resume

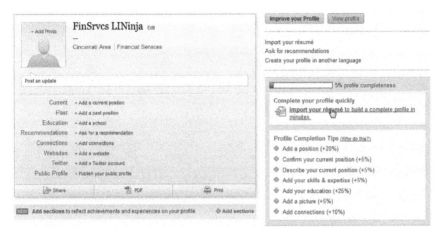

FIGURE 16.5 Add a Position

company because you will become attached to that company page and you want to be certain you're attached to the right page.

If you are an independent or have your own DBA (Doing Business As), even though you're with a larger broker-dealer, then type the name in as you want it to appear. You will see the drop-down populate as you type. If you see your company name and you know that you didn't add it, then that is an existing company page that was created by someone else. You'll need to differentiate the name of your company in some way from that which has already been created because there can't be two company pages with the exact same name.

FIGURE 16.6   Company Name

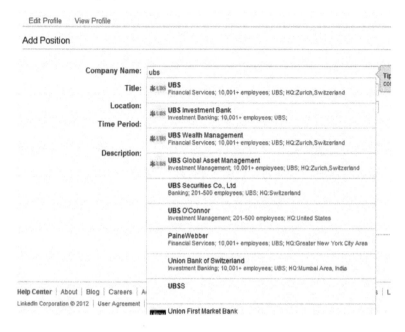

Figure 16.7 shows an example of a completed financial advisor position. I'll walk you through why I did things this way.

The title *wealth advisor, financial planner, president, and founder* is a title that I have used for a client who was an independent advisor who referred to himself as a wealth advisor. Because of the issues with people not likely searching for a *wealth advisor*, we are positioning him as both. Additionally, because he works with small businesses, he wanted to also highlight himself as a small business owner, hence the *president and founder*. I know that some broker-dealers are very picky about what you use as your title so you may not be able to add these other phrases.

There are two boxes in the image that are checked by default. The first says, *Update my headline to:* and the second says, *Let my connections know about this job change via email.* I recommend *unchecking* these boxes before you save this position. We don't want your title as your headline (we will address the reasons for this later). Additionally, we haven't finished your profile yet, so you don't want to be sending any messages to any of

FIGURE 16.7 Add Position—Filled

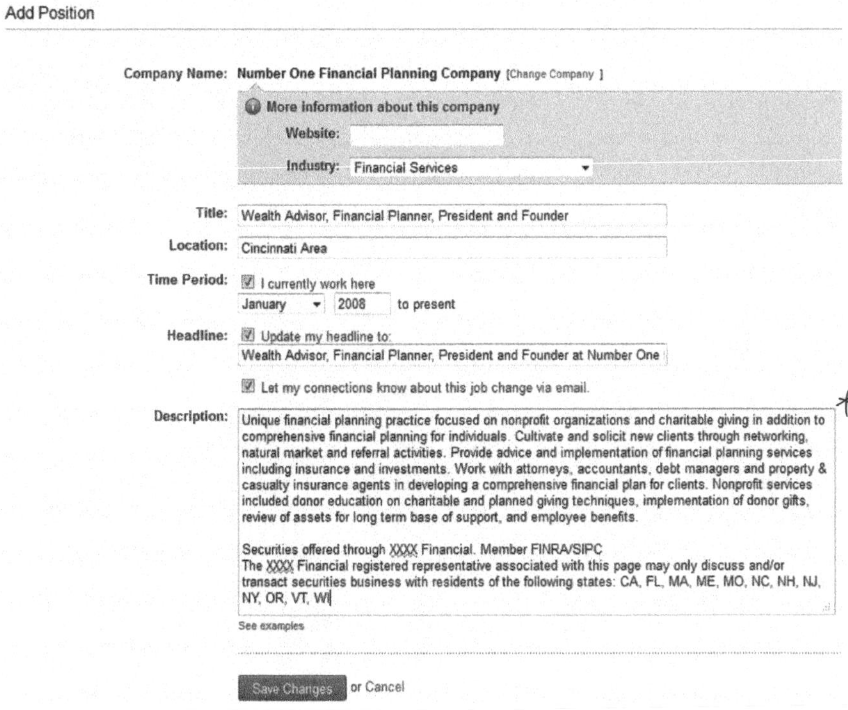

Add Position

Company Name: **Number One Financial Planning Company** [Change Company]

ⓘ More information about this company

Website:

Industry: Financial Services

Title: Wealth Advisor, Financial Planner, President and Founder

Location: Cincinnati Area

Time Period: ☑ I currently work here
January ▾ 2008 to present

Headline: ☑ Update my headline to:
Wealth Advisor, Financial Planner, President and Founder at Number One

☑ Let my connections know about this job change via email.

Description: Unique financial planning practice focused on nonprofit organizations and charitable giving in addition to comprehensive financial planning for individuals. Cultivate and solicit new clients through networking, natural market and referral activities. Provide advice and implementation of financial planning services including insurance and investments. Work with attorneys, accountants, debt managers and property & casualty insurance agents in developing a comprehensive financial plan for clients. Nonprofit services included donor education on charitable and planned giving techniques, implementation of donor gifts, review of assets for long term base of support, and employee benefits.

Securities offered through XXXX Financial. Member FINRA/SIPC
The XXXX Financial registered representative associated with this page may only discuss and/or transact securities business with residents of the following states: CA, FL, MA, ME, MO, NC, NH, NJ, NY, OR, VT, WI

See examples

Save Changes or Cancel

your existing connections encouraging them to look at your profile before we're finished.

The *Description* should clearly outline what it is that you do as a financial advisor. What's your process, who do you work with, and what services do you offer? You want to take advantage of this space for secondary search terms. If you notice, in the example shown in Figure 16.7, *financial planning* was used three times in addition to other key terms like *charitable giving, insurance,* and *investments.* Finally, this is a great place to add your required disclosure statement. Some broker-dealers have their advisors put them in the *Summary* section. You're limited by the number of characters you get in the summary, so try to get this in your position description, if at all possible, so you don't waste valuable space.

Now that you've got your current position listed, simply repeat those steps for all of your past positions. In the past positions, you want to try and work in any key phrases into the titles without telling lies. For example, the client I mentioned above was a tax accountant before he became a financial planner. He had some tax positions early in his career and then moved into roles of asset and portfolio manager before his present role, which he's held for more than 20 years. So where his title was *financial consultant*, we made it *financial consultant and financial advisor*. Where the title was *tax accountant*, we made it *tax accountant and financial advisor*. Because financial advisor is such a general title, you can often make it work with other financial positions, which helps your SEO.

Education

The education section is pretty straightforward. Simply click on *Add a school*. In this section, shown in Figure 16.8, you only want to include education and training programs. There is a separate section for certifications, designations, and licenses. There is also a separate section for courses and classes that were not part of a degree program but that may highlight additional knowledge and expertise.

All of the recognized colleges and universities are prelisted and as you start typing the name, they will automatically fill in (see Figure 16.9). Simply select the appropriate school from the drop-down menu when it appears. If your school is not listed, you can still add it, you'll just have to type in the full name as it would be recognized by others.

As you fill out the *Degree* and *Field of Study* sections, other drop downs will pop up based on terms that have been frequently used by others (see Figure 16.10). You do not have to use these suggestions; they are provided simply for ease of use.

I know that many people don't like to enter the years they attended college because it shows people how old you are. Reality check: Between listing the numbers of years of experience and adding a photograph of what you look like right now, people are going to likely be able to guess your age

FIGURE 16.8 Add Education

FIGURE 16.9 Education School Name

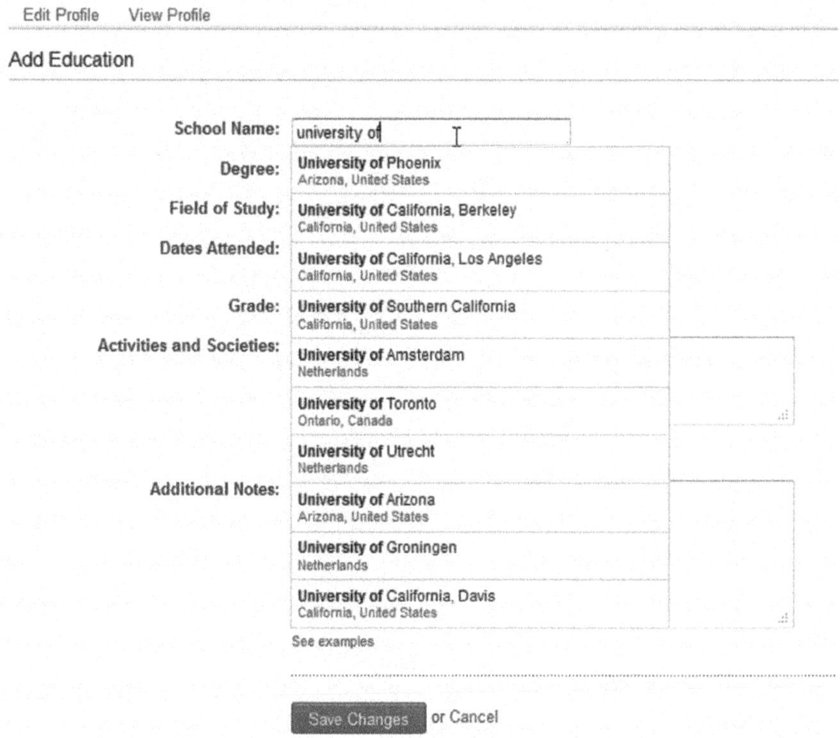

Edit Profile   View Profile

Add Education

School Name: | university of |

Degree: **University of** Phoenix
Arizona, United States

Field of Study: **University of** California, Berkeley
California, United States

Dates Attended: **University of** California, Los Angeles
California, United States

Grade: **University of** Southern California
California, United States

Activities and Societies: **University of** Amsterdam
Netherlands

University of Toronto
Ontario, Canada

University of Utrecht
Netherlands

Additional Notes: **University of** Arizona
Arizona, United States

University of Groningen
Netherlands

University of California, Davis
California, United States

See examples

Save Changes   or Cancel

anyway. I highly recommend including the dates you attended the school. LinkedIn has a function for you to search for past classmates to connect with and for others to find you. This function only works based on dates. So if you don't include the dates, then you won't get the benefit of connecting with important people from your past who could help your business today.

The *Grade* field is a fairly new field. To be honest, I'm ambivalent regarding whether to fill this out unless you're fresh out of school. So that's your call. As for activities, I do recommend entering these. When you're trying to connect with past classmates or they are trying to connect with you, the activities list can help trigger the memory of how you knew each other and who you are—especially if it's been many years since you've been in contact with them!

FIGURE 16.10 Education—Additional Sections

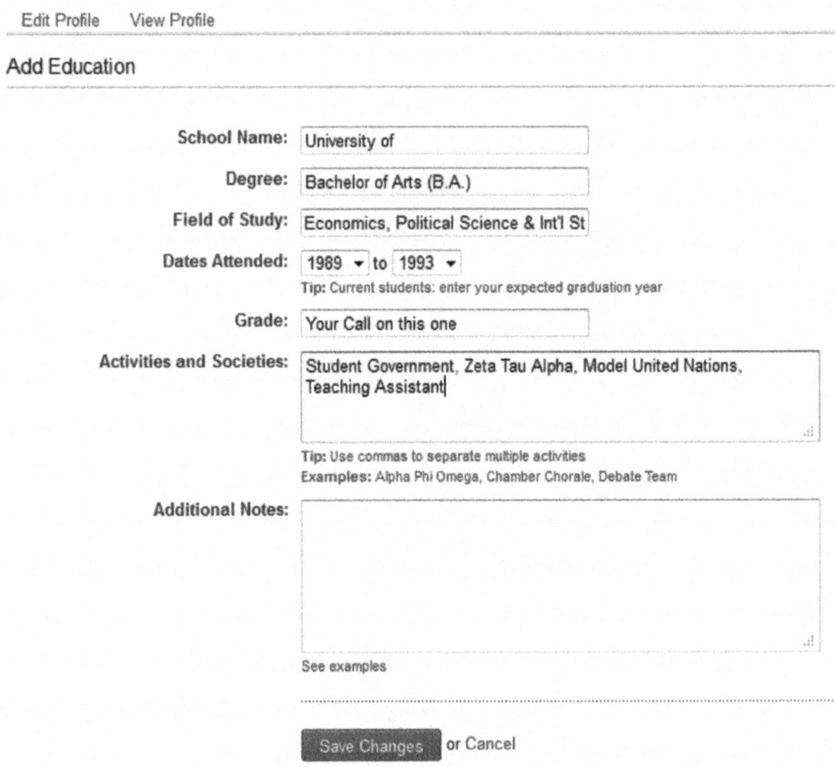

Edit Profile   View Profile

Add Education

School Name:	University of
Degree:	Bachelor of Arts (B.A.)
Field of Study:	Economics, Political Science & Int'l St
Dates Attended:	1989 ▾ to 1993 ▾
	Tip: Current students: enter your expected graduation year
Grade:	Your Call on this one
Activities and Societies:	Student Government, Zeta Tau Alpha, Model United Nations, Teaching Assistant

Tip: Use commas to separate multiple activities
Examples: Alpha Phi Omega, Chamber Chorale, Debate Team

Additional Notes:

See examples

Save Changes or Cancel

Adding Certifications, Designations, and Licenses

The section to add these important pieces of information is a section that was added to the LinkedIn profile later and is not a default section because not everyone has a need for it. Therefore, we're going to have to turn it on in order to use it. To find it, look just under the bottom of the profile box at the top. You'll see a link to *Add sections*, as is shown in Figure 16.11. Click on it.

You'll get a pop-up box with the sections that you can add (see Figure 16.12). If nothing happens after you click on the link, then check your pop-up blocker settings. You'll want to make certain that pop ups are allowed when you're on www.linkedin.com (they currently aren't using pop-up advertising, so this shouldn't be a problem).

FIGURE 16.11   Add Sections

FIGURE 16.12   Add Sections Pop Up

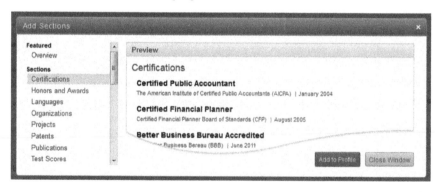

The section we're most interested in right now is *Certifications*. While you're here, if you know you're going to want to use some of the other special sections, you might want to go ahead and add them now. Some of those sections include *Honors and Awards* (there is another default section in the profile called *Honors and Awards*, but this newer version is much better and I recommend using it instead of the older default version), *Courses* (for nondegree/noncertification/nondesignation education that you might want to add), *Organizations* (to highlight community and volunteer positions that are more involved than donating a few hours per year, such as board positions), *Projects* (great for community projects such as those done in leadership classes or electoral campaigns that aren't ongoing organizations),

Publications (you can use this section for articles and books authored by you or about you), and finally, *Volunteer Experience and Causes* (this is a great catchall for smaller organizations and missions that are important to you, but in which you haven't held leadership positions).

The one special section that *every* financial advisor should complete is the Certifications section for your licenses and designations. As you can see in Figure 16.13, the form requires basic information including an actual license number if it is given.

Figure 16.14 is what a completed Certifications section looks like with many of the most common licenses and certifications.

Now, let's go back to the very top of your profile (see Figure 16.15) and work your way down.

Name

Out of all of the complexity that is a LinkedIn profile, you would think that the one part that would be completely straightforward would be the name field. You would think. For the most part, it *is* straightforward unless you try to make it more than what it is. You may see other people adding more content in the name fields than just their name and decide to give it a try. Don't!

FIGURE 16.13 Add a Certification—Blank

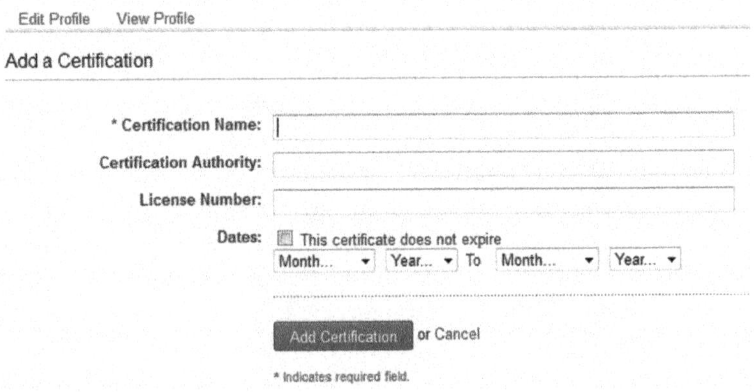

Edit Profile   View Profile

Add a Certification

* Certification Name: |

Certification Authority:

License Number:

Dates: ☐ This certificate does not expire
Month... ▼   Year... ▼ To   Month...   ▼   Year... ▼

Add Certification   or Cancel

* Indicates required field.

FIGURE 16.14   Certifications Section—Sullivan

Certifications

CPA - Certified Public Accountant
AICPA | June 1983

PFS - Personal Financial Specialist
AICPA | August 1994

CFP - Certified Financial Planner
Certified Financial Planner Board of Standards | License ██████ | October 1994

Series 7 & 24
FINRA SIPC

Life and Health Insurance
Commonwealth of Massassachusetts

FIGURE 16.15   Name, Photo, and Headline

Crystal Thies
Online Networking Trainer, Consultant & Speaker
helping companies & sales pros use LinkedIn to find
prospects
Cincinnati Area | Marketing and Advertising

The name is made up of two fields: first name and last name. I recommend that you keep your name to exactly that. The first name should be the name that most people know you by (especially your business colleagues). You want to minimize usage of any initials before or after the first name. You also want to keep any alphabet soup that would go after your last name to the Certifications section we just discussed. Essentially, what this means is that the name at the top of your LinkedIn profile may not look the same as your name on your business cards.

There's an important reason I recommend this and it's not to destroy your branding efforts. The most searched terms in LinkedIn are names. Any additional information beyond what people would think to use to search for you could result in you not showing up in the search results. The one search you want to guarantee you show up in is a search for *you*. I have tried searching for people by name and not been able to find them because of the extra content they had in their name fields. So keep it clean!

To edit the appearance of your name, click on the *Edit* link next to your name (see Figure 16.16). This edit link also gives you access to editing your headline, location, and industry.

As you can see in Figure 16.17, LinkedIn also has a field for a *Former/Maiden Name*. For the most part, this is for women whose name may have

FIGURE 16.16 Edit Name Link

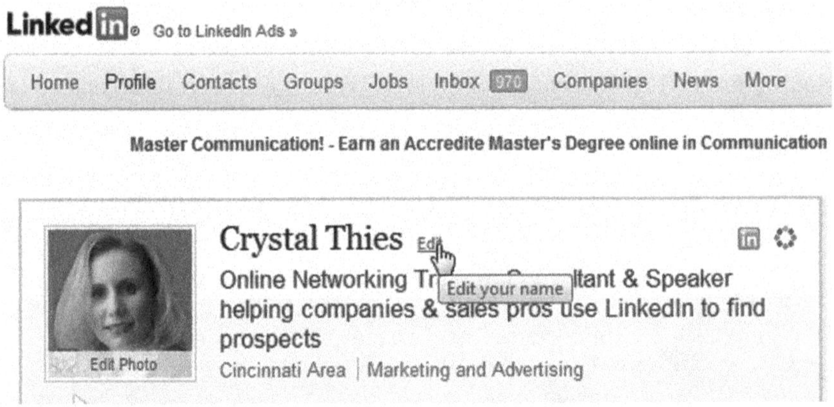

FIGURE 16.17 Edit Name

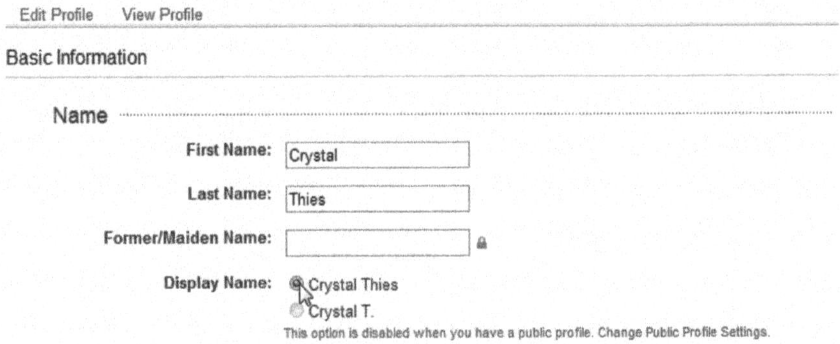

changed as a result of marriage or divorce, but it is applicable for anyone who has legally changed their name for any reason. If your name has changed and you want people to be able to find you who knew you by a past name and who may not be aware of your current name, then you do want to take advantage of this field. However, if it has been a long time since you've been known by that former name or it's a name that you don't want to be affiliated with anymore—as in the case of a divorce—then you may elect not to use it. Yes, you're limiting the ability of some people to possibly recognize or find you, but it may be a sacrifice worth taking. You have to make that decision.

If you use this field, you may want to adjust a privacy setting. You'll notice that there is a lock next to the field box (see Figure 16.18). If you click on that lock, it will pull up the privacy settings associated with that field. Essentially, you have the ability to set who can see that former name. I always recommend being as open as possible if your purpose to use LinkedIn is sales and business development. When you close off any profile visibility, you're limiting the ability of a prospect who doesn't know you or isn't in your network to consider you. For this reason, I recommend at least the *My Network* option.

Lastly, there is the ability to set whether or not people can see your last name or only your last initial. If you have a public profile, then this option is disabled because your last name will be listed on your public profile. You can only hide your last name if you do not have a public profile. To be honest, most people outside your network (beyond the 2nd degree) won't see your

FIGURE 16.18   Former/Maiden Name

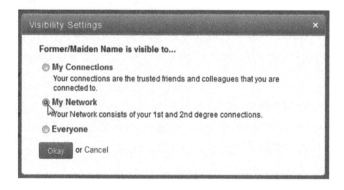

last name on your LinkedIn profile because it's now a benefit available to only the highest-level premium members.

Industry and Location

Affiliating your profile with the correct industry is very important because it is one of the most widely used search filters that are available to all members— basic (free) and premium. The industry field may seem as straightforward as your name and it can be. I have seen some broker-dealer compliance policies that require you to use the industry *financial services*, which is the industry used by the vast majority of financial advisors. If that's the case, then your industry selection is about as straightforward as it can get. However, if you have a financial advisory practice that may cover many different types of financial services or if you specialize in a particular area, then you may consider some of the other industries that could potentially be a better fit for you.

The other available industries that are relevant and related to financial services are: accounting, banking, capital markets, insurance, investment banking, investment management, and venture capital & private equity. So, which should you choose? Being found by the people looking for your services is the number one determining factor in selecting the industry with which to affiliate (if you have the latitude to do so). So, ask yourself the question, "Based on how I've branded and positioned my financial services practice, which industry would someone who doesn't know me select to find the services that I'm offering?"

Now, there could potentially be multiple answers to this query, but LinkedIn only allows you to pick one industry at this time (see Figure 16.19). I recommend going with the numbers and the service that is most impor-tant to your practice. Where you may likely find this a problem is deciding between *financial services* and *insurance* if you work for an insurance company but are also licensed to sell investments. Those who are RIA may also have a hard time deciding between *financial services* and *investment management*. My suggestion would be to either go with the business line that is the most dom-inant and/or broad or select the business line that you want to grow in the most.

As for the location, you always want to enter the actual zip code where your office is located. As with industry, the ability to search by zip code is a benefit available to everyone on LinkedIn. If you live in a major metro-politan area, then any zip code in that metropolitan area will affiliate you

FIGURE 16.19   Add Industry

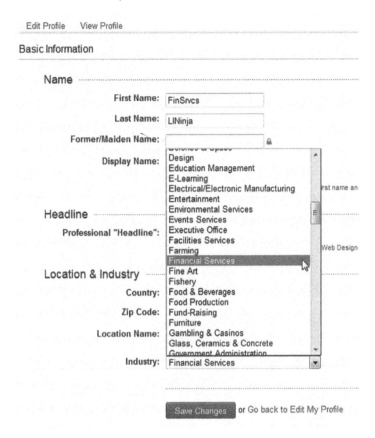

with that metropolitan area. However, people can search as small a geographic radius as 10 miles, which is significantly smaller than most major metropolitan areas. Therefore, by using your exact zip code, you are able to be found by those looking within a small portion of a major metropolitan area.

If you do find yourself in this situation, then LinkedIn may give you the option of affiliating with your actual city or the larger metropolitan area (see Figure 16.20). There are pros and cons to both options. You will need to make the decision that is best for your practice.

FIGURE 16.20 Edit Location

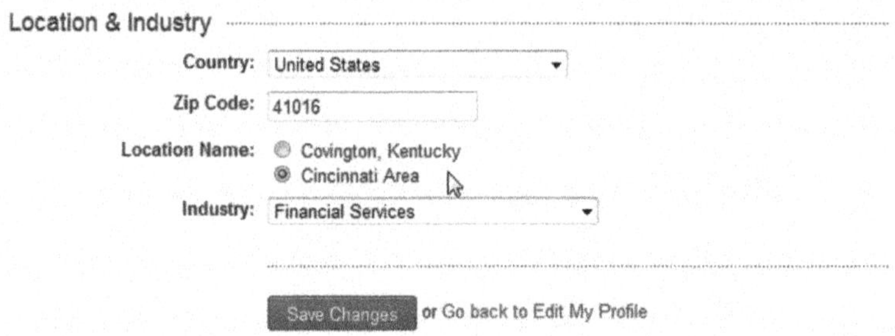

⸙ Headline

The *Headline* is one of the *most important* parts of your LinkedIn profile. This is the only information that shows up in search results that *you* control. It's the only piece of information that says, "Pick me!" The analogy I often use is to picture yourself standing in front of a newsstand. At the top of every newspaper it says, "Newspaper." How are you to know which one to choose? The same thing happens when a prospect runs a search in LinkedIn and everybody's profile says "Financial Advisor." You have the power to set yourself apart.

You may have noticed that many people have their title and company name as their Headline. The sad part is that even though this isn't how LinkedIn intends this field to be used, it encourages you to do so. If you recall, when we added your current position, there was a box that was checked telling LinkedIn to change your headline from whatever it was to your new title and company. As a result, most people don't know to uncheck it and we have lots of people with their titles as headlines. Additionally, I have also seen some broker-dealer compliance policies requiring this field to be your official title.

So, what should your headline say? I recommend that you use this space to answer three questions: (1) what you do from a functional standpoint; (2) who you serve; and (3) what results you get. Additionally, it's very important that you fit in your primary search phrase, and if possible, any secondary phrases. Finally, keep in mind that LinkedIn limits the length of the headline to 120 characters (see Figure 16.21).

FIGURE 16.21 Add Headline

Edit Profile   View Profile

Basic Information

Name

First Name: FinSrvcs

Last Name: LINinja

Former/Maiden Name: [   ] 🔒

Display Name: ⦿ FinSrvcs LINinja
○ FinSrvcs L.

Tip: For added Privacy, you can display only your first name and last initial. (Your connections will still see your first and last name.)

Headline

Professional "Headline": Financial Planner helping |

Examples: Experienced Transportation Executive, Web Designer and Information Architect, Visionary Entrepreneur and Investor...See more

Headline Examples: ⌐

- Wealth Advisor helping small business and real estate owners manage their intertwined finances to maximize personal wealth
- Certified Financial Planner helping busy professionals achieve their financial goals
- Financial Advisor helping parents plan for the future to give their children the education of their dreams
- Financial Planner helping people nearing retirement optimize their assets to live the lives they've always wanted

Photo

Your photo is a very important part of your profile. People want to see you and get to know you. It is also your brand when you appear in your connections' news feed. Some of you may not want to have an actual photo of your face and decide to use your logo instead. Not only is this a bad idea, but it's also against LinkedIn's terms of service. If you use a logo instead of a photo, you could find your account shut down if the LinkedIn police notice it.

Your photo doesn't necessarily need to be a super formal, professional photo. A friend with a decent digital camera or smartphone, a good eye, and a nice or plain background can save you a lot of money. You want the photo to be close up of your face with little background. You want to have a warm and inviting smile. As long as your face is good, the rest can be changed and optimized by a friend, employee, or freelancer with some graphic design expertise.

To see for yourself why the photo is so important, go to your LinkedIn home page. Go down to your news feed. Now with a quick pace, scroll through all of the status updates and activity from your network (even if you just created your account, you should find your news feed populated with other people in your industry in your geographic location that have their status updates visible to everyone even though you're not connected to them). Who stood out? Whose photos made you want to slow down and see what they said? I've found that headshots with bright, solid background colors or with the background completely removed stand out the most. Muddled, busy backgrounds are the worst. Additionally, I recommend against having alcoholic drinks visible in your hand or in the background. You don't want to include anything that could result in some prejudice before people get to know you. Finally, your LinkedIn photo is not the place to include kids, other people, or pets. Keep those types of photos for your Facebook account. So, let's walk through adding your photo to your profile. Click on the link, as shown in Figure 16.22, where your photo will go that says, *Add Photo.*

LinkedIn will bring up a box where you can browse your computer's files to locate the file of your photo (see Figure 16.23). Most standard image files (JPG, GIF or PNG) are accepted, with a file size allowance of up to 4 MB, so don't be afraid of using a higher resolution image if you have it available.

FIGURE 16.22   Add Photo Link

FIGURE 16.23 Add Photo File

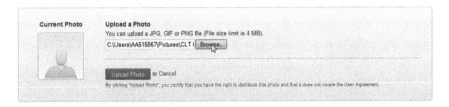

FIGURE 16.24 Add Photo Edit

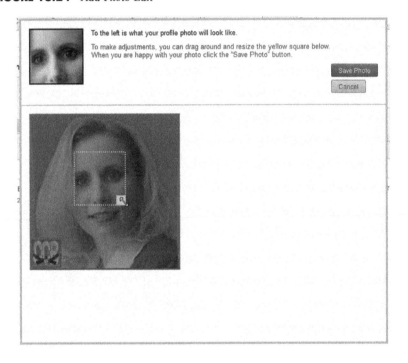

When you click on *Upload Photo*, LinkedIn will bring up an editor allowing you to specify which part of the photo you want to appear on your profile (see Figure 16.24). What is great about this is that it allows you to zoom in so that your smiling face fills the bulk of the photo space. The amount of my face that is selected in the image below is not what is recommended, it's simply to demonstrate how small of a piece of the photo you can grab if you use a photo where you are with other people or that is far away.

BRANDING YOUR PHOTO

If you notice, I've added some branding to my photo. What you see in the lower left-hand corner is the LinkedIn Ninja Black Belt Badge that my students can have added to their LinkedIn photo after they are certified in my course. If you have access to graphic designers, you can add branding or a logo to your headshot—LinkedIn has no rules against this as long as it is actually a photo of you. If you do this, I recommend that you avoid adding the branding or logo in the lower right-hand corner. When the LinkedIn API pulls your photo into other programs that interact with and use data from LinkedIn (like the Outlook Connect Tool), they add a LinkedIn logo in that corner of your photo. So your logo would be covered up if that is where it is located.

Websites

LinkedIn allows you to have three website links on your profile. One common thread I've seen in the different broker-dealer compliance policies is that you're only allowed to use links to FINRA approved sites. That's not to say that you will be limited, but I share this to let you know that you might be. So, you may be thinking you'll only have use for one of the three website links. That's where you're wrong!

So what can you use your website links for? First, use your broker-dealer's main website. Second, use your personal company website (which could be a sub-domain of your broker-dealer's website or your own domain). Third, drive them to a specific page within either of those other two websites (or use two specific pages if you're an independent advisor) or if you do have a Facebook business page (not a personal profile), use that link.

What types of specific pages could you use? The first idea that comes to mind is the sign-up page for a newsletter or an email list. A second idea would be a page for changing news or market commentary. Most importantly, you want to make these links go to content that helps build your business and would be interesting and compelling to potential clients.

Adding website links sounds like it should be pretty easy, but most people don't add their links in the optimal way. Whenever you see website links on someone's profile and they say, *Company Website* or *Personal Website* or *Blog*, then they haven't done it right. I'm going to show you how to do it right!

To add one or more website(s), simply click on *Add a website* in the profile box or *Edit* if you already have a link set up. (see Figure 16.25). Next, you'll see the space for three websites with two fields each as shown in Figure 16.26. The first is a drop-down box and the second is the

FIGURE 16.25 Add a Website Link

FIGURE 16.26 Add Websites

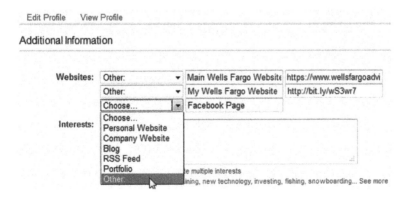

space to type the address. However, if you click on that drop-down box and select the option that is all the way at the bottom of the list, called *Other*, then you'll see a third box appear—almost like magic! This third field allows you to type in your own text for what the link will actually say.

If you notice, one of those links is a Bitly link. Earlier in this book, we discussed Bitly links and their value. Another smart trick if you want to track the number of clicks would be to use Bitly or some other trackable type of link in these fields.

So, no more generic links like *Company Website*. Your links now have the name of your own websites or whatever websites you choose to share (see Figure 16.27).

Twitter

LinkedIn offers complete integration with your Twitter account. Right below your website links, you will find the link to attach your Twitter account. There are several reasons why you should add your Twitter account. First, it makes it easy for your LinkedIn connections to also follow you on Twitter. Additionally, anyone who lands on your profile may decide to follow you on Twitter even if it's not appropriate to connect on LinkedIn. Second, you can send your LinkedIn status updates into the twittersphere at the same time.

FIGURE 16.27   Custom Website Links

FinSrvcs LINinja
Financial Planner helping people nearing retirement optimize their assets to live the lives they've always wanted
Cincinnati Area | Financial Services

Current	**Wealth Advisor, Financial Planner, President and Founder** at **Number One Financial Planning Company**
Education	University of
Connections	0 connections
Websites	Main Wells Fargo Website
	My Wells Fargo Website
	Facebook Page

So after you click on *Authorize app*, as shown in Figure 16.28, you'll get a pop-up window requiring you to log in to your Twitter account and authorize LinkedIn to access your Twitter account information. If your computer saves your log-in information, then it will fill this in for you. If your computer doesn't save your log-in information, make certain you have your Twitter password handy.

Summary

Next to your headline, the *Summary* is the most important part of your profile. It's what compels people to want to contact you and get to know you

FIGURE 16.28   Authorize Twitter Account App

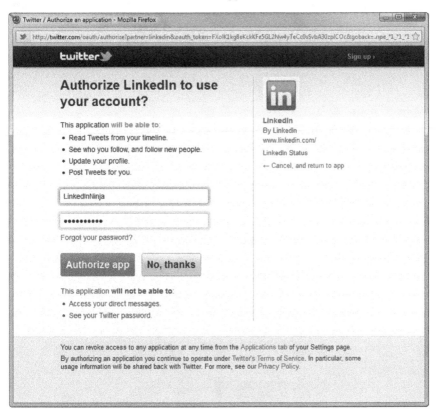

and possibly do business with you. It essentially takes what you've started in the headline and delves deeper.

It is *not* your bio! It is your elevator speech! It's telling people what you do, who you serve, what results you get, and what sets you apart from the thousands of other financial advisors out there. You should already have some type of elevator speech that you use, so this will give you a chance to really refine it and nail it down. Also, chances are that you've never put your elevator speech through the compliance review process. Technically, if it's something that you're repeating over and over, then it really should be reviewed by compliance anyway. Therefore, you can be more confident going forward knowing that the words you're using most often in your daily business have been blessed by the compliance gods.

As you develop your summary, don't forget your search optimization. You want to try to use your primary phrase two to three times or more in your summary. Additionally, this is the place to work in those secondary phrases.

LinkedIn currently allows 2,000 characters for your summary with blank lines counting as two characters (see Figures 16.29 and 16.30).

FIGURE 16.29   Add Summary

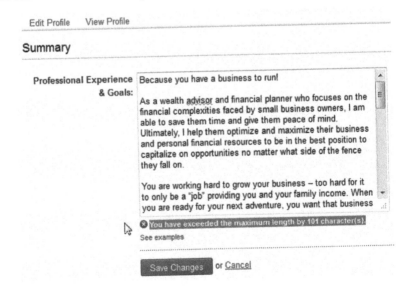

FIGURE 16.30 Sample Summary

Summary

Because you have a business to run!

As a wealth advisor and financial planner who focuses on the financial complexities faced by small business owners, I am able to save them time and give them peace of mind. Ultimately, I help them optimize and maximize their business and personal financial resources to be in the best position to capitalize on opportunities no matter what side of the fence they fall on.

You are working hard to grow your business – too hard for it to only be a "job" providing you and your family income. When you are ready for your next adventure, you want that business to be an asset that can either be passed on to another family member or converted into wealth. However, the wealth of a business does not result in a single "harvest" at the end of your career. And, if you wait too long to harvest, the crop may have disappeared!

I help my clients know when and how to properly "harvest" the wealth that is growing in their business to help achieve their personal financial goals. However, that harvesting can be very costly if not handled appropriately. My education and experience in financial planning, investing, and accounting allows me to see the full financial picture and tax consequences.

I can help guide you on making good investments and knowing when that investment needs to be reconsidered – whether the investment is putting capital back into your business or into your personal portfolio. We'll also closely look at the tax ramifications from both the business and personal perspective to make the overall best decisions for you and your family.

Whether you're looking for your first wealth advisor / financial planner or a different perspective from your current wealth advisor / financial planner, please feel free to contact me so that together we can get you focused on running your business and not so much on trying to figure out how to run your finances!

This will give you 300 to 400 words depending on average word length. Although the blank lines cost you extra characters, I do recommend using them and building in sufficient white space. People don't like to read long, dense paragraphs. So, if you want them to read your summary, make it easy for them to read through or skim easily with several short paragraphs. You can even create bulleted lists by using a dash (−) or plus sign (+).

If you created your LinkedIn account a while back, you will also have a *Specialties* subsection of the summary. LinkedIn is no longer including this section in new accounts, so if you just created the account you won't see it on your profile, though you will see it on many others. There is no way to add it. However, if you recall at the beginning of this chapter, I mentioned that many broker-dealers weren't allowing use of this section anyway because they don't like the implications of the word *specialties*. LinkedIn has recently added a new section called *Skills & Expertise*. With the elimination of the Specialties section, I can only assume that Skills & Expertise is meant to take its place.

Recommendations

Have I shocked you? Are you starting to wonder if I even know what I'm talking about? We all know that client testimonials are verboten, so why even bring them up? Well, not all of your connections are clients and I know that many—if not the majority—of you have likely had more than one career.

Recommendations are very important on LinkedIn. The number of recommendations that you have and the words that people use when they write your recommendations do affect your search rankings. Additionally, having others speak on behalf of your skills, accomplishments, and character always increases your credibility.

Therefore, if you have had past positions before you became a financial advisor, I highly recommend trying to get as many recommendations attached to them as possible. To request a recommendation, go to the *Profile* drop-down menu and click on *Recommendations* (see Figure 16.31).

You'll see all of the positions you've added to your profile in addition to all of your education listed, with links to ask to be endorsed. Click the link next to the position for which you want to request a recommendation (see Figure 16.32). All recommendations are tied to a specific position. Unfortunately, there is no such thing as a general or freestanding recommendation.

Next, you'll have to select who it is you want to ask for the recommendation. LinkedIn allows you to request the recommendation from up to

FIGURE 16.31   Recommendations

FIGURE 16.32 Request a Recommendation

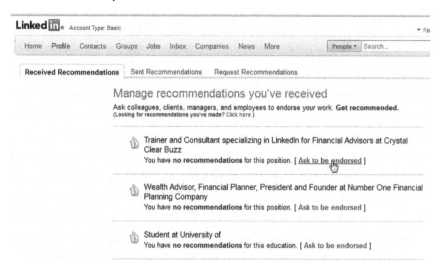

200 people at a time. Personally, I think this is excessive given the personal nature of recommendations. Therefore, I recommend requesting your recommendations either one at a time or in small batches.

If you know who you're going to ask, you can start typing their names in the *Your connections* box (you must be connected to the person on LinkedIn in order to get a recommendation from them) and LinkedIn will pull up the person's name as you're typing. If you are asking multiple people, you can click on the LinkedIn logo to the left of that box and it will pull up your entire list of connections and you can just check the box next to those you want to ask (see Figure 16.33).

The message you see in the image is the default message that LinkedIn provides. You *never* want to send just this message. You always want to personalize it. Also, to get the best results for your recommendations, I always recommend coaching your connection on what to include in addition to offering to write it for them if they are too busy.

By coaching, I mean suggesting that they address a particular project, skill or expertise you have. Oftentimes, I find that people are unhappy because something in particular wasn't mentioned. Chances are that it wasn't mentioned because the person simply didn't think about it and not because they didn't have positive comments to share in its regard.

FIGURE 16.33 Request a Recommendation 2

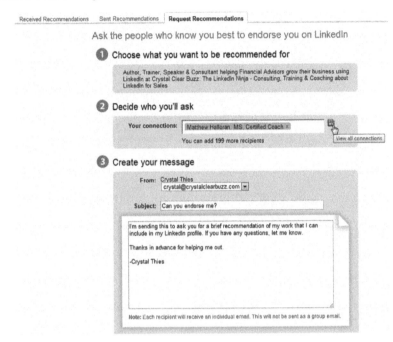

You should recall that I've said that the words used in your recommendations do have an effect on your LinkedIn search rankings. You may be wondering how that can help you if these recommendations aren't tied to your current financial advisor role and these people aren't writing about your accomplishments as a financial advisor. Well, that's why we coach! If this is someone you still have a good or ongoing relationship with, ask that person to finish up the recommendation with something like, "Jane was a great tax accountant and I can only imagine how great of a job she's doing now as a financial planner. Her clients are lucky to have her."

Some of you may not necessarily be comfortable with that because although it is allowable within the letter of the law, it may not appear so within the spirit of the law. I don't agree. Actually, the Commonwealth of Massachusetts doesn't agree, either. They recently released new guidelines on social media for the approximately 600 independent investment advisors that they regulate. These guidelines specifically stated that recommendations attached to your position as a financial advisor were not forbidden—only those written by clients providing testimonials to your work as a financial advisor.

Therefore, if you're one of those 600 people, you are allowed to ask for and display recommendations on your profile from connections who are not clients providing direct testimonial of your actual work as a financial advisor. Massachusetts stated that they hope their guidelines will become the model for all other states. So, if you are an RIA in another state, you may want to take the risk and do the same as long as your state regulatory body has not provided guidelines to the contrary. For those governed by FINRA, I can see FINRA possibly moving in the same direction, but the broker-dealers may be a different story. I can easily see them deciding that the monitoring may be too much of a headache to allow it. I could also see a multitiered policy where only advisors of certain experience or accomplishment are given the latitude and the oversight support to have such recommendations.

So, to wrap things up, those who can get recommendations on past, non-regulated positions should and should try to get those people to try to extrapolate that recommendation to what they're doing now while being clear that they have no first hand knowledge of your abilities as a financial advisor. Additionally, if you are allowed to, you want to try and get character recommendations from those who aren't clients. They can refer to knowing that you're a financial advisor, but should also mention that they are not clients. Coaching with those giving you recommendations is extremely important—even more so than regular people. It's the only way you can get a recommendation that you'll be able to use. Also, think of it from the recommender's point of view. The more you tell me what you want, the easier it is for me and the last thing I want to do is waste my time writing you a recommendation that you cannot use.

Finally, if the recommendation is attached to your current position as a financial advisor, have your compliance review department review it to be certain that it is clear that it is not a client testimonial *before* you accept the recommendation. If compliance is unhappy with any of the wording, then you can reply back to the person who wrote the recommendation and request the necessary changes to display it on your profile. Once you click on the "Accept Recommendation" button, you will have to delete the recommendation and your connection will have to start over. A best practice when you receive such recommendations is to send the connection a note letting them know that it is being reviewed and that you may have to ask for

FIGURE 16.34   Add Additional Information

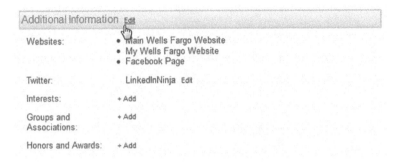

changes depending on the review. Your note will also keep your connection from wondering why there is a delay in posting it to your profile.

Additional Information

We've already talked about the website links and Twitter account, which make up part of the *Additional Information* section. There are a few more fields in this section: *Interests, Groups and Associations,* and *Honors and Awards* (see Figure 16.34).

Honestly, I'm ambivalent about the interests section. If you feel like sharing personal interests and hobbies, then do so. If not, then don't. The groups and associations area is where the LinkedIn groups that you join will show up. However, if there are some names of community organizations that people may search for, then you may want to add them here in text format. As for the honors and awards section, there is a newer version of this under the *Add sections* tab, which, in my opinion, is better. You can still use the basic one provided, but I would recommend using the updated version.

Personal Information

The *Personal Information* section shown in Figure 16.35 is for you to provide your contact information for your connections. Only your 1st degree connections can see your phone number and address, so I *always* recommend that these be filled in with your business contact information. Since instant

FIGURE 16.35 Add Personal Information

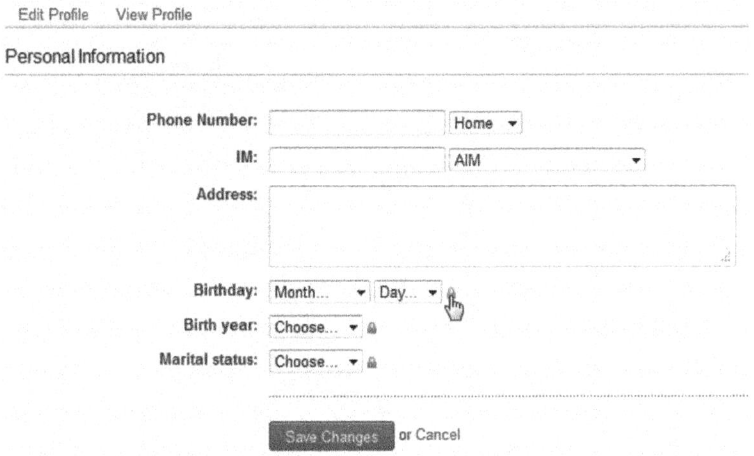

Edit Profile   View Profile

Personal Information

Phone Number: [   ] [Home ▼]

IM: [   ] [AIM   ▼]

Address: [   ]

Birthday: [Month... ▼] [Day... ▼]

Birth year: [Choose... ▼] 🔒

Marital status: [Choose... ▼] 🔒

[Save Changes] or Cancel

messaging (IM) isn't a compliance-approved communication method at this time, I recommend leaving that field empty, even if you have an IM account.

As for the birthday and marital status fields, I've never been a big fan. After all, this isn't Facebook. You'll want to make your own decision about whether you want to include that information. If you do, you will want to verify the privacy settings. If you notice, there are little locks next to each of those fields and the default setting for each one isn't your connections only. If you don't adjust these privacy settings, then other people can and will see that information.

Skills & Expertise

As I mentioned earlier, the *Skills & Expertise* section is taking the place of the old specialties section (see Figure 16.36). Technically, this section is still undergoing some beta testing. As a result, we're unsure of its full effect on search results. The one thing I do know for certain is that it can't hurt. You'll find this section all the way at the bottom of the profile. You can add up to 50 skills.

When you start typing in your first skill, you'll see a drop-down list appear with all of the prefilled terms that include the skill you're typing

FIGURE 16.36 Add Skills

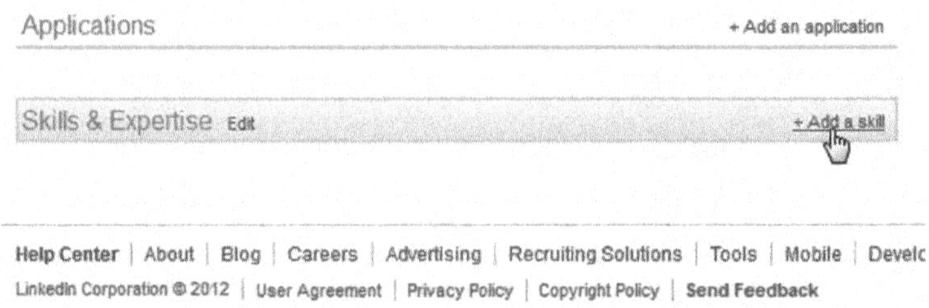

FIGURE 16.37 Skills and Expertise 1

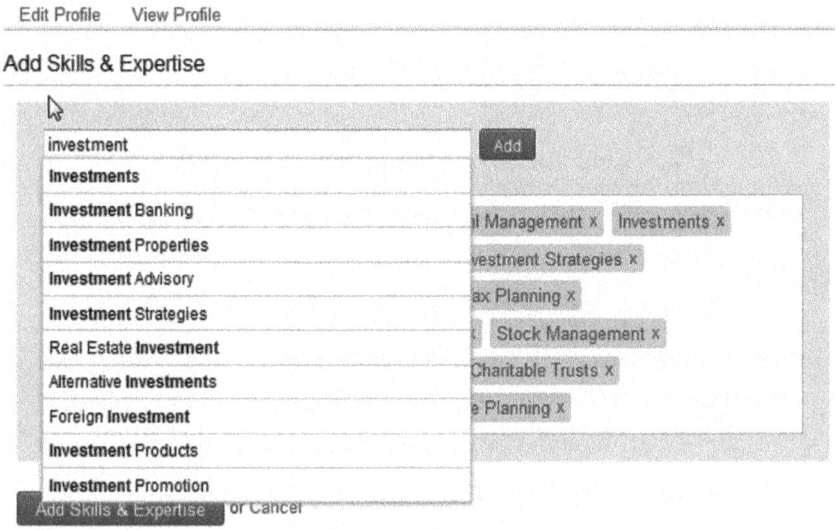

(see Figure 16.37). These lists may suggest skills and expertise that you hadn't thought of and can quickly add.

However, you also don't have to be tied to the prefilled suggestions. If you find that your skill isn't listed or you want to describe it in a different way, you can. Just make sure you capitalize all of the words to stay consistent in style with the prefilled terms (see Figure 16.38).

What you end up with is a word cloud of keywords on your profile (see Figure 16.39).

FIGURE 16.38 Skills and Expertise 2

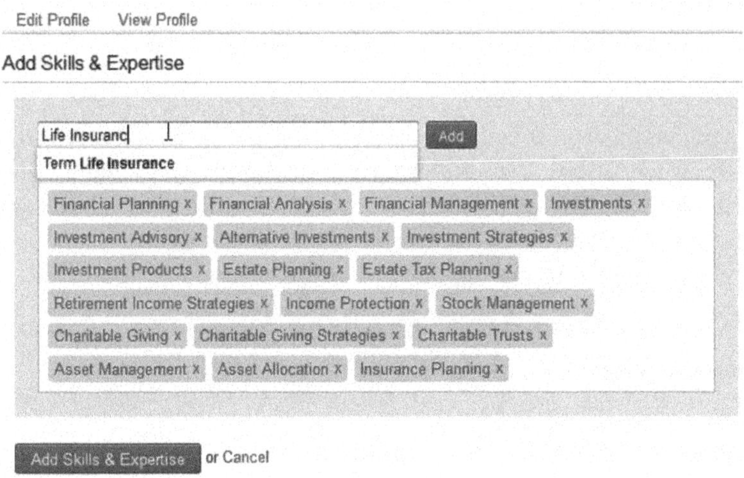

Edit Profile   View Profile

Add Skills & Expertise

| Life Insuranc| | Add |

Term **Life Insurance**

Financial Planning x   Financial Analysis x   Financial Management x   Investments x

Investment Advisory x   Alternative Investments x   Investment Strategies x

Investment Products x   Estate Planning x   Estate Tax Planning x

Retirement Income Strategies x   Income Protection x   Stock Management x

Charitable Giving x   Charitable Giving Strategies x   Charitable Trusts x

Asset Management x   Asset Allocation x   Insurance Planning x

Add Skills & Expertise   or Cancel

FIGURE 16.39 Skills and Expertise on Profile

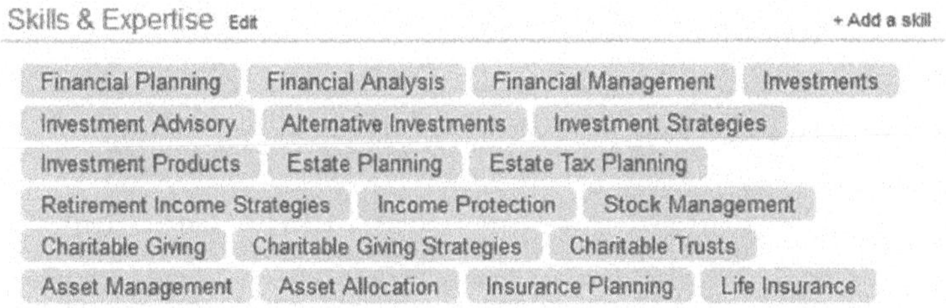

Skills & Expertise Edit   + Add a skill

Financial Planning   Financial Analysis   Financial Management   Investments

Investment Advisory   Alternative Investments   Investment Strategies

Investment Products   Estate Planning   Estate Tax Planning

Retirement Income Strategies   Income Protection   Stock Management

Charitable Giving   Charitable Giving Strategies   Charitable Trusts

Asset Management   Asset Allocation   Insurance Planning   Life Insurance

Special Sections

If you recall from earlier in the chapter, we've already used one of the special sections—*Certifications*. There are several other special sections that can really enhance your profile and we're going to quickly cover some of the more advantageous sections. Some of these sections were actually originally created for students and those just out of school to highlight important accomplishments that were not job related. However, they have equal applicability to those long out of school. As a reminder, you find the link to add these sections just below the big profile box at the top of your profile when you're in the *Edit Profile* function.

Volunteer Experience & Causes

This section allows you to be as general or as specific as you want to be in identifying what types of nonprofit causes and organizations you support. As you can see in Figure 16.40, there are checkboxes with general categories of causes; you can type in and list specific organizations that you support; and finally, you can list actual volunteer positions that you've had or still have.

FIGURE 16.40   Add Volunteer Experience

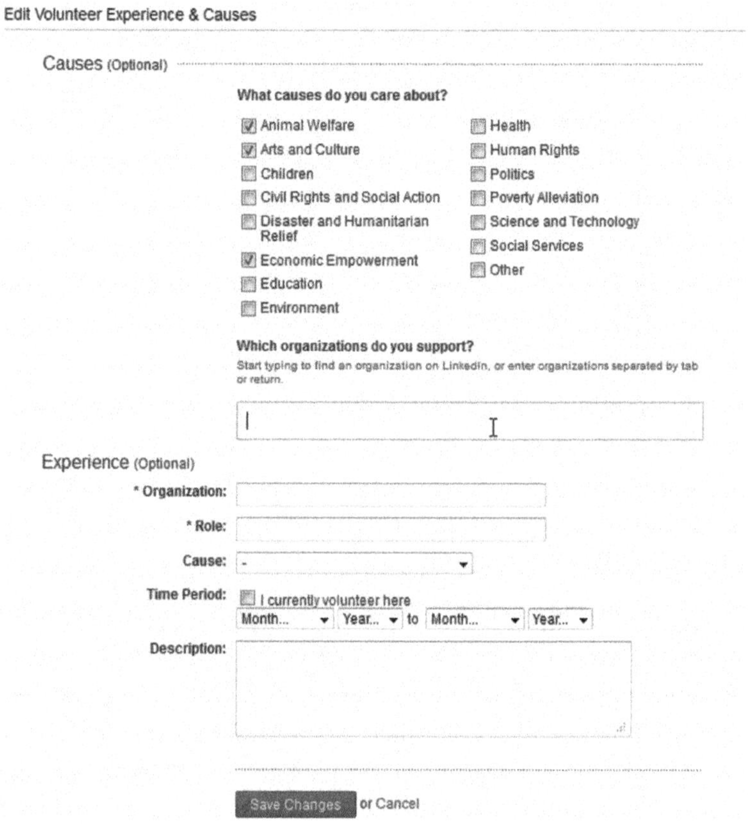

FIGURE 16.41 Add an Honor or Award

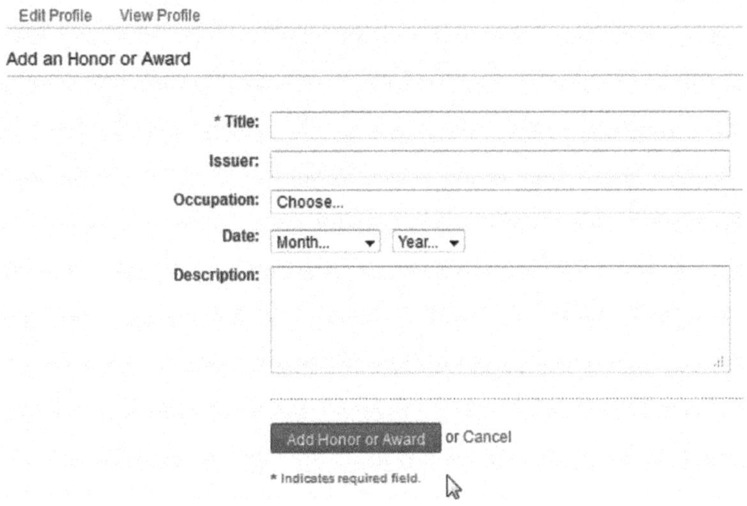

Honors and Awards

This is the *Honors and Awards* section (shown in Figure 16.41), which I recommend using instead of the Honors and Awards section under Additional Information. First, the new version ties the award to a specific position. Therefore, when people are reading about that job description, they'll see below it that you received an award and there is a hyperlink that will hop down to it.

Second, it's titled *Honors* and Awards. Who's to say what is and isn't an honor? In addition to actual awards, I use this field to list pro bono speaking opportunities for significant organizations. To me, that's an honor. So, think of things that have happened in your professional life that you consider an honor but that don't fit nicely into another category. Use the field shown in Figure 16.42 to highlight such distinctions.

Organizations

The *Organizations* section is a little different than the volunteer section. When I think of volunteer work, I think of mission-oriented work with the

FIGURE 16.42 Honors and Awards

Honors and Awards

Speaker: LinkedIn Ninja Black Belt for Sales and Small Business
The Circuit: Information Technology association for the Greater Cincinnati tri-state region
April 2011 | Crystal Clear Buzz: The LinkedIn Ninja - Consulting, Training & Coaching about LinkedIn for Sales
A sold out speaking engagement to teach IT companies how to leverage LinkedIn for sales and business development.

Speaker for Tech Tuesday
Clermont Chamber of Commerce
August 2011 | Crystal Clear Buzz: The LinkedIn Ninja - Consulting, Training & Coaching about LinkedIn for Sales
Yes! You Can Do That on LinkedIn!

President's Award for Quality Financial Advice
American Express Financial Advisors
1998 | Ameriprise Financial Advisors

sole purpose of giving back to the community. These aren't positions or activities meant for professional development or to increase my business in any way.

There are leadership positions, projects, and organizations that I participate in that may technically be with nonprofit organizations, but they are meant to increase my credibility as a professional, my reach within the community for business purposes, and ultimately, help grow my business. I see these types of positions as more fitting within the Organizations rather than the Volunteer section (see Figure 16.43). These types of leadership positions and organizations would be professional associations, networking groups, political organizations, and the like.

A benefit that the organizations section has for these types of positions that the volunteer section doesn't have is that you can tie these leadership positions directly to jobs and education (see Figure 16.44). In a way, that's almost how you can tell which section is best for the particular non-paid leadership position. If it's directly related to or impacts any of your jobs or educational experience, then put it here.

Projects

The *Projects* section (Figure 16.45) may or may not have a place in your LinkedIn profile. Originally created for students to highlight special

FIGURE 16.43   Add an Organization

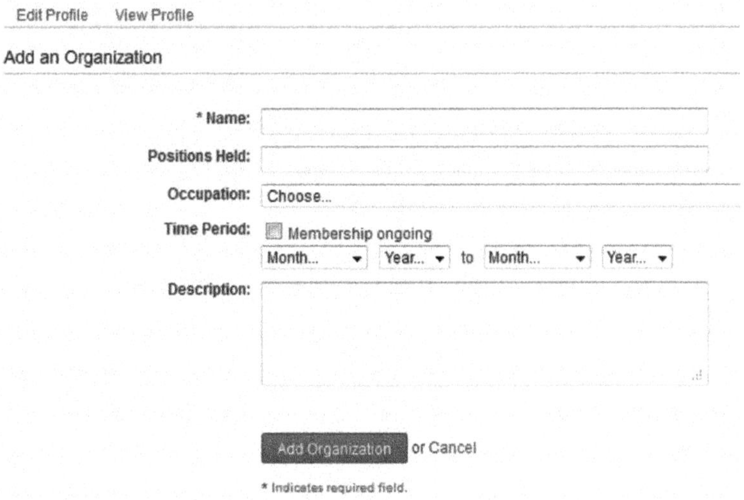

Edit Profile   View Profile

Add an Organization

* Name:	
Positions Held:	
Occupation:	Choose...
Time Period:	☐ Membership ongoing
	Month... ▼ Year... ▼ to Month... ▼ Year... ▼
Description:	

[Add Organization] or Cancel

* Indicates required field.

FIGURE 16.44   Organizations

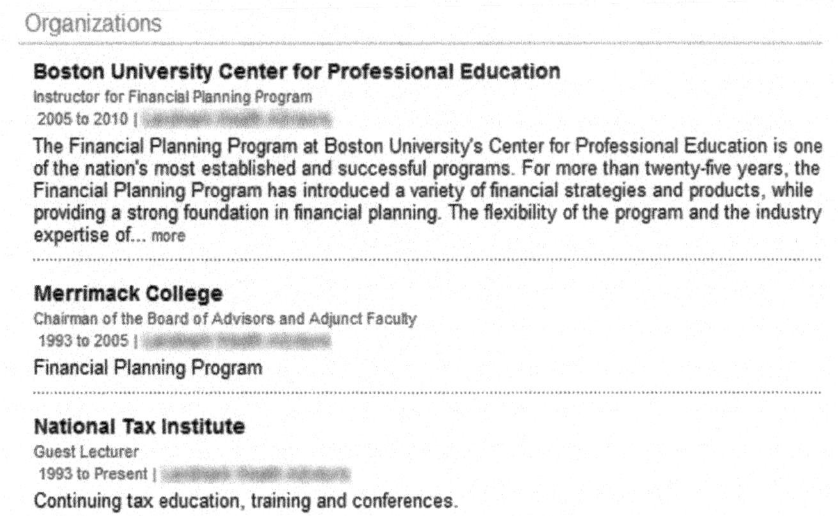

Organizations

Boston University Center for Professional Education
Instructor for Financial Planning Program
2005 to 2010 |
The Financial Planning Program at Boston University's Center for Professional Education is one of the nation's most established and successful programs. For more than twenty-five years, the Financial Planning Program has introduced a variety of financial strategies and products, while providing a strong foundation in financial planning. The flexibility of the program and the industry expertise of... more

Merrimack College
Chairman of the Board of Advisors and Adjunct Faculty
1993 to 2005 |
Financial Planning Program

National Tax Institute
Guest Lecturer
1993 to Present |
Continuing tax education, training and conferences.

FIGURE 16.45   Add a Project

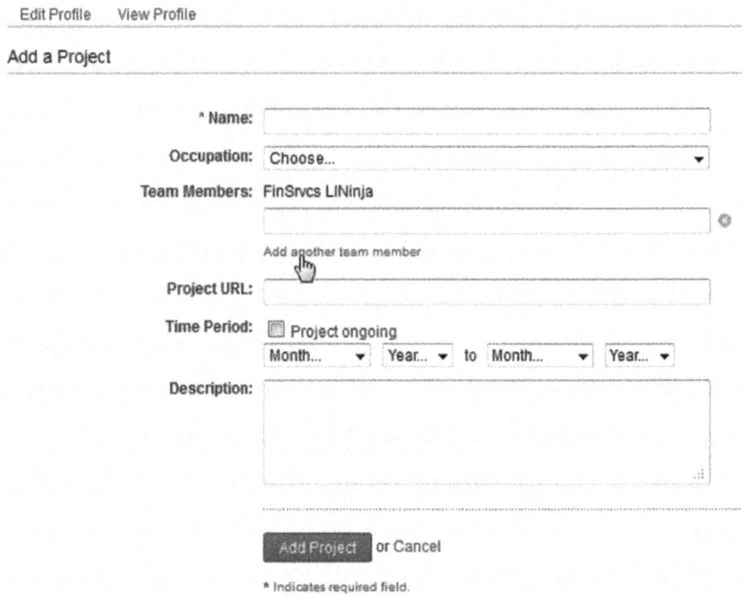

projects, it is relevant for those of us well out of school too. Some of the projects that would be perfect for this section may also be related to the leadership positions and activities already mentioned in the Volunteer and Organizations sections.

One of the things that you will notice with the Projects section is that you can tie the project to a specific job or school, but you can pull in and tag the other project team members if they are on LinkedIn and you are connected to them (see Figure 16.46).

Some of the types of projects or activities that would work well here include:

- Special Event Committee
- Class Project for a City Leadership Program
- Election Campaign
- Major Fundraising Campaign
- Major Community Project

FIGURE 16.46 Projects

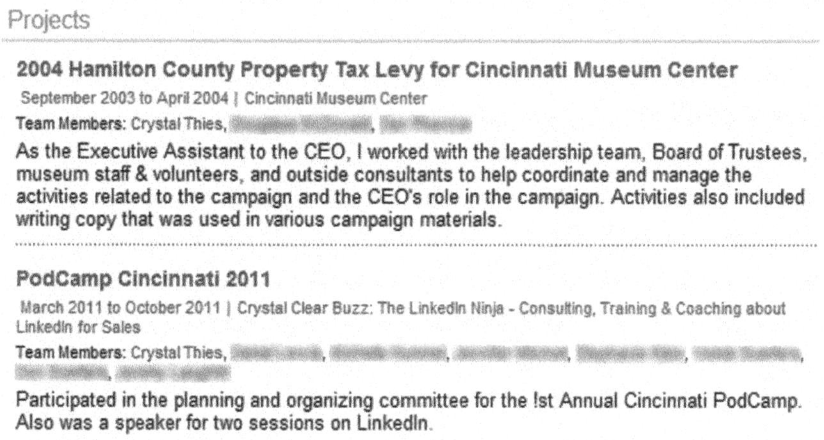

Projects

2004 Hamilton County Property Tax Levy for Cincinnati Museum Center
September 2003 to April 2004 | Cincinnati Museum Center
Team Members: Crystal Thies, ▓▓▓▓▓▓▓, ▓▓▓▓▓▓
As the Executive Assistant to the CEO, I worked with the leadership team, Board of Trustees, museum staff & volunteers, and outside consultants to help coordinate and manage the activities related to the campaign and the CEO's role in the campaign. Activities also included writing copy that was used in various campaign materials.

PodCamp Cincinnati 2011
March 2011 to October 2011 | Crystal Clear Buzz: The LinkedIn Ninja - Consulting, Training & Coaching about LinkedIn for Sales
Team Members: Crystal Thies, ▓▓▓▓▓▓, ▓▓▓▓▓▓, ▓▓▓▓▓▓, ▓▓▓▓▓▓, ▓▓▓▓▓▓, ▓▓▓▓▓▓, ▓▓▓▓▓▓
Participated in the planning and organizing committee for the !st Annual Cincinnati PodCamp. Also was a speaker for two sessions on LinkedIn.

Publications

The final special section that we will discuss is *Publications*, as shown in Figure 16.47. Technically, this section is meant for publications that you've authored, but I've found you can also make it work for publications about you or where you're mentioned or quoted. The only downside is that you will appear as an author—which won't be true—but you can add the name of the real author even if you're not connected to that person.

If the publication is an article, you can provide the URL for people to read it online (see Figure 16.48). If the publication is a book, you can provide the URL for people to go and purchase it.

Applications

If you liked all of the extra special content you could add to your profile with the special sections, then you're going to really like what you can do with the different profile applications you can add. The profile applications are mostly developed by third parties to bring added functionality to LinkedIn. All of the third-party applications do require you to sign up for an account on their site in order to take full advantage of them. The majority of these

FIGURE 16.47   Add a Publication

Edit Profile   View Profile

Add a Publication

* Title:	
Publication/Publisher:	
Publication Date:	Month... ▾ Day... ▾ Year... ▾
Publication URL:	
Author:	FinSrvcs LINinja
	Add another author
Summary:	

Add Publication   or Cancel

* Indicates required field.

third-party applications provide a free membership to be able to use them in LinkedIn.

I do have to tell you that I have seen several broker-dealers that block the ability to access the applications for use on your profile, which results in blocking the applications from being visible in anyone's profile. As a result, the usage of the applications may not be allowed by your compliance policy. The issue is that you're free to add content to these applications and your management may be concerned that the content you add hasn't been properly reviewed or that you can easily change it or add to it after review.

As a result, the main thing to keep in mind is that all of the content you share either needs to be reviewed by your compliance department or provided by a product company that has submitted it to FINRA/SEC for review, and that it must be clearly labeled suitable for distribution to the public.

It would be too much to give full how-to instructions for every application you could possibly use on your profile, but I'm going to highlight the most valuable among them. Between LinkedIn's Help Center and the help

FIGURE 16.48 Publications

Publications

Five Ways to Ninja-ize Your LinkedIn Experience
IT Martini | April 18, 2011
Authors: Crystal Thies, Angela Slezak
IT Martini recently caught up with the Crystal "The LinkedIn Ninja" Thies to learn how Information Technology Professionals can optimize their networking experience on LinkedIn.

The Secret Life of LinkedIn
Financial-Planning Magazine | Practice Perfect Blog | November 1, 2011
Authors: Crystal Thies, Donna Mitchell
It starts with the profile. Advisors should skip broad descriptions that state the obvious, according to Crystal Thies, CEO of Crystal Clear Buzz, a consulting firm based in Ludlow, Ky. Advisors also should be aware of regulatory prohibitions against making recommendations to buy specific products, says Thies, who helps professionals maximize their use of LinkedIn, among other consulting services.

The Social Media Handbook for Financial Advisors: How to Use Facebook, Twitter, and LinkedIn to Build and Grow Your Business (Bloomberg Financial)
Bloomberg Press/Wiley Publishing
Authors: Crystal Thies, Matthew Halloran, MS, Certified Coach
Social media is everywhere. 3.5 billion pieces of content are shared on Facebook each week, 22 million professionals are networking on LinkedIn, and 140 million tweets are posted every day. The opportunities these platforms present for financial advisors are huge, but most advisors have no idea how to use them to build bigger, stronger client bases. The Social Media Handbook for Financial Advisors... more

instructions available from the third-party application sites, you should be able to figure out how to make them work.

To access and add the applications to your profile, go to the *More* menu item at the far right of the navigation bar (see Figure 16.49). At the bottom of the drop-down menu, you'll see *Get more applications.* Click on it.

Simply select the application you want to add. A more detailed description will appear with a button to add it to your profile.

File Sharing—Box

With the *Box.net* application (see Figure 16.50), you can share any files with anyone who visits your LinkedIn profile. These files could be marketing collateral such as brochures and flyers, and expertise content like white papers and articles. You could include podcasts, newsletters, and even common client forms.

FIGURE 16.49   Get More Applications

FIGURE 16.50   Box.net

Box.net Files
by Box.net

Add the Box.net Files application to manage all your important files online. Box.net lets you share content on your profile, and collaborate with friends and colleagues.

FIGURE 16.51   SlideShare

SlideShare Presentations
by SlideShare Inc

SlideShare is the best way to share presentations on LinkedIn! You can upload & display your own presentations, check out presentations from your colleagues, and find experts within your network.

Presentations and Videos—SlideShare

SlideShare allows you to show PowerPoint presentations or play a video directly in your LinkedIn profile without leaving the page.

SlideShare is actually another social network where people regularly search for information (see Figure 16.51). In addition to presentations, you can embed a YouTube video, upload and embed a video that is not on YouTube, and even upload an audio file, time your slides to the audio file, and convert the entire thing to a video file.

Blogs—WordPress and BlogLink

If your website has a blog or you're using a blog on a separate platform, then you have two options to pull the blog articles directly into your profile.

The WordPress application (Figure 16.52) only works for blogs on a WordPress platform. You can only have one blog feed coming into your profile.

The Blog Link application (Figure 16.53) is powered by TypePad, which is a premium blog platform. However, it will pull in the blog feeds from any blog platform. Additionally, it will pull in the feeds of multiple blogs. Basically, it looks at the website links that you have attached to your profile and it pulls in any feeds associated with those links. One thing to keep in mind is that blogs are not the only sites that have feeds attached

FIGURE 16.52 WordPress

WordPress
by WordPress

Connect your virtual lives with the WordPress LinkedIn Application. With the WordPress App, you can sync your WordPress blog posts with your LinkedIn profile, keeping everyone you know in the know.

FIGURE 16.53 Blog Link

Blog Link
by SixApart

With **Blog Link**, you can get the most of your LinkedIn relationships by connecting your blog to your LinkedIn profile. Blog Link helps you, and your professional network, stay connected.

to them. Your Facebook page and profile are also feeds, as is your Twitter account. So if you list them in your websites or use the Twitter application, then everything you post there will also be pulled into this application and will be displayed on your LinkedIn profile.

There are many other existing applications, and applications are regularly being added and taken away. Explore your options and consider how you can make the best use of what is available.some of this content that you would use in these applications may be available on your website and you may be thinking that you'd rather people go to your website to get to it. Chances are greater that they won't go to your website and therefore will never see the content. If you get them to your LinkedIn profile, give them everything they may possibly want while they are there, because it may be your only shot.

Changing the Order

LinkedIn has put all of the content in its own default order. If you don't like that order, you can change it (see Figure 16.54). You can move the different sections around while in the Edit Profile function by simply taking your cursor to the top of a main content section. You'll see the cursor change from an arrow to a plus sign, indicating that you can drag and drop the section to a different location. Additionally, if you have more than one current position listed in the experience section, you can drag and drop them in the order that you want them to appear. By default, LinkedIn always puts the newest position at the top.

As a financial advisor, any of the content that is more marketing related is the most important — so you want it as close to the top as possible. If you're using the applications, you'll see that LinkedIn currently adds them to the bottom of the profile. You're going to want to move them from the very bottom of your profile because many people won't scroll down that far to find them. I recommend moving the applications to just below your

FIGURE 16.54   Changing the Order

summary. In my opinion, unless you're looking for a job, the experience section is one of the least important sections. Look at the content you've added to your profile objectively and put it in the order that would be most compelling to a prospective client.

Finalizing Your Profile

Once you've finished your profile, you'll need to follow your compliance policy and submit it for review. Based on my experience with multiple compliance departments, you're likely to have some changes, edits, and possibly even deletions. Make the required changes.

Once your profile has been approved, you'll want to go in and change the *Public Profile* setting to make your profile completely visible (see Figure 16.55). Google only indexes the public profile, so your LinkedIn profile will only show up in Google searches (for your name or keywords) if you change this setting.

If you recall, in order to change your public profile setting, go into *Edit Profile* and the *Publish your public profile* link is the last line inside the profile box.

This time around, you'll be clicking *Make my public profile visible to everyone*. Additionally, you'll want to put checks in all of the sections that are listed below (see Figure 16.56).

You're also going to want to customize the URL for your public profile. Once you've customized the URL, then it will be really easy to share your LinkedIn profile via your business cards, email signature, and website. You can see the link to set your custom URL in the upper right-hand corner.

FIGURE 16.55 Publish Your Public Profile

FIGURE 16.56   Public Profile Options

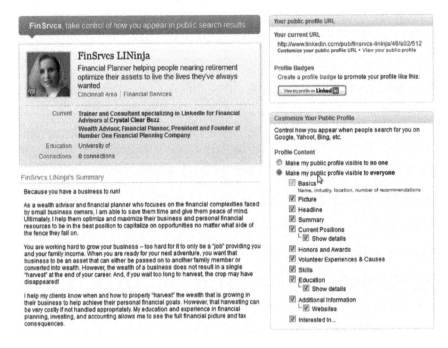

I recommend simply making your URL your first and last name together (www.linkedin.com/in/firstnamelastname). However, since every URL must be unique, if you have a common name, then yours may be taken. You can add a middle initial or something else about your name that would create a unique URL (see Figure 16.57).

Final Thoughts

I tell my nonfinancial clients that your profile should never be finished; it's a work in progress. This is because you want to keep your profile fresh and current. Additionally, your network is notified every time you make changes to your profile, which drives traffic back to check it out. Another important consideration is that any changes you make to your profile after your

FIGURE 16.57   Public Profile URL

compliance review will require a new compliance review. Now, that doesn't mean that you should never make changes, but it does mean you want to be smart and strategic when making those changes. I would recommend a quarterly update or an update when there is anything new and of great significance—like a publication—that you want to share and highlight in a timely fashion.

CHAPTER 17

Building Your LinkedIn Network to Create a Self-Referral Machine

Crystal Thies

Where LinkedIn really shines for financial advisors is in its ability to help you take more control over the referral process. A 100 percent referral business is what every financial advisor strives for because the conversion is high and it takes the least amount of effort. A properly built LinkedIn network will increase the quantity of opportunities because you will be able to self-refer to potential clients instead of waiting for referrals to come to you.

Networking Philosophy

There is a spectrum of networking philosophy of which you should be aware. On the one end are closed networkers and the other open networkers. Closed networkers have a very high standard of whom they will connect with, which usually requires having met in person or had significant inter-action; *quality* of connection is what is most important. Open networkers, on the other hand, value *quantity* and are looking to build the largest possible network regardless of whether each person in their network is

219

interested in or able to help them. Open networkers always identify themselves, often with the acronym LION (LinkedIn Open Networker).

For financial advisors, I recommend being closer to the closed end of the spectrum. Let's face it; there is an enormous amount of competition in this industry and the likelihood of a referral being successful from someone who doesn't know you is very low. The trust factor has to be very high before most people would consider talking to a financial advisor, which usually starts with someone they know vouching for you.

Who Should Be in Your Network?

Building your network with everyone you know who would be willing to help you is the first part of creating a strong and effective network. The first people on your list should be your clients. It surprises me that many people think they shouldn't have their clients in their LinkedIn network. Aren't they your best referrers? Wouldn't you like to be able to see who they know? As long as you're not connecting with competitors, there should be no issue. Besides, your network is going to have many more people than just clients, so how is anyone to know who is or isn't a client?

The second part of that equation is competitors. Given the sometimes vicious nature of competition among financial advisors, I always recommend against connecting with competing financial advisors—even in the same office. Unless you trust them 100 percent or are partnering with them in some manner, I just don't think it's worth the risk. I recommend keeping your connections visible to your network because it is one of the main reasons for LinkedIn (and there are some people who will disconnect if they find that your connections are closed). A competitor may not steal a client, but your network could give them prospect ideas—the people you've been working as prospects.

Adding Connections

To add connections, go to the *Contacts* tab and select *Add Connections* from the drop-down menu (see Figure 17.1).

The fastest way to grow your LinkedIn network is by importing your contact database. Chances are that your clients are—and should be—part of your contact database. I've seen several compliance policies that forbid the

FIGURE 17.1   Add Connections

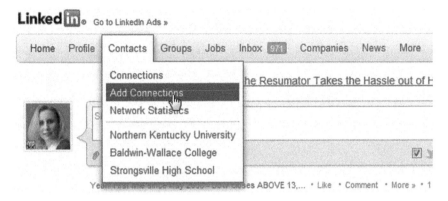

transferring of any client data to any external system. If that's the case, then I do recommend removing them from the exported list and only including non-client contacts at this stage. You'll simply have to search for your clients by name one by one to stay compliant in adding them to your LinkedIn network.

If you use a webmail program for your personal email messaging (Gmail, Yahoo!, AOL, etc.), LinkedIn will log in, crawl through your contact list, and pull them in for you.

For non-web-based contacts, see the link I've circled at the bottom of Figure 17.2 to manually import contacts. When exporting your contacts from your database, CRM, or Outlook file, save it as a CSV file, which stands for comma separated values. Each database has its own export procedure, but they all offer an option to export as a CSV file. See your program's user guide for instructions on how to export.

One step inbetween exporting and importing that I highly recommend is removal of nonessential fields. When you export a contact database, it will include all contact record fields. LinkedIn only needs three fields: first name, last name, and email address (see Figure 17.3). If you open the file in Microsoft Excel before importing it into LinkedIn, you can delete all columns that are not needed by LinkedIn. This will ensure that your import goes smoothly. The extra fields can cause LinkedIn to read the file incorrectly, and it will either not import the file or import it incorrectly. After your remove the extra fields, be certain to resave it as a CSV file. Excel will try to convince you to change it with warnings that formatting won't be preserved, but ignore these warnings and save it as a CSV.

FIGURE 17.2 Import Webmail Contacts

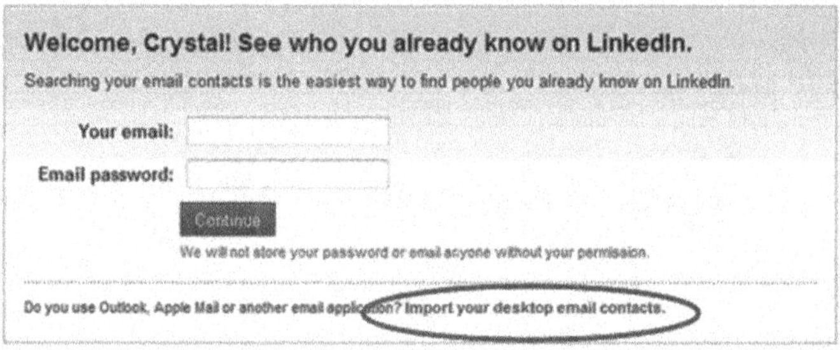

Welcome, Crystal! See who you already know on LinkedIn.
Searching your email contacts is the easiest way to find people you already know on LinkedIn.

Your email:
Email password:

Continue

We will not store your password or email anyone without your permission.

Do you use Outlook, Apple Mail or another email application? Import your desktop email contacts.

FIGURE 17.3 Invite Imported Contacts

Invite 152 Contacts to Connect

You have 152 contacts that can be invited and 9 are already using LinkedIn. Select which contacts you wish to invite to connect.

Select all

Member since March 2009 | 50 connections

Member since August 2008 | 1 connection

Member since January 2009 | 3 connections

Member since January 2010 | 1 connection

Member since August 2004 | 500+ connections

Member since September 2006 | 0 connection

Send Invitations or Cancel

The great part about the importing process is that LinkedIn will match up your contacts with the people who have already joined and tell you who is already on LinkedIn!

Anyone whose name has the LinkedIn logo attached to it has been found to be on LinkedIn already. All you have to do is put a check mark in the box next to their name and you can invite everyone you know who is on LinkedIn already to connect at one time.

Some very important things to keep in mind when using the import function: First, you will *not* be able to add a personal note explaining how you know the contact or are connected, so only include them in the bulk invitation if there is absolutely no question that they will know who you are. Second, if there isn't a LinkedIn logo next to their name, and you leave them checked, they will get a message inviting them to join LinkedIn and then connect instead of the simple message to connect. Third, if you see someone listed that you know is on LinkedIn and there isn't a LinkedIn logo next to them, then that means they do not have the email address you are using associated with their profile (which is why it's important that you connect all of your active email addresses to your profile, because you may be missing invitation-to-connect opportunities from people you know who have a different email address). You will have to search for them individually and send a separate invitation to connect.

In addition to the import contacts function, LinkedIn will run specific searches based on the content you've added to your profile to make it easy to find others that you have worked with in past jobs and have gone to school with (see Figure 17.4).

The function to find past work colleagues (see Figure 17.5) actually keeps track of when you last looked.

The feature that enables you to find alumni (see Figure 17.6) gives you the chance to search each school you've attended by those who were also in attendance during the range of dates you attended. There is also an option for you to search by graduation year.

The fourth way LinkedIn helps you find connections actually involves the use of an algorithm, which will recommend people it thinks you may know (see Figure 17.7). These are people who are connected to your connections—particularly multiple connections—in addition to being from your past schools and companies.

FIGURE 17.4 Add Connections Tabs

FIGURE 17.5 Add Colleagues

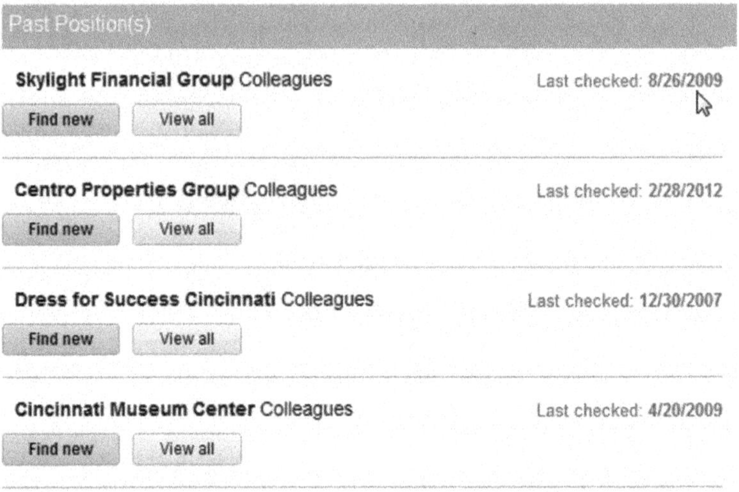

Past Position(s)

Skylight Financial Group Colleagues   Last checked: 8/26/2009

[Find new] [View all]

Centro Properties Group Colleagues   Last checked: 2/28/2012

[Find new] [View all]

Dress for Success Cincinnati Colleagues   Last checked: 12/30/2007

[Find new] [View all]

Cincinnati Museum Center Colleagues   Last checked: 4/20/2009

[Find new] [View all]

FIGURE 17.6 Add Alumni

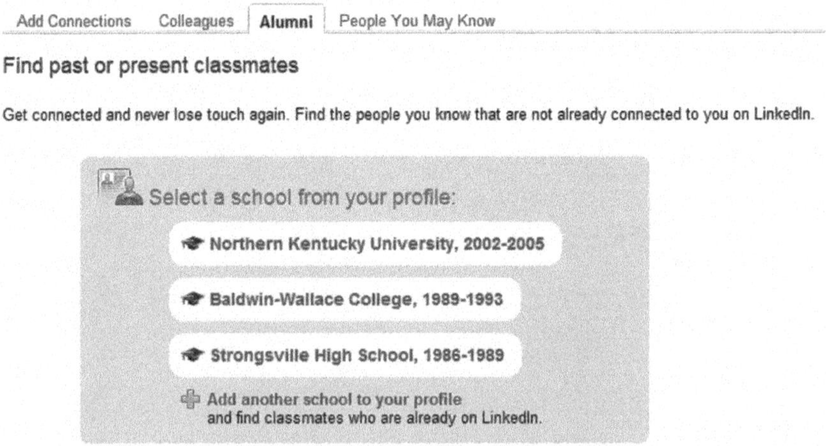

Add Connections   Colleagues | **Alumni** | People You May Know

Find past or present classmates

Get connected and never lose touch again. Find the people you know that are not already connected to you on LinkedIn.

Select a school from your profile:

🎓 **Northern Kentucky University, 2002-2005**

🎓 **Baldwin-Wallace College, 1989-1993**

🎓 **Strongsville High School, 1986-1989**

➕ Add another school to your profile
and find classmates who are already on LinkedIn.

I recommend checking these occasionally because new people are joining LinkedIn every day (more than two people every second!).

Remember: You're trying to connect with as many people as possible who know who you are and who would be willing or likely to help you if you asked. These are not necessarily prospects themselves. Someone may be a barista working in a coffee shop and appear, on the surface, to be not worth having in

FIGURE 17.7   People Connections

your network. But that barista may be handing out coffee to CEOs and high-level executives all day long and could end up being a great referral source. So don't judge someone's usefulness based on their status or position. You can never tell just how connected a person may be until you look under the hood!

Sending Individual Invitations to Connect

After you've done your initial network build out, then it's very important to regularly be adding new people to your network. In the next chapter, we're going to be looking at searching for prospects. The best prospects are in the 2nd degree of our network. However, if we don't keep growing our 1st degree network, we'll quickly burn through our 2nd degree. So, how do you keep your network growing?

The easiest way is to be diligent about inviting every new person you meet to connect (assuming they are on LinkedIn). I have my students actually put a time in their calendars as a standing weekly appointment to make certain that they are inviting the new people they meet at networking events. I recommend that you do the same.

There is a proper etiquette to inviting people to connect that isn't followed by many and it includes personalized invitations to connect. This requires using LinkedIn's messaging system, so you will need to have an archiving software program in place that captures LinkedIn messages in order to be allowed to customize these invitations to connect.

LinkedIn's philosophy is that you should only be connecting to people you know. Therefore, you must have the person's email address to invite him to connect *unless* you worked with him in the past, you went to school with him in the past, you've done business with him (meaning that either you are that person's client or he is yours), or you're in a LinkedIn group with him (see Figure 17.8). You want to be certain that you pick the proper relationship or reason to connect (there are people who pick a false reason just to get the invitation sent and it can cause your account to be restricted if they report you).

As you can see, LinkedIn claims that the personal note is optional. I don't believe it should be. Ninety-nine percent of the time, you should be adding at least a sentence or two of personalization. The only exception is if you're 200 percent certain that this person knows exactly who you are and that you have a close enough relationship that you know them personally. The note doesn't need to be much unless you're trying to connect with

FIGURE 17.8 Invitation to Connect

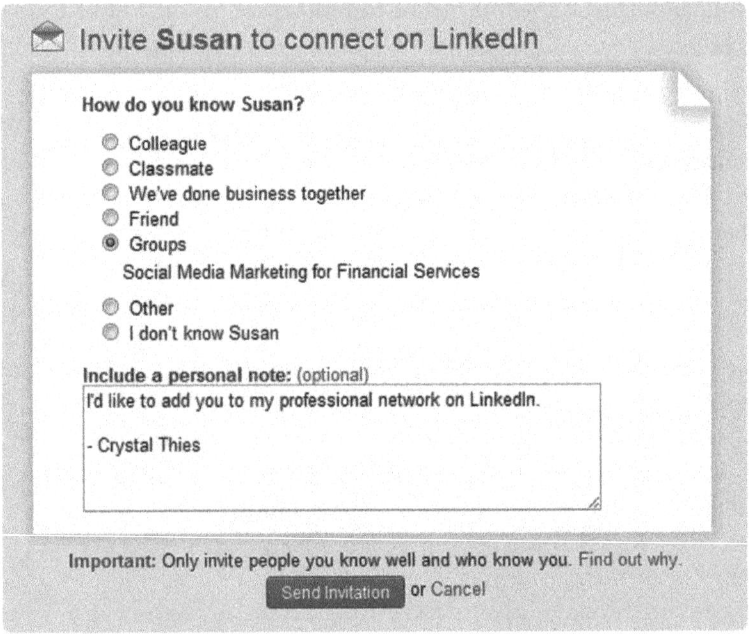

someone you've never met. Besides, LinkedIn only gives you 300 characters, so you don't have much space to be verbose.

Sample messages:

Susan,

It was great meeting you at the Chamber networking event. I'd love to connect and stay in touch via LinkedIn. If there is ever anything I can do to help you, please let me know.

Warmest regards,

Crystal Thies

Susan,

I've enjoyed the comments you've been making in the group discussions and am interested in getting to know you better. If there is anything I can do to help you or your business, please do not hesitate to ask.

Warmest regards,

Crystal Thies

To me, the number one thing you should focus on in your note to connect is being a giver and focused on demonstrating a benefit for them— not you. You may be trying to connect with them because of something you want out of the new relationship, but you never phrase it that way. Additionally, you need to be genuine about wanting to help the other person and be focused on doing that first. Finally, you'll find that your wording for many of these invites tends to be the same. From a compliance standpoint, any letter sent to more than 25 people needs to be reviewed. A best practice would be to create invitation message templates for the most common reasons you connect with new people and send them through compliance review. Although they are being captured by the archiving service you are using, they still will need to be reviewed.

Final Thoughts

Your LinkedIn network isn't only an asset; it's a portfolio. This is how you should approach it. Nurture your network. Be strategic about who you bring in. Be smart about not letting in people who could diminish its value. Get to know those who enter and invest in their livelihood and growth. First, *give* to them, and you will eventually *get* in return.

CHAPTER 18

Finding Prospects Using LinkedIn: Creating Your Self-Referral Machine

Crystal Thies

This is likely the chapter you've been waiting for. Whenever I speak on LinkedIn and give the audience a chance to decide what I'm going to talk about, they *always* pick this topic. I first found LinkedIn when I was looking for new online tools that I could use if I decided to take a big risk and go back into financial planning again after being out for almost a decade. This was back in 2007 and LinkedIn didn't have half the capabilities it has today. What it did have (and what I saw that helped convince me to take the risk and jump in and take the Series 7 for the second time in my life) was this ability to search out to the 3rd degree of your network to see how you were connected to prospects. This is because when you know how you're connected, you don't have to cold call. I'd done my hours of dialing for dollars back in the 1990s, and I wasn't going to build a second practice like that. The new practice would be built by relationships—not by strong-arming people who didn't know me.

The LinkedIn Advanced Search: Free versus Premium

The LinkedIn Advanced Search has a lot of complexities. This is also where you see the biggest differences between the basic (free) and the premium memberships. Back in 2010, LinkedIn added several advanced search filters that were only available to premium members. When I saw these filters and their capabilities, it was then that I switched from being a free LinkedIn member to a premium LinkedIn member.

In addition to the advanced search filters, premium members get more search results. Free members only get the first 100 search results. Premium members start with 300 search results and increase based on level of membership.

One hundred search results may seem like a lot, but as you'll see in a couple of examples, when combined with the basic search filters, it can be difficult to get highly targeted search results and you end up with a lot of *junk* in the results. Often, you're not able to get to some of the best prospects at the free level.

The advanced search page (see Figure 18.1) is too large to capture and print to be readable. To access and see for yourself, look for the link to the far right of the menu bar after a basic search box that says *Advanced*.

Search filters available to all members:
- Keywords
- Name—first and last
- Location—up to 100 mile radius around zip code
- Title—current, past, or both
- Company Name—current, past, or both
- School
- Industry—select one or many
- Relationship—1st Degree, 2nd Degree, Group, or 3rd Degree & Everyone Else
- Language—all foreign languages LinkedIn recognizes

Search filters available to all premium members:
- Company Size—1–10; 11–50; 51–200; 201–500; 501–1000; 1001–5000; 5001–10000; 10000+
- Seniority Level—manager, owner, partner, CXO, VP, director, senior, entry, students & interns, volunteer
- Interested In—potential employees; consultants/contractors; entrepreneurs; hiring managers; industry experts; deal-making contacts; reference check; reconnect
- Fortune 1000—Fortune 50; Fortune 51–100; Fortune 101–250; Fortune 251–500; Fortune 501–1000

FIGURE 18.1   Advanced Search Link

Search filters available to only the highest-level premium members:

- Groups—select specific groups of which you're a member
- Function—multiple functions based on the role the person plays in an organization
- Years of Experience—less than 1 year; 1 to 2 years; 3 to 5 years; 6 to 10 years; more than 10 years
- Recently Joined—1 day ago; 2–7 days ago; 8–14 days ago; 15–30 days ago; 1–3 months ago

One other significant benefit of premium membership that affects active prospecting on LinkedIn is the *Profile Organizer.* LinkedIn came out with the profile organizer about six to eight months before the new advanced search filters and it *almost* made me upgrade to premium. The profile organizer allows you to save the profiles of people you're not connected to. Holding onto a prospect when you see them is more important than you may think. I have literally run a search one day, seen a great prospect, and then ran the search the next day and couldn't find the same person! Think about it—more than one person joins LinkedIn every second. Add to that the fact that people are always changing their profiles and learning how to better optimize their profiles and it's actually pretty easy to see how the first 100 search results could change so drastically from one day to the next.

Developing Good Searches

Creating good and effective searches is both an art and a science. LinkedIn's search functionality recognizes a handful of Boolean operators that can help you develop highly targeted searches. The image shown in Figure 18.2 comes from LinkedIn's Help Center and explains the Boolean operators that you can use.

FIGURE 18.2   Boolean Operators

> **Boolean searches** - The site doesn't support wildcard searches, but you can use advanced search operators and Boolean logic. You can also use these Boolean search types to refine your results:
>
> - Quoted searches - For an exact phrase, enclose the phrase in quotation marks (e.g. "product manager").
> - NOT searches - To exclude a particular term, type that term with an uppercase NOT immediately before it (e.g. NOT computer).
> - OR searches - To see results that include just 1 of 2 or more terms, separate those terms with an uppercase OR (e.g. sales OR marketing).
> - AND searches - To get results that include 2 or more terms, you can use the upper-case word AND as a separator (e.g. manager AND director). Note: You don't need to use AND. If you search 2 or more terms, you'll automatically see results that include all of them.
> - Parenthetical searches - To do a complex search, you can combine terms using parentheses. For example, to find people who have "VP" in their profiles, or have director AND division in their profiles, type: VP OR (director AND division).

If you've never used Boolean search operators before, you do need to keep in mind that they must be capitalized to work; otherwise, they are seen as just another search word. Additionally, in replace of the NOT operator, you can also use a minus sign (−) (i.e., instead of: NOT computer, you could use: −computer). Lastly, you can use multiple operators together. One of the upcoming examples we will look at has the search phrase: "in transition" OR "new opportunity". If you wanted to exclude people in transition who were financial advisors, you could use the search phrase: "in transition" OR "new opportunity" −"financial advisor" −investments.

Finding 401(k) Rollover Opportunities

I know I've been teasing you about this, so here it is! LinkedIn really is a gold mine for finding 401(k) rollover opportunities. Of course, I can show you how to find the opportunities, but you're the one who is going to have to have the relationship building and sales skills to get to the opportunity and seal the deal.

Essentially, all you have to do is put the terms in the last paragraph in the *Keyword* box of the *Advanced Search*. Then, set the *Location* filter to your zip code and set the radius for as wide an area as you want (up to 100 miles).

The third filter you need to adjust is the *Relationship* filter. Assuming that you've already vetted your 1st degree network for client opportunities, you're going to want to focus on the 2nd degree level of your network. With the 2nd degree, you are dealing with your 1st degree's connections. That means that these are people for whom you at least have an email address and possibly even a phone number. Therefore, you can take your communications out of LinkedIn (especially important if you're using LinkedIn personally because your broker-dealer doesn't allow you to use social media) and use your approved communications methods. If you get to a point that you've exhausted your 2nd degree prospects or you're comfortable with cold prospecting, you can also focus on the group-level relationship. As you'll see in Chapter 19, you have the capability to send messages to group members you're not connected to even if you're not a premium member. Therefore, they are also especially valuable.

Figure 18.3 shows what this looks like.

Next, I'm going to show you my search results. Keep in mind that my search results are based on my 1st degree network, which is currently about 1,500 people. If you're just getting started and your network is small, then you're not going to have these same results. However, if you keep growing your network, it will get there. (See Fig. 18.4.)

FIGURE 18.3 In Transition Search

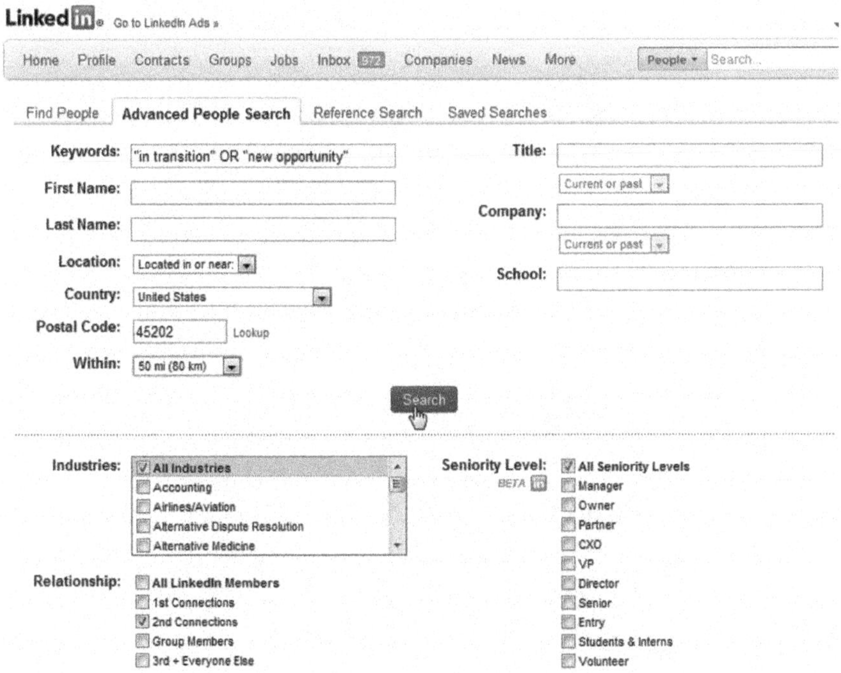

FIGURE 18.4 In Transition Search Results

If you look at the top of the results, you'll see that I have 188 2nd degree connections with those terms in their profiles within a 50-mile radius of downtown Cincinnati, Ohio.

At the bottom of each person's record, it will tell you how many shared connections you have. If you click on that link, it will show you up to three of those shared connections. To see the remaining shared connections, you'll need to go and look at the full profile. When you look at the full profile, that's where you can see where they worked last to determine the likelihood of an existing 401(k) and what type of job history they have had to estimate their income potential. Essentially, you're qualifying the prospect to see if it appears that they would meet your minimum client guidelines. If they do, then it's time to start strategizing.

When it comes to developing the strategy, you want to see if there is more than one way to get to the person. Ultimately, you want to get the *best* person to introduce you. The best person is someone who knows you really well and is willing to make the referral *and* knows the prospect well enough that when they ask that person to talk to you, he or she will.

Small Business Owner Search

Next, let's look at another search that is a common target market among financial advisors that will allow us to look at some of the differences in the search filters and results between the free and premium memberships.

Essentially, our goal is to find small business owners of established companies in our geographic region who are in our 2nd degree network. For the free member search, we will be using keywords in the *Title* field (see Figure 18.5). For the premium member search, we'll be using the company size and seniority filters.

FIGURE 18.5 SBO Search

Figure 18.5 is for the free member search. Since small business owners refer to their titles in many different ways, you will want to include all possible options. Therefore, anyone who has at least one of the four words (owner, president, CEO, founder) in their current title who is also a 2nd degree connection within 50 miles of downtown Cincinnati, Ohio, will show up in my search results, as shown in Figure 18.6.

This search provided 12,309 results. But remember: I can only access the first 100 at the free level. One other thing to keep in mind with these results is that there are a lot of *solopreneurs*—consultants and people running multilevel marketing (MLM) companies that refer to themselves as small business owners with those keywords. Now, you may be happy to have those types of business owners as clients, but I know that some of you are focused more on small business owners with brick-and-mortar operations and multiple employees.

For the premium-level search, we're not going to be using any keywords. Instead, we're going to set the *Company Size* search filter for companies with

FIGURE 18.6   SBO Search Results

either 11 to 50 or 51 to 200 employees. This way, we'll get smaller companies, but not the sole proprietors and MLMers. We're also going to set the *Seniority* filter to only pull owners, partners, and CXO-level people. Figure 18.7 shows what this looks like.

What you'll see in the results, as shown in Figure 18.8, is that we went from more than 12,000 search results in that free member search to 1,644. Also, we can see the first 300 of them. So we ended up with more targeted and qualified search results, and we can access more of them.

If we want, we can continue to whittle and adjust the search variables in the right-hand column. What's even better is that LinkedIn tells us how

FIGURE 18.7   SBO Search Premium

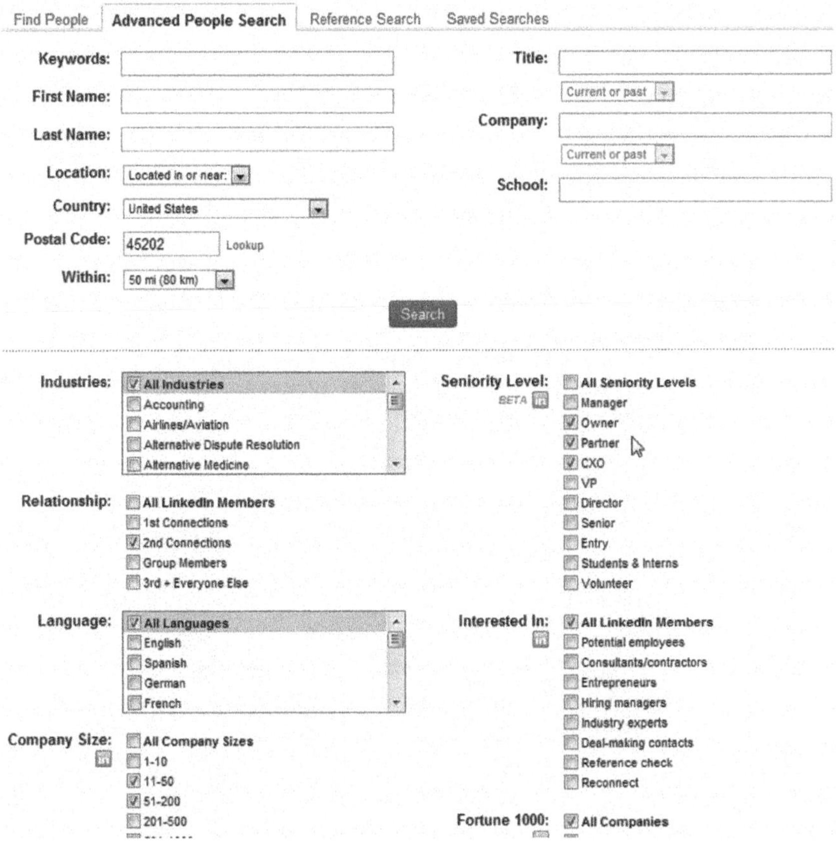

FIGURE 18.8   SBO Search Premium Results

many search results we have for each variable. So simply checking and unchecking the boxes of these search filters will allow us to see *all* of the search results. See Fig. 18.9.

Once you have tweaked the search in such way that you know you'll want to duplicate it, you can save the search. Free members get three saved searches. Premium members get a minimum of five saved searches with the total number depending on their level of membership. See Fig. 18.10.

Can it get any better than this? Actually, it can. Not only can you save these elaborate searches, but LinkedIn will also email you new search results every week! Imagine that—prospects landing right in your inbox.

FIGURE 18.9 Search Variable Column

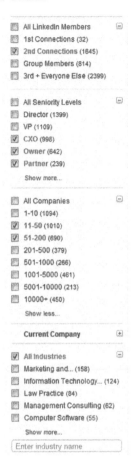

Connecting with the Prospects

LinkedIn does have an introduction function that you can use to ask your connections to introduce you to these prospects. For 2nd degree prospects, I don't recommend using it. You do need to use it to get to a 3rd degree prospect because there's a missing link/connection that you can't see. Technically, you're asking for an introduction, but I recommend that you use your own email or just pick up the phone to ask for the introduction.

FIGURE 18.10 Saved Searches

| Find People | Advanced People Search | Reference Search | **Saved Searches** |

Saved Searches (5)

Search Name	New Results	Email Alert	Date Created
sales managers b2b 41016 [Edit | Delete]	7 [view]	Weekly	October 21, 2010
FA 100 mi Group [Edit | Delete]	88 [view]	Weekly	November 9, 2010
Sr Execs Cincy [Edit | Delete]	None	Never	November 30, 2010
Sales Sr Fortune 1000 [Edit | Delete]	184 [view]	Weekly	March 6, 2011
marketing mgr small tech [Edit | Delete]	118 [view]	Weekly	September 28, 2011

An email message would look something like this:

Dear 1st Degree Connection,

I see that you are connected to Ms. Prospect on LinkedIn. Based on what I know of Ms. Prospect and can see on her profile, I think that my services may be of benefit to her. Would you be open to talking to me about possibly introducing me to her? I would be happy to schedule a phone call at your convenience or maybe we could meet for coffee sometime to discuss it in greater detail. I look forward to hearing from you.

Warmest regards,

Financial Advisor

Final Thoughts

So, have I opened your eyes to the true value of LinkedIn? Was I lying when I said *self-referral machine*? I really like and value Facebook and Twitter, but LinkedIn is the *only* social network that allows you to search through the outer rings of your network in this particular way. Remember: It all comes down to relationships. How you approach these prospects is what will ultimately determine your success. You have to be humble and appreciative. As I mentioned in the earlier chapters of the book, you have to be giving back to your network heavily because these will be some pretty big favors you'll be asking for. The last thing you want is for any of your connections to feel used and abused. If even one feels taken advantage of, word will get around and you'll be dead in the water. Do it right and make me proud. I'd love to hear your success stories, so please feel free to contact me and share them.

CHAPTER 19

Using LinkedIn Groups for Visibility and Prospecting

Crystal Thies

LinkedIn *Groups* can be the most valuable part of your LinkedIn strategy to grow your business, but a groups strategy can be the most difficult to understand and implement. Add to that the fact that it also takes the most time; needless to say, I hear a lot of groans and moans when I suggest it.

The Opportunity in LinkedIn Groups

A recent study from LeadFormix on traffic from LinkedIn to their business-to-business (B2B) client websites found that 38 percent of the people coming to the site from a LinkedIn group resulted in a completed form on their websites! True, tangible leads are coming from LinkedIn groups!

According to an infographic from Lab 42, 81 percent of LinkedIn members belong to at least one LinkedIn group and 52 percent of group members participate in group discussions. However, not only can you interact with people to whom you're not connected inside the groups; you can also send them messages. Other than groups, the only way you can send messages to people who aren't 1st degree connections is to become a premium member and use InMails.

LinkedIn currently has more than 1.2 million groups! And more are being started every day. Some LinkedIn groups are big and some are small. Some are super active and some are dead. LinkedIn allows each member to belong to 50 groups. Finding the right LinkedIn Groups for you and your business—let alone the right discussion opportunities within those groups—can be a very daunting task.

Currently, FINRA considers participation in forums, bulletin boards, and groups of this nature as public appearances and pre-approval is not required, but filing and archiving is required (it will be called retail communications once FINRA Rule 2210 passes, but the treatment is still the same). As a result, many broker-dealers still are not allowing participation in groups (because they don't have the archiving software in place), so please check your compliance policy before diving in.

Two Types of Groups—Open and Closed

LinkedIn's groups used to be all closed—meaning that only the group members could see anything that happened in the groups. There are now open groups that allow everyone to see the activity regardless of whether they are in the group or not. Additionally, some of the open groups even let people participate without fully joining the group. If you're using a social media archiving program, then your activity and participation will be captured and archived regardless of whether the group is open or closed. If you're not using a social media archiving program, then your broker-dealer will only be able to see your activity in a closed group if they happen to be a member of it. Therefore, you need to be responsible for printing and preserving your activity if it is to be filed and archived. It's simply impossible for them to do it for you because they cannot see the discussions in which you're posting or commenting.

Choosing the Right Groups

First and foremost, the LinkedIn groups you select should be the groups where your target clients are spending their time. Depending on how the group is set up and who is allowed to participate, you sometimes may not be able to get into all of the groups that would be most valuable. An example would be if you had a niche market working with physicians and there was a LinkedIn group for physicians to discuss business practices. Since you're not a physician yourself, you likely wouldn't be allowed to join.

Much of the time, I see sales people belonging to mostly industry-related groups, and they are wondering why they aren't finding any new clients and customers. The answer is that they're spending all of their LinkedIn group time with their competitors! A few of those groups are great for professional development, but I would recommend limiting the number to only those that are actually helping you.

Essentially, you have to evaluate each group you join and decide how you're going to use it. You have to be an opportunist. I have three main purposes for the groups I'm in.

1. *Market reach to prospects*—What's important is match to target market, size of the group, and a low level of duplicate members in other groups. I'm using these groups mostly for prospecting and if allowed by the group owner, advertising.
2. *Establishing myself as an expert*—These are groups of my target market where there are good discussions happening and I can demonstrate that I really *know* what I say I do. These are groups like *Top Recommended People*. I don't have too many of these because they take a lot of time, so I'm very selective.
3. *Groups for broadcasting and advertising*—These are large groups that are a bit more general in their makeup so as to pull in some prospects in need of my services that I may not have otherwise thought about. They would be the large local groups and the like, which address many different topics.

You probably aren't going to like this, but the bottom line is that you have to look at and evaluate each group individually to develop the strategies that will work within that group.

Since the owners have free reign to decide who can be in their group, what they can post, and how everything operates, you have to abide by their sandbox rules. In some groups, blatant self-promotion is fine and in others, it's not.

Salesperson Groups

One type of group I recommend you look into is those created for sales-people. There are several *good* sales groups. By *good*, I mean they are large, have great and active discussions, include members from many geographic locations, and are well managed and moderated. The sales groups are the one type of group where you can find prospects and get professional develop-ment at the same time. The discussions are usually around being a better salesperson (professional development), but the sales people talking about it come from all walks of life and industries (prospects).

Even better, since the discussions are about sales techniques and experiences, you're not selling financial services or even talking about them (compliance isn't an issue), and you're building relationships with people who could become great referral sources or even clients.

One of my clients is both a financial advisor and a sales coach. He's found great success on LinkedIn by gaining interest in group discussions with sales people, building a relationship, and then letting them know the full extent of his business as both the coach and advisor. He has converted coaching clients into financial advisory clients. Though most of you don't have the in-between step that he does, that doesn't mean that you wouldn't be able to convert sales group members to clients.

Searching for Groups

The tool that enables searching for groups isn't very sophisticated though they have made some recent improvements. You can search by keyword and category and you can use the same Boolean connectors that we discussed in Chapter 18. The search results, however, are always listed by group size (large to small) and not by relevance. With more than a million groups, you can see why it may be time consuming to find all of the best groups.

To search for groups, go to the *Groups* tab and select *Groups Directory* from the drop-down menu (see Figure 19.1).

In the search box, you can search for terms like the name of your city to find locally oriented groups, or terms like "small business owner"; and you can even combine them—"New York" AND "small business owner"—for even more targeted results (see Figure 19.2). As you will see in the image, you can now filter the group results based on groups that have people from

FIGURE 19.1   Find Groups

the different levels of your network—1st, 2nd, or 3rd. Additionally, you can specify if you want open or closed groups as well as the language of the groups.

Our search results (see Figure 19.3) show us that we have more than 1,200 groups with that phrase. The largest—On Startups—has almost 259,000 members and there were 12,393 discussions posted this month. That tells me this group is great for accessing a lot of potential prospects on LinkedIn, but with more than 12,000 postings already this month, I'm not likely to get much visibility because it is too active.

Some of the other groups, however, still have a great membership base in the thousands, but their activity base is much lower. Therefore, I would have a chance at some visibility in these groups in addition to good prospecting opportunities. Depending on where I'm at with my 50-group membership

FIGURE 19.2   Search Groups

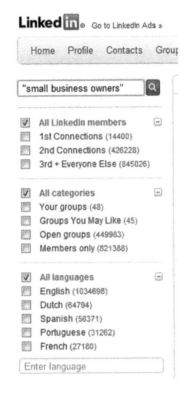

FIGURE 19.3   Group Search Results

limit, I may join all or I may be more selective. The one thing to keep in mind is that you can always leave a group, so if you join and don't find it valuable—or find another group that you think will be more valuable—then don't hesitate to leave and join the new group.

Posting in Groups

It is important to learn the rules for each group before posting. Whoever owns the group sets their own guidelines. They get to say who can join the group and what you can and cannot post in the group. Some groups have stringent rules and are highly moderated (see Figure 19.4). Other groups are like the Wild, Wild West; anyone can post anything he or she wants and there is often more advertising and self-promotion happening in these groups than valuable discussions (these are often referred to as spam groups). *If* the group owner has set group rules and posting guidelines, you'll find them in the upper right-hand corner (they will pop up when you click on the link). If there is no link, then there are no rules.

As you can see in Figure 19.4, LinkedIn has three available tabs for categorizing the different information that can be posted in the groups. The only required tab is *Discussions*. The other available tabs are *Promotions* and *Jobs*. Group owners have the power to elect not to have the promotions and jobs tabs visible. Additionally, in the discussions tab, it is now possible to post polls in addition to discussion items or article links.

Where permitted and appropriate, post your blog articles (if you write your own blog) or other interesting financial planning related articles. To get more traction, add a discussion provoking questions to try and engage the group members. Not only is this a best practice; it is also sometimes a

FIGURE 19.4   Group Rules

requirement before you are allowed to post article links in some groups. Ideally, you don't just want to post links to articles unless you're only interested in driving traffic back to your own website and you're doing it in a spam group.

Post discussion-provoking questions based on real-life situations. I've found that people are more likely to engage when they feel there is a real problem to tackle. Take a situation from one of your clients that had an unanticipated outcome or resulted in something out of the norm, and ask for help to brainstorm how it could be approached differently in the future or why it may have happened. When starting a discussion, make sure you do it when you know that you will be able to respond if things get moving. It's in the comments after the initial question where you'll be able to demonstrate the most expertise and value while building relationships and credibility.

Post opportunities like seminars, webinars, and white papers. You have to be careful with these and the rules of the group. Some group owners see this as advertising and this should go in the promotions tab. Some group owners don't care as long as it is pertinent to the group members. I always scan through the most recent postings in the main discussion tab to see if there is something similar that was allowed to stay. If there is, then post it there. If not, put it in promotions. If the group owner doesn't like it, they can move it, delete it, and even kick you out of the group. If others are doing it, it's usually all right.

One other thing to consider is that if you're posting content that is more of an advertisement—like an invitation to a seminar or webinar—you should have that post pre-approved by the compliance department. You're going to have to submit your other promotional content for the event to compliance anyway. So be smart and think ahead to include what you plan to post as status updates about the seminar (whether on your profile or in groups) along with the rest of the materials at the same time and you're covered.

Joining Others' Conversations

Posting something new isn't always the most advantageous way to participate in a group. When you post a discussion to a group, you automatically *follow* that discussion. When you comment on a discussion, you also automatically follow the discussion. Whenever anyone adds a comment to a discussion, everyone who is following the discussion receives your comment as an email message immediately after you post it.

Therefore, if you have to add a comment to a running discussion that has over 100 comments, then every person who has commented will receive an email message with your comment. When a discussion gets that involved, people normally make multiple comments, but in that 100-comment instance, there would likely be about 70 to 80 people receiving the email message with your comment. I don't know what you're thinking right now, but I'm thinking that's pretty darn good visibility.

Many groups have *introduce yourself* discussions, which are often the most popular discussions in the group. Given what I said happens in the previous paragraph, the effects would be exponentially greater if that introduce yourself discussion received over 2,000 comments. Yes, people can stop following a discussion and they won't get your message, but you still can't beat having a personal introduction sent out via email to tens or hundreds or even thousands of people to whom you're not even connected.

Of course, you should only be doing this activity if you're compliantly using LinkedIn for business purposes. Recently, I was going through my news feed when I noticed that one of my clients posted a comment to an "introduce yourself" discussion item in a large group. I clicked on the comment and it turned out to be a full blown advertisement for his services as a financial advisor. I freaked out and sent him a message that he had to delete it immediately. His broker-dealer is only letting them use LinkedIn for personal use. His activity isn't being archived anywhere so using those "introduce yourself" discussions as an advertisement is a huge no-no. To be honest, any "introduce yourself" post in a group is an advertisement and a posting that you will likely duplicate in multiple groups, so it is recommended that you write an introduction of yourself for your groups and send it through the compliance pre-approval process. Even though LinkedIn groups fall within the interactive content of social media that technically doesn't need compliance pre-approval, this usage of that platform is an advertisement that will be seen by more than 25 people. LinkedIn group discussions don't disappear, so your compliance department will definitely find these comments if you are set up on an archiving system and will likely find them if they are posted in an open group. Bottom line is to be smart.

While you're at it, look for old, popular discussions that may have gone dormant. A well-thought-out comment added to these old discussions can get them revitalized and bring in new people. A new discussion isn't always best. However, if you can start a discussion that turns into one of these super popular and long running discussions, then you've hit gold. Ask yourself: What type of question would do that?

Connecting with Group Members

Look for members in your groups who could be strategic connectors and not just prospects (but also not competitors). Begin to build a relationship with them and then engage them to connect.

The best time to invite them to connect is just after they have posted or commented on a discussion because they have made themselves visible. Simply send them an invitation to connect with a note similar to the following:

Dear Group Member,

I read your comment/post in XYZ group and found it very interesting. When I see valuable and knowledgeable people such as you, I like to reach out and connect. This way we can begin to build a relationship and hopefully be in a position to help each other down the road. If there is ever anything I can do to help you, please do not hesitate to ask.

Sincerely,
Crystal

However, not everyone is active in the groups and you may find someone you want to connect with who doesn't post regularly. When it comes to connecting with people like this, I recommend sending them a message to gauge their interest in connecting before sending an actual invitation to connect (see Figure 19.5). Now, it is possible for a group member to block receipt of messages from group members, so if you don't see a link to send a message or connect, then that means that they have made the decision to put that boundary in place.

In the message to the group member you want to connect with, explain why you want to connect and then offer to either accept their invitation to connect or to send them an invitation if they respond to your message that they would like to connect.

FIGURE 19.5 Message Group Member

Final Thoughts

The best places on LinkedIn to find opportunities, increase your sphere of influence, and truly engage are in LinkedIn groups. Find and join groups of your target market, engage, participate, and give back. Be sure to follow the rules and capture the people you begin to develop relationships with by connecting. You get what you give by participating in groups. I have gotten multiple clients through my participation in LinkedIn groups and you can, too.

Also keep in mind compliance. Although LinkedIn groups by default as a public appearance under the old rules and as an online interactive electronic forum under the new rules does not require pre-approval, if you're promoting a product or service (including business development events), then it is still an advertisement and should be put through compliance approval before posting. Be smart. If it sounds anything like an advertisement, get it approved first.

CHAPTER 20

Gaining Visibility on LinkedIn

Crystal Thies

When you look at LinkedIn's sharing features, you may think it's very similar to Facebook and Twitter. LinkedIn integrates with Twitter and it has a *Like* function that it obviously borrowed from Facebook. However, it's not the same—it's better. When you interact with status updates and your network's activity, you actually get more visibility than the other social networks. In addition to the news feed, we'll cover a couple other features in LinkedIn that you can use for visibility and awareness. One thing to keep in mind is that as you're building this visibility, you'll also uncover some prospects. Keep an eye out and you can find some opportunities. Think of it like a reverse Whack-a-Mole. All of the different posting activities will cause some prospects and others to pop their heads up. However, instead of bashing them on the head, you want to grab them by the neck and yank them out of their holes. Now, with that image in mind. . . .

Working the News Feed

If you don't do anything else in this chapter, you need to do this. And you need to do it at least five minutes a day.

FIGURE 20.1   Status Update—Cho

You may be too busy to get a lot of status updates composed and processed through compliance review (if required by your compliance policy) on a regular basis—or at least, as often as you would like. One of the easiest things you can do that won't require compliance review is to build off of the nonfinancial status updates from your network. What's great about it is that it gives both you and them visibility.

What do I mean by *build off?* I mean either clicking on the *Like* link at the bottom of a connection's status update or adding a comment to their status update (see Figure 20.1). By adding a comment, you can get a conversation going across networks. I once commented on one of my connection's status updates and we ended up with over 30 comments from people across about eight different networks.

Liking a status update is the quickest and easiest way to do this (see Figure 20.2). Liking is different in LinkedIn than Facebook. At one time, the *Like* action went into the main news feed of Facebook, but it hasn't for quite a while. In LinkedIn, when you like a status update, it's almost like *you* did a full status update to your network. As you see in the image, it says that you like the status update and then the full status update is below that.

An added benefit is that when it goes out to your network, your connections can hover over and see the connection who posted the original status update (see Figure 20.3).

They can also comment on the status update even if they aren't connected to that person. In Figure 20.4, Tom liked Chris' status update so I saw it in my news feed. I'm connected to Tom, but I'm not connected to Chris, yet I was

FIGURE 20.2   Status Update—Like

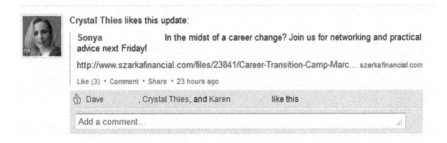

FIGURE 20.3   Status Update—Like and Hover

able to comment on Chris' status update and begin a dialogue with him. Additionally, if there are multiple comments by multiple people, each person who commented will get email messages with the new comments. LinkedIn wants to make certain that these interactions are seen and acted on.

What's really great about this type of activity is that it's easy, quick, and fun. If you have a smartphone with the LinkedIn app, you can literally interact with your network via the news feed whenever you have a couple of minutes in between meetings and have nothing else to do.

Company Status Updates

Interactive company pages are a recent addition to LinkedIn. It is possible for people to follow a company page, and it is also now possible for the

FIGURE 20.4   Status—Like and Comment

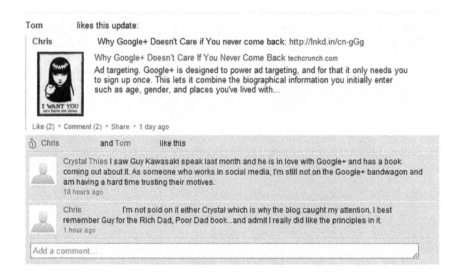

Tom   likes this update:

Chris   Why Google+ Doesn't Care if You never come back: http://lnkd.in/cn-gGg

Why Google+ Doesn't Care If You Never Come Back techcrunch.com
Ad targeting. Google+ is designed to power ad targeting, and for that it only needs you
to sign up once. This lets it combine the biographical information you initially enter
such as age, gender, and places you've lived with...

I WANT YOU

Like (2) • Comment (2) • Share • 1 day ago

Chris   and Tom   like this

Crystal Thies I saw Guy Kawasaki speak last month and he is in love with Google+ and has a book
coming out about it. As someone who works in social media, I'm still not on the Google+ bandwagon and
am having a hard time trusting their motives.
18 hours ago

Chris   I'm not sold on it either Crystal which is why the blog caught my attention. I best
remember Guy for the Rich Dad, Poor Dad book...and admit I really did like the principles in it.
1 hour ago

Add a comment...

company pages to do status updates that go out into the news feed of everyone following them.

What does that mean for you? Well, you can interact with the status updates the same way you can a person's status update. You can like it and you can comment on it (see Figure 20.5). You are then visible to everyone who follows the company in addition to being visible within your network. Chances are, this visibility is to people you don't know and to whom you are not connected. Isn't that a good thing?

The strategy is to find companies that your target market would follow—companies with a large number of followers and that are actively doing status updates from their company page. Follow those companies and then look for status updates in which you can engage.

The bottom line in interacting with status updates, whether from a person or a company, is that such activity will be one of the biggest traffic drivers to your profile. As a premium member, I get to see more of the people who visit my profile as well as statistics over a 90-day period. After I've been commenting on status updates, I can see that the people who check out my profile are often connected to the people whose status updates I commented on.

FIGURE 20.5 Company Status Update

Learn iT! Feb 29 is the last day to snag the $99 introductory rate for Learn iT! Anytime -- will be $125 on March 1! Use code "linkedin" for an additional 5% off. Don't sleep on this one friends!
Smarter Video-Based Learning
learnitanytime.com
The most important part of any video-based class is the teacher. We've all had bad instructors, and none of us wants another one. Learn iT! Anytime self-paced video courses are exclusively taught by the same top-tier...

Like • Comment (1) • Share • 1 day ago

Crystal Thies Hey Network! If you need some training on Microsoft Office programs, Adobe Acrobat, html, css and more, you need to check out this special offer! You're not going to find training this cheap. They even have a monthly option of $12.99!
1 day ago

FIGURE 20.6 Polls

LinkedIn Polls

One of the more interesting applications available in LinkedIn, which was not developed by a third party and has real potential, is the LinkedIn *Polls* application. LinkedIn Polls (see Figure 20.6) is simply the ability to ask a simple question with five multiple-choice answers that anyone can answer. To access the polls, go to the *More* tab and you'll find it in the drop-down menu.

On the polls home page, you can review your open and closed polls and their results, see the polls you've answered, find new polls to answer, and

FIGURE 20.7 Polls Home

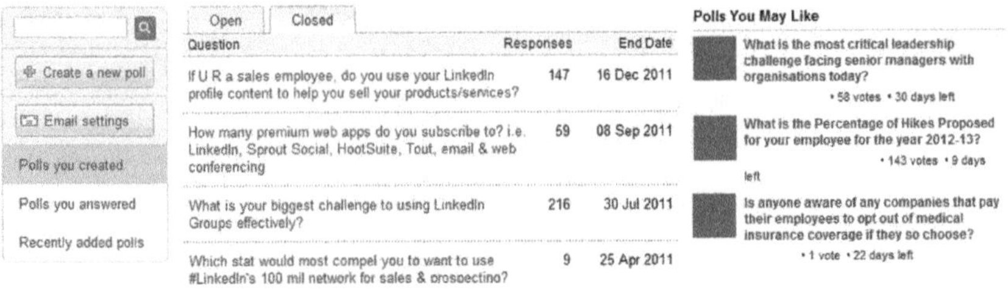

create a new poll (see Figure 20.7). If you're interested in answering or seeing polls on specific topics, you can search by keywords.

When you click on the *Create a new poll* button, you're taken to a form that both creates and shares the poll at the same time (see Figure 20.8). These polls are designed to be shared. The length of the question is 120 characters, so there is space to fit it and the link back to the poll in a tweet. You must have a minimum of two answer choices and can have up to five answer choices. The text for each answer is limited to 40 characters. As a result of the tight character limits, you may find that you have to use text slang to make things fit. In my opinion, it is appropriate in this usage since it is meant to be shared in social media, even though this is business communication.

Just below the answers, you'll see *Runs until*, which sets the end date of the poll. The default time is a month; however, if you click on the calendar icon, you will see that you can extend the run of the poll for two months. In my opinion, longer is always better, but I can envision situations where the poll is used for a specific purpose and you end it sooner.

As you can see below the question and answers, you can share this poll with all three social networks (see Figure 20.9). The polls app is one of only two functions in LinkedIn with direct Facebook integration at this time. Be certain to compose each share appropriately for the social network. You can see in the tweet that I added a hashtag in the hope of achieving greater visibility among those following the hashtag.

After you've created the poll, you'll have access to many sharing tools to continue using throughout the run of the poll.

In addition to sharing on the three social networks that were addressed when you created the poll, you will also be given a direct link that you can use to direct people to the poll via regular email and other communications (see Figure 20.10). It will also give you the *embed* code to add the poll

FIGURE 20.8   Create Polls

directly to your website (I've used this as a pop up on my site for everyone visiting and it's a great way to get lots of answers). Also, the LinkedIn *Share* function is a lot more comprehensive than in other social networks, as it allows you to not only share it as a status update, but also to share directly in groups and to send to individuals via LinkedIn's message system.

Once people start answering your poll, you can see detailed results information with demographic breakdown by answer. Additionally, people can leave comments—whether they've answered the poll or not, and even after the poll closes. The comments section is a great area to build new relationships and even find some prospects.

FIGURE 20.9   Share This Poll

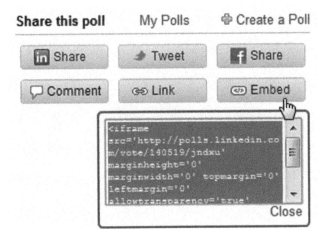

FIGURE 20.10   Share

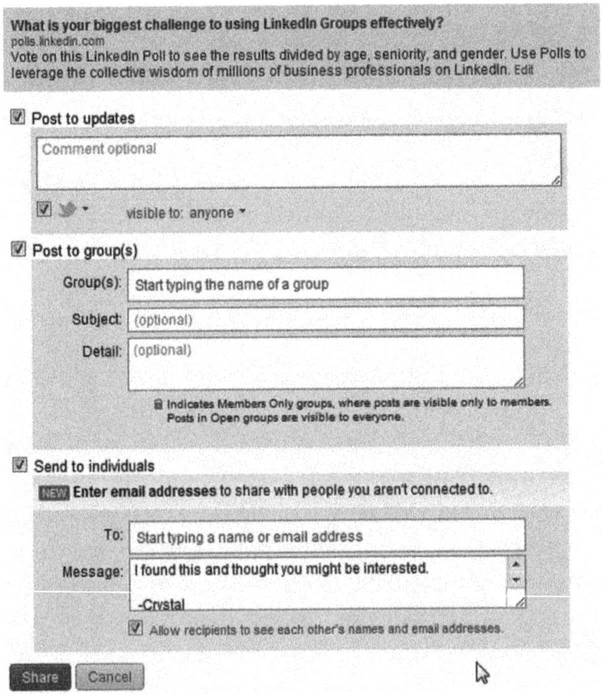

What is your biggest challenge to using LinkedIn Groups effectively?
polls.linkedin.com
Vote on this LinkedIn Poll to see the results divided by age, seniority, and gender. Use Polls to
leverage the collective wisdom of millions of business professionals on LinkedIn. Edit

☑ Post to updates

    Comment optional

    ☑ 🐦 ▾   visible to: anyone ▾

☑ Post to group(s)

    Group(s):   Start typing the name of a group

    Subject: (optional)

    Detail: (optional)

                🔒 Indicates Members Only groups, where posts are visible only to members.
                Posts in Open groups are visible to everyone.

☑ Send to individuals

    NEW Enter email addresses to share with people you aren't connected to.

    To: Start typing a name or email address

    Message: I found this and thought you might be interested.

               -Crystal

               ☑ Allow recipients to see each other's names and email addresses.

    Share   Cancel

Figure 20.11 shows the results from one of my past polls. I had a total of 216 votes and 18 comments, with which I was very pleased. In addition to getting great visibility, I also got some great market research out of it.

Asking good and engaging questions is going to be the biggest challenge for you as financial advisors. Your topic matter isn't the most fun and is actually stuff that a lot of people tend to avoid. Also, when I look at the types of questions advisors have been asking, they are often salesy and cliché. There have been several past polls asking people if they have a financial advisor, talk to their financial advisor, like how they pay their financial advisor, and with the exception of less than a handful, very few of these polls drew any significant numbers of participants. So, you're going to have to be thoughtful and creative to get highly participatory polls around financial topics.

Use current events that get people talking. Instead of asking, "Why aren't you using a financial advisor?" ask something like, "Has the Bernie Madoff situation played into your decision not to use a financial advisor?" Just the Madoff name alone is going to grab peoples' attention and make them want to participate.

From a compliance standpoint, the LinkedIn Polls feature falls into a gray area. While it is interactive content, it also doesn't disappear. It's also a feature that is so small that most compliance departments may not think to address it in a compliance policy. Before using LinkedIn Polls for the first time, I would recommend getting a ruling from your compliance department on how they want them treated from a review and oversight perspective. Most LinkedIn Polls aren't time sensitive, so think ahead and plan for the review process.

LinkedIn Events

Recently, LinkedIn completely revamped the *Events* application. To be honest, I liked the older version better than the new version and had more success with it. I also have noticed that it appears as though fewer people are using the new events application. That very well could be because they eliminated one of my favorite functions, which was the ability to publicly say that you were interested in an event. Now you can *Follow* the event, but it's a private follow and there is no other way to essentially say *maybe*.

With that being said, the events application can play a very big role in getting people to share and attend any events that you have. It's a perfect tool to share networking events, educational seminars, and any other events that

FIGURE 20.11   Polls Result

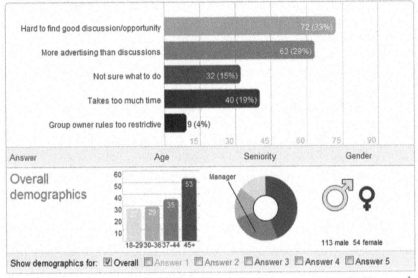

What is your biggest challenge to using LinkedIn Groups effectively?

By Crystal Thies Online Networking Trainer, Consultant & Speaker helping companies & sales pros use LinkedIn to find prospects • 216 votes • 18 comments • Ended 30 Jul 2011

are open to the public (whether free or paid). You'll find the events application just above the polls in the *More* drop-down menu.

In addition to posting your own events, you can also use this application to find interesting events to attend. You can search by keyword, location, and industry.

For each event, in addition to the date, time, and location, you can include a logo, detailed description, and a link to register and/or get more information. Just like with the polls, there are share buttons to easily share on LinkedIn, Twitter, and Facebook, in addition to a custom link for easy sharing outside of social media. Lastly, there is a running dialogue box and activity feed to share updates of people who will be attending in addition to simply adding comments, introductions, questions, and anything else you want to share with people attending or thinking about attending the event.

One of the new features with this update that I do like is the ability to simply click on a link and have the event added to your calendar

FIGURE 20.12 Search Events

(see Fig. 20.12). Additionally, it will recognize which of the attendees you're not connected to and suggest them as people for you to meet.

Keep in mind that LinkedIn Events is static content and not interactive, so you will need to get compliance approval before posting an event on LinkedIn. However, this shouldn't be a big deal because there are other promotional materials that will have to be approved by compliance as well. Simply think ahead and alter your invitation or email marketing materials to what is needed for the LinkedIn Events listing and submit it all together.

The updated events application has a lot of potential and is definitely something you want to utilize for any events you hold, including any virtual events like webinars and teleconferences. If your event is free for attendees and is more casual, where all you need to know is who is attending, you could even use it to fully manage your RSVPs (see Fig. 20.13).

FIGURE 20.13 Events

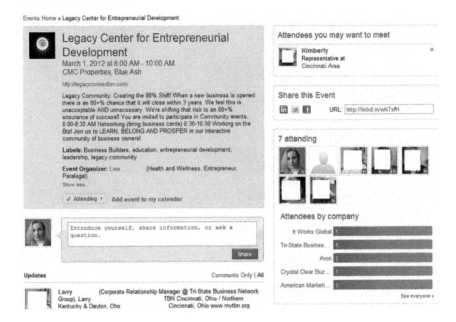

Final Thoughts

These are only three of many available strategies and tools you can use on LinkedIn. Keep in mind that LinkedIn is ever evolving, and watch for new applications and features that you can use to your advantage. When I first got started on LinkedIn, none of this was available to me. LinkedIn has been like a train picking up steam and it's currently going full speed ahead. Follow LinkedIn's blog—as well as my own—to stay up to date with the latest strategies and techniques to maximize and optimize the time you spend on LinkedIn.

PART V

Next Steps

CHAPTER 21

The Future
of Social Media

Crystal Thies

The breadth, depth, and velocity of social media is mind boggling. People have been telling me to write a book for a couple of years and I've always responded that most printed books on social media are a waste of time because they are out of date on the day of their release. Even as we write this, Matt and I are struggling to make major changes to the text as a result of the addition of Timeline to Facebook and some feature changes in LinkedIn while meeting the deadlines of the publisher. The book isn't scheduled to hit the shelves for another three months; what else will change by then?

There's Much More than the Big Three

We've covered a lot of material, but we've only covered a fraction of a fraction of the tip of the iceberg. We didn't talk about blogging. We didn't talk about Google+. We didn't talk about YouTube. And, we didn't talk about the latest newcomer that is the talk of the town, Pinterest. Honestly, there are thousands of social networks available and new players are entering the game all the time. Oh, and we didn't even talk about LinkedFA which is a social network created specifically for financial advisors and their clients.

To cover everything in social media, we would be looking at writing an encyclopedia at this point. As a financial advisor, you'll likely always be behind the times — which isn't necessarily a bad thing. Many of the latest flavors of the month don't end up having holding power, so that keeps you from jumping in too soon and wasting time and energy.

Careful evaluation is needed before expanding your social media efforts. Is your target market well represented in that social network? Is the new social network offering something that you can't do or get from your existing social media activities? Can you afford — time and money — to add this new social media activity to your entire marketing plan? You need to carefully answer these questions before deciding to expand beyond the scope of this book. It really is too much for one person to do on their own, so you must be smart about your social media activity.

Staying Up To Date

We are developing a companion website with more information, tips, tools, and strategies. This website will have links to the tools discussed in this book as well as others we didn't have time to share or that have come onto the scene in the meantime. Since we know that the book is out of date already, the website will also be the place where we can let you know what has changed in regards to social media and compliance regulations.

http://socialmediahandbookforfinancialadvisors.com

You are also encouraged to connect with both of us on social media.

Crystal Thies

www.linkedin.com/in/crystalthies
www.twitter.com/linkedinninja
www.facebook.com/CrystalClearBuzz
www.linkedin.com/company/crystal-clear-buzz
www.youtube.com/linkedinninja

Matthew Halloran

www.linkedin.com/in/mattthelifecoach
www.twitter.com/GIVEStrategy
www.facebook.com/GIVEStrategy
www.facebook.com/personaltelescope

About the Authors

Matthew Halloran

Matthew Halloran first became interested in social media when Myspace was the place to be. With over 80,000 Twitter followers with a 99 percent effectiveness rating, 1,000 LinkedIn connections, and 700 Facebook fans, he knows how to gain followers and do it in a way to help build business.

Having coached and consulted hundreds and spoken to thousands of financial advisors, Matthew knows how an FA practice runs and needs to market using new and effective (low-cost) strategies. He feels that social media is the new marketing frontier, which if used wisely, can transform the prospecting aspect of any financial services practice.

Matthew is now the director of national development for GIVE Strategies, a mission-driven company that focuses on helping connect financial advisors, CPAs, estate planning attorneys, clients, and planned giving directors to redirect $1 billion to charity. He is the president and founder of Top Advisor Coaching, a coaching program for top producers in business, finance, legal, and philanthropy using a proven approach that has transformed people's businesses and their lives.

Crystal Thies

Crystal Thies first became a financial advisor in 1997 with American Express Financial Advisors. She was quickly recognized as an emerging leader and a technology advocate. Her enthusiasm for technology and computer software knowledge made her the natural choice to help roll out and train all regional advisors on the company's first advisor managed financial planning software program. Crystal exceeded the goals of the new advisor program and received the President's Award for Quality Advice in 1998.

As a financial advisor, Crystal had started specializing in charitable giving. When relocation ended her financial planning practice, Crystal entered the nonprofit sector full time. She also returned to graduate school and received a Master's of Public Administration and Nonprofit Management Degree in 2004.

In 2007, Crystal found LinkedIn® and decided to re-enter financial planning to develop a highly niche market around charitable giving and nonprofits. After being out of financial planning for several years, Crystal saw tools like LinkedIn® as perfect for financial advisors with tight marketing budgets to grow their businesses quickly. Unfortunately, social media was too far ahead of the compliance curve and Crystal decided to follow her new passion for social media.

As the founder and CEO of Crystal Clear Buzz, LLC, Crystal is known as the LinkedIn® Ninja. Her company is focused on helping companies and individuals utilize social media for sales and business development—particularly LinkedIn. Crystal Clear Buzz provides training, custom strategy development, consulting, and other services related to maximizing the use of LinkedIn® to find clients and grow revenue. In addition to many independent financial advisors, Crystal has worked directly with Wells Fargo, UBS, and Fifth Third Bank.

Index

271